21世纪国际商务教材教辅系列

编写委员会

21世纪国际商务教材教辅系列

中国教育发展战略学会终身教育工作委员会
职业技能认证研究中心指定培训用书

总 主 编　余世明
副总主编　袁绍岐　张彬祥　何　静

DOCUMENTS & CREDIT FOR INTERNATIONAL BUSINESS

国际商务单证实务练习题及分析解答

（第三版）

主编　余世明　　副主编　张少辉　张小彤

暨南大学出版社
JINAN UNIVERSITY PRESS
中国·广州

图书在版编目（CIP）数据

国际商务单证实务练习题及分析解答/余世明主编；张少辉，张小彤副主编．—3 版．—广州：暨南大学出版社，2009. 10（2013. 1 重印）
（21 世纪国际商务教材教辅系列）
ISBN 978 - 7 - 81079 - 646 - 0

Ⅰ. 国…　Ⅱ. ①余…②张…③张…　Ⅲ. 国际贸易—票据—解题　Ⅳ. F740. 44 - 44

中国版本图书馆 CIP 数据核字(2008)第 054262 号

出版发行：暨南大学出版社

地　址：中国广州暨南大学
电　话：总编室（8620）85221601
营销部（8620）85225284　85228291　85228292（邮购）
传　真：（8620）85221583（办公室）　85223774（营销部）
邮　编：510630
网　址：http：//www. jnupress. com　http：//press. jnu. edu. cn

排　版：广州市天河星辰文化发展部照排中心
印　刷：湛江日报社印刷厂

开　本：787mm × 960mm　1/16
印　张：16
字　数：402 千
版　次：2006 年 1 月第 1 版　2009 年 10 月第 3 版
印　次：2013 年 1 月第 11 次
印　数：34001—37000 册

定　价：23. 00 元

目　录

编写说明

国际商务单证实务是一门实践性相当强的课程。虽然近年来全国推行国际商务单证员和国际商务操作员的培训认证，但有关的实训材料较少。本书作为《国际商务单证实务》教材的配套练习册，力求使学生在学好教材的同时有针对性地进行训练，达到巩固、强化的目的。本书的编写具有如下特点：

（1）内容新。以最新的国际贸易惯例（如《UCP600》、《2010年通则》等）进行解释，采用的单证材料和案例也是近几年外贸公司的实际业务资料，力求贴近实际。

（2）题型全。练习题中包括了中英文术语、短语互译，单项选择题，多项选择题，判断题，阅读理解，单据填制，单据改错和案例分析题等，保证学生能得到全面的训练。

（3）单证真。书中的单证大多数来自公司的实例，除客户名等资料改动外，其他全部保留，力求给学生更直观的感觉。

（4）解答简明。书中的练习题全部配有参考答案，对单项选择题、多项选择题、判断题等客观题型的答案，还配有简明的分析解答，方便学生理解。

（5）针对性强。本书以国际商务单证员、国际商务操作员、外销员、报关员和国际货运代理从业人员等统考的内容和题型为基础，有助于学生顺利通过上述各种认证考试。

本书的编写分工如下：第一章、第二章的第三节和第五节、第三章的第三节和第四节由余世明编写，第二章的第四节和第六节、第三章的第一节和第二节由张少辉编写，第二章的第一节和第二节、第六章、第七章由张小彤编写，第四章、第八章由杨子电编写，第五章由陈夏鹏编写，第九章由邓棣嫦编写。全书由余世明负责总纂和修审。

本书不仅可作为高职高专和中等职业技术学校国际商务专业和其他相关财经类专业学生学习《国际商务单证实务》的配套用书，而且可作为涉外各类考证和各类干部培训国际商务基本知识的实训用书。

本书在编写过程中参考了大量的资料，特别是现行国际商务单证各版本的教材，还引用了很多外贸公司的实际单证，在此谨向各位作者和外贸公司的经理、业务员、单证员表示衷心的感谢！由于水平有限，错误之处敬请批评指正。

编　者

2012年1月

第一章
信 用 证

一、练习题

（一）中英文术语、短语互译

1. 中译英

（1）不可撤销信用证
（2）开证日期
（3）电汇索偿
（4）一切银行费用
（5）佣金
（6）出票根据
（7）正本单据
（8）通知行
（9）账户
（10）保兑行

2. 英译中

（1）Applicant
（2）Beneficiary
（3）Negotiation Bank
（4）Drawee Bank
（5）Expiry Date
（6）Documentary Credit
（7）Documents Required
（8）Special Conditions
（9）Up to an Aggregate Amount of
（10）The Full Name and Address of the Openers

（二）单项选择题

1. 不可撤销信用证在信用证的有效期内，未经（　　）的同意，开证行或开证人不得撤销或修改。

A. 受益人
B. 开证人
C. 开证行
D. 受益人、开证人以及有关银行

2. 根据《UCP600》的规定，若信用证没有注明（　　）字样，则认为该信用证为不保兑信用证。

A. Confirmed
B. Revocable
C. Revolving
D. Transferable

3. 在进料加工贸易中，经常先向外商购买原材料或配件，我方加工成品后再卖给该外商。为了避免上当受骗，我方应采用（　　）比较稳妥。

A. 保兑信用证
B. 可转让信用证
C. 预支信用证
D. 对开信用证

4. 下列对信用证有效期的描述，属于直接写明具体日期的是（　　）。

A. Documents must be presented for negotiation within 10 days after the on board date of bill of lading.

B. Negotiation must be on or before the 15th day of shipment.

C. This L/C is valid for negotiation in China until Oct. 1, 2002.

D. Documents to be presented to negotiation bank within 15 days after shipment.

5. 根据《UCP600》的规定，如使用“于或约于”之类词语限定装运日期，银行将视为在所述日期前后各（　　）内装运，起讫日包括在内。

A. 3天　　B. 5天

C. 7天　　D. 10天

6. “Transshipment permitted, part shipments allowed, but part shipment of each item not allowed”的中文意思是（　　）。

A. 转运允许，分运允许，但每个品种的货物不得分运

B. 转运不允许，分运允许，但每个品种的货物不得分运

C. 转运允许，分运允许，但每个品种的货物必须分运

D. 转运允许，分运不允许，但每个品种的货物不得分运

7. 下列信用证有关费用的条款，要求卖方负担有关费用的是（　　）。

A. All banking charges for seller's account.

B. Port congestion surcharges, if any, at the time of shipment is for opener's account.

C. All banking charges outside Hongkong are for account of accountee.

D. Drawee bank's charges and acceptance commission are for buyer's account.

8. 下列属于信用证条款中开证行保证文句的是（　　）。

A. Letter of guarantee and discrepancies are not acceptable.

B. We hereby undertake to honour all drafts drawn in accordance with terms of this credit.

C. One copy of commercial invoice and packing list should be sent to the credit openers 15 days before shipment.

D. Drafts to be drawn for full CIF value less 5% commission, invoice to show full CIF value.

9. 下列英文词或词组中，表示“议付行”的是（　　）。

A. Confirming Bank　　B. Opening Bank

C. Negotiation Bank　　D. Advising Bank

10. 根据《UCP600》的规定，若信用证没有特别说明，则信用证（　　）。

A. 未注明“Transferable”字样或条款，即为可转让信用证

B. 未注明“Irrevocable”字样，即为可撤销信用证

C. 未注明“Confirmed”字样，即为不保兑信用证

D. 未注明是否即期付款，即为远期付款信用证

（三）多项选择题

1. 信用证中，表示开证人的常见词或词组有（　　）。

A. Principal　　B. Opener

C. Applicant　　D. account of...

E. Accountee

2. 信用证中，表示受益人的常见词或词组有（　　）。

A. Beneficiary　　B. in favour of...

C. Opener　　D. in your favour

3. 对于保兑信用证，承担第一性付款责任的有（　　）。

A. 通知行　　B. 议付行

C. 开证行　　D. 保兑行

4. 下列信用证条款中，属于佣金条款的是（　　）。

A. Port congestion surcharges, if any, at the time of shipment is for opener's account.

B. Signed invoices must show 5% commission.

C. 5% commission to be deducted from the invoice value.

D. Beneficiary's drafts are to be made out for 95% of invoice value, being 5% commission payable to credit opener.

5. 对 SWIFT，下列表述正确的是（　　）。

A. 使用 SWIFT 系统的银行必须加入该协会，方可使用 SWIFT 系统

B. 使用 SWIFT 信用证，必须遵守 SWIFT 使用手册的规定，使用 SWIFT 手册规定的代号

C. SWIFT 信用证必须按国际商会制定的《UCP600》的规定处理

D. SWIFT 系统具有自动收发储存信息、自动加押和核押等功能

E. SWIFT 系统可每周 24 小时连续不停地运转

（四）判断题

1. 2005 年 6 月 18 日在 SWIFT 电文中表示为 180605。（　　）

2. 在 SWIFT 信用证中，数字"2584678.36"表示为"2584678,36"。（　　）

3. 信用证不准分批，又没有数量增减条款，则实际装运数量允许有 5% 的增减幅度。（　　）

4. 信用证规定起运港为 CHINA PORTS，若信用证禁止分批，则信用证中装运港 CHINA PORTS 的实际意义与 CHINA PORT 相同。（　　）

5. 信用证没有规定有效期或装运期，则该信用证为无效信用证。（　　）

6. 信用证修改通知书的内容，受益人可根据实际情况，接受其中的一部分，拒绝其中的另一部分。（　　）

7. 信用证修改通知书必须由原通知行转递或通知。（　　）

8. 信用证的性质是银行信用，因此，信用证项下使用的汇票必定是银行汇票。（　　）

9. 背对背信用证是指交易的一方开出第一张信用证，但暂不生效，须在对方开来一定金额的回头信用证经受益人表示接受时，才通知对方银行两证同时生效。（　　）

10. 对于不可撤销信用证，如果开证人提出申请，开证行可随时撤销该信用证。（　　）

（五）案例分析

1. 某公司从国外某商行进口一批钢材，货物分两批装运，支付方式为不可撤销即期信用证，每批分别由中国银行开立一份信用证。第一批货物装运后，卖方在有效期内向银行交单议付，议付行审单后，即向该商行议付货款，随后中国银行对议付行作了偿付。我方在收到第一批货物后，发现货物品质与合同不符，因而要求开证行对第二份信用证项下的单据拒绝付款，但遭开证行拒绝。问：开证行这样做是否合理？为什么？

2. 我某轻工业进出口公司向国外客户出口某商品一批，合同中规定以即期不可撤销信用证为付款方式，信用证的到期地点规定在我国。为保证款项的收回，应议付行的要求，我方商请香港某银行对中东某行（开证行）开立的信用证加以保兑。在合同规定的开证时间内，我方收到通知银行（即议付行）转来的一张即期不可撤销保兑信用证。我出口公司在货物装运后，将有关单据交议付银行议付。不久接保兑行通知：“由于开证行已破产，我行将不承担该信用证的付款责任。”问：（1）保兑行的做法是否正确？为什么？（2）对此情况，我方应如何处理？

（六）阅读理解

1. 阅读理解一

*KRUNG THAI BANK PUBLIC COMPANY
*LIMITED
*BANGKOK

User Header	Service Code	103:
	Bank. Priority	113:
	Msg User Ref.	108:
	Info. from CI	115:
Sequence of Total	*27	: 1 / 1
Form of Doc. Credit	*40 A	: IRREVOCABLE
Doc. Credit Number	*20	: BL 120197
Date of Issue	31 C	: 010123
Expiry	*31 D	: Date 010422 Place CHINA
Applicant Bank	51 D	: KRUNG THAI BANK PCL.,SUANMALI IBC.
Applicant	*50	: METCH THAI CHEMICAL COMPANY LIMITED 45-7 MAITRICHITR RD., BANGKOK,THAILAND.
Beneficiary	*59	: SINOCHEM GUANGDONG IMPORT AND EXPORT CORPORATION 58 ZHANQIAN ROAD.GUANGZHOU,CHINA
Amount	*32 B	: Currency USD Amount 16,264
Available with/by	*41 D	: ANY BANK BY NEGOTIATION
Drafts at ...	42 C	: SIGHT
Drawee	42 D	: KRUNG THAI BANK PCL.,SUANMALI IBC.
Partial Shipments	43 P	: PROHIBITED
Transshipment	43 T	: ALLOWED
Loading in Charge	44 A	: GUANGZHOU, CHINA
For Transport to ...	44 B	: BANGKOK,THAILAND
Latest Date of Ship.	44 C	: 010412
Descript. of Goods	45 A	: 42.80 MT LITHOPONE 30PCT ARROW BRAND USD380.- PER MT DETAILS AS PER PROFORMA INVOICE NO.01TH44GD176A3-032 DATED JAN.22,2001. C I F. BANGKOK,THAILAND
Documents required	46 A	:

+ SIGNED COMMERCIAL INVOICE IN 10 COPIES SHOWING SEPARATELY F.O.B.VALUE,FREIGHT CHARGE,INSURANCE PREMIUM, C.I.F.VALUE AND COUNTRY OF ORIGIN.
+ FULL SET OF CLEAN ON BOARD OCEAN BILLS OF LADING TO ORDER OF KRUNG THAI BANK PUBLIC COMPANY LIMITED MARKED FREIGHT PREPAID PLUS TWO NON-NEGOTIABLE COPIES,NOTIFY : APPLICANT
+ MARINE INSURANCE POLICY OR CERTIFICATE IN DUPLICATE,ENDORSED IN BLANK,FOR FULL INVOICE VALUE PLUS 10 PERCENT STATING CLAIM PAYABLE IN THAILAND COVERING INSTITUTE CARGO CLAUSES (A) AND WAR RISKS.
+ PACKING LIST IN 5 COPIES.
+ CERTIFICATE OF ANALYSIS IN 5 COPIES.
+ ONE FULL SET OF NON-NEGOTIABLE SHIPPING DOCUMENTS MUST BE SENT TO THE APPLICANT BY AIR COURIER WITHIN 3 DAYS AFTER SHIPMENT AND BENEFICIARY'S CERTIFICATE TO THIS EFFECT IS REQUIRED.
+ BENEFICIARY'S CERTIFICATE CERTIFYING THAT ONE COPY EACH OF INVOICE,N/N B/L HAVE BEEN FAXED TO BUYER TO FAX NO.662-225 WITHIN 3 DAYS AFTER SHIPMENT.

```
2001AN31   07:19:37                                      Logical Terminal GDPF
MTS700                  Issue of a Documentary Credit             Page 00002
                                                                  Func JSRVPR1
Addtional Cond.        47 A :
                 + ALL DOCUMENTS MENTIONING THIS L/C NO.
                 + BOTH AMOUNT AND QUANTITY PLUS OR MINUS 5PCT ACCEPTABLE.
                 + IF ANY DISCREPANCY,WE SHALL DEDUCT USD50.- BEING OUR FEE
                 FROM THE PROCESS.
                 + THE NAME, ADDRESS, TELEPHONE NUMBER OF SHIPPING AGENT IN
                 BANGKOK MUST BE MENTIONED ON B/L.
Details of Charges     71 B : ALL BANK CHARGES OUTSIDE
                              THAILAND INCLUDING COST OF WIRE
                              AND REIM.CHARGE ARE FOR
                              BENEFICIARY'S ACCOUNT.
Confirmation          *49   : WITHOUT
Instructions           78   :
                 + UPON RECEIPT OF SHIPPING DOCUMENTS
                 IN STRICT CONFORMITY WITH L/C TERMS,WE WILL COVER YOUR ACCOUNT
                 AND LESS OUR COST OF WIRE IF ANY ACCORDING TO YOUR INSTRUCTION.
                 + DRAFT(S) AND DOCUMENTS TO BE SENT TO US BY COURIER SERVICE
                 MAILING ADDRESS(SUANMALI IBC.,20 YUKHON 2 RD.,POMPRAB,BANGKOK
                 10100,THAILAND.)
                 + THIS ADVICE IS OPERATIVE WITH NO CONFIRMATION TO FOLLOW AND
                 SUBJECT TO ICC 1993 REVISION PUB 500.
Send. to Rec. Info.  72   : KINDLY ACKNOWLEDGE RECEIPT THIS
                            CREDIT BY RETURN SWIFT WILL BE
                            MUCH APPRECIATED.
Trailer                     Order is <MAC:> <PAC:> <ENC:> <CHK:> <THG:> <PDE:>
                            MAC:642A77D3
                            CHK:4111579499C7
```

请从上面信用证中找出以下内容：

（1）开证人：

（2）受益人：

（3）信用证号码：

（4）开证日期：

（5）信用证有效期及到期地点：

（6）装运港：

（7）目的港：

（8）装运期限：

（9）分批和转船的要求：

（10）商品数量及名称：

（11）要求单据：

（12）交单期限：

（13）信用证金额：

（14）信用证数量和金额增减百分比：

（15）信用证特殊条款：

（16）单据不符点扣费额：

（17）形式发票号码及日期：

（18）贸易术语：

2. 阅读理解二

```
98OCT22   17:15:23                                          Logical Terminal P5A7
MT S700                 Issue of a Documentary Credit                 Page 00001
                                                                      Func GZPRQ
MSGACK  DWS765I Auth OK, key B1980419F862E4A3, BKCHCNBJ SAIBJPJT record652333
Basic Header           F  01 BKCHCNBJA400 8954 778732
Application Header     O 700 1624 981022 SAIBJPJTCXXX 4970 776422 981022 1524 N
                                             *ASAHI BANK LTD. THE (FORMERLY.THE
                                             *KYOWA SAITAMA BANK, LTD.)
                                             *TOKYO
User Header                Service Code     103:
                           Bank. Priority   113:
                           Msg User Ref.    108:
                           Info. from CI    115:
Sequence of Total          *27     : 1 / 1
Form of Doc. Credit        *40 A   : IRREVOCABLE
Doc. Credit Number         *20     : LC-410-046405
Date of Issue               31 C   : 981022
Expiry                     *31 D   : Date 990115 Place CHINA
Applicant                  *50     : SUMITOMO CORPORATION
Beneficiary                *59     : GUANGDONG YUEFENG TRADING CO.
                                     NO.31 ZHEN'AN ROAD GUANGZHOU,
                                     CHINA.
Amount                     *32 B   :            Currency USD Amount 98.000,00
Pos. / Neg. Tol.(%)         39 A   : 5  / 5
Available with/by          *41 D   : ANY BANK
                                     BY NEGOTIATION
Drafts at ...               42 C   : DRAFTS AT SIGHT FOR FULL INVOICE
                                     VALUE
Drawee                      42 A   : SAIBJPJT
                                    *ASAHI BANK LTD, THE (FORMERLY THE
                                    *KYOWA SAITAMA BANK, LTD.)
                                    *TOKYO
Partial Shipments           43 P   : ALLOWED
Transshipment               43 T   : ALLOWED
Loading in Charge           44 A   :
                      SHIPMENT FROM CHINESE MAIN PORT
For Transport to            44 B   :
                         OSAKA, JAPAN
Latest Date of Ship.        44 C   : 981231
Descript. of Goods          45 A   :
                      HALF DRIED PRUNE 1998CROP
                      GRADE    SPEC                QNTY     UNIT PRICE             SHIPMENT
                                                  (CASE)    (USD/CASE)
                       B    L:700CASE  M:700CASE  1,400     21.0  C AND F OSAKA    NOV.,1998
                       A    L:700CASE  M:700CASE  1,400     26.0  C AND F OSAKA    DEC.,1998
                       B    L:700CASE  M:700CASE  1,400     21.0  C AND F OSAKA    DEC.,1998
                      PACKING:IN WOODEN CASE, 12KGS PER CASE
                      TRADE TERMS: C AND F OSAKA
Documents required          46 A   :
                      +2/3 SET OF CLEAN ON BOARD OCEAN BILLS OF LADING MADE OUT TO
                      ORDER OF SHIPPER AND BLANK ENDORSED AND MARKED ''FREIGHT
                      PREPAID'' AND ''NOTIFY SUMITOMO CORPORATION OSAKA.''
                      +MANUALLY SIGNED COMMERCIAL INVOICE IN TRIPLICATE(3) INDICATING
                      APPLICANT'S REF. NO. SCLI-98-0474.
                      +PACKING LIST IN TRIPLICATE(3).
                      +MANUALLY SIGNED CERTIFICATE OF ORIGIN IN TRIPLICATE(3).
                      +BENEFICIARY'S CERTIFICATE STATING THAT CERTIFICATE OF
                      MANUFACTURING PROCESS AND OF THE INGREDIENTS ISSUED BY GUANGDONG
                      YUE FENG TRADING CO., SHOULD BE SENT TO SUMITOMO CORP ESCLZ
                      SECTION.
                      +CERTIFICATE OF WEIGHT AND QUALITY IN TRIPLICATE.
Additional Cond.            47 A   :
                      1. INSURANCE TO BE EFFECTED BY BUYER.
                      2. TELEGRAPHIC REIMBURSEMENT CLAIM PROHIBITED.
```

```
98OCT22  17:15:44                                              Logical Terminal P5A7
MT S700                  Issue of a Documentary Credit                  Page 00002
                                                                        Func GZPRQ
                    3. 1/3 ORIGINAL B/L AND OTHER SHIPPING DOCUMENTS MUST BE SENT
                       DIRECTRY TO APPLICANT SUMITOMO CORP ESCLZ SECTION IN 3 DAYS
                       AFTER B/L DATE. AND SENT BY FAX.
                    4. AMOUNT AND QNTY 5PCT MORE OR LESS ALLOWED.
                    5. THIS COMMODITY FREE FROM RESIN.
Details of Charges    71 B : ALL BANKING CHARGES OUTSIDE JAPAN
                             ARE FOR ACCOUNT OF BENEFICIARY.
Presentation Pariod   48   : DOCUMENTS TO BE PRESENTED WITHIN 15
                             DAYS AFTER THE DATE OF SHIPMENT,
                             BUT WITHIN THE VALIDITY OF THE
                             CREDIT.
Confirmation         *49   : WITHOUT
Instructions          78   :
                  THE NEGOTIATING BANK MUST FORWARD THE DRAFTS AND ALL DOCUMENTS BY
                  REGISTERED AIRMAIL DIRECT TO US (INT'L OPERATIONS OFFICE MAIL
                  ADDRESS: C.P.O.BOX NO.800 TOKYO 100-8691 JAPAN) IN TWO
                  CONSECUTIVE LOTS. UPON RECEIPT OF THE DRAFTS AND DOCUMENTS IN
                  ORDER, WE WILL REMIT THE PROCEEDS AS INSTRUCTED BY THE
                  NEGOTIATING BANK.
Trailer                      Order is <MAC:> <PAC:> <ENC:> <CHK:> <TNG:> <PDE
                             MAC:9E9080D4
                             CHK:AEFC879GF339
```

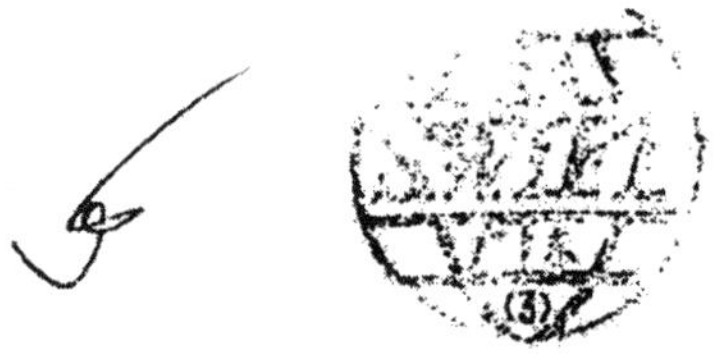

请从该信用证中找出下面的内容：

（1）开证人：

（2）受益人：

（3）信用证号码：

（4）开证日期：

（5）信用证有效期及到期地点：

（6）装运港：

（7）目的港：

（8）装运期限：

（9）分批和转船的要求：

（10）商品数量及名称：

（11）要求单据：

（12）交单期限：

（13）信用证金额：

（14）信用证数量和金额增减百分比：

（15）信用证特殊条款：

（七）信用证审核

1. 信用证审核一

根据下面的合同审核信用证：

售 货 合 同
SALES CONTRACT

卖 方：GUANGDONG LIGHT ELECTRICAL
Sellers: APPLANCES CO., LTD.

Contract No.: 98SGQ468001
Date: APR. 22, 1998
Signed at: GUANGZHOU
Telex: 0835
Fax: 83556688

地 址：
Address: 52 DEZHENG ROAD SOUTH, GUANGZHOU, CHINA

Buyers: ABC CORP.
Address: AKEDSANTERINK AUTO P. O. BOX 9, FINLAND

Telex:
Fax:

This Sales Contract is made by and between the Sellers and the Buyers, whereby the Sellers agree to sell and the Buyers agree to buy the under-mentioned goods according to the terms and conditions stipulated below:

（1）货号、品名及规格 Name of Commodity and Specifications	（2）数量 Quantity	（3）单位 Unit	（4）单价 Unit Price	（5）金额 Amount
HALOGEN FITTING W500	9,600PCS	PC	CIF HELSINKI USD3.80/PC	USD 36,480.00
10% more or less both in amount and quantity allowed	Total Amount			USD 36,480.00

（6）Packing: 12PCS IN A CARTON （7）Delivery from GUANGZHOU to HELSINKI （8）Shipping Marks:

（9）Time of Shipment:

Within 30 days after receipt of L/C allowing transshipment and partial shipment.

（10）Terms of Payment:

By 100% Confirmed irrevocable Letter of Credit in favor of the Sellers to be available by sight draft to be opened and to reach China before MAY 1, 1998 and to remain valid for negotiation in China until the 15th days after the foresaid Time of Shipment. L/C must mention this contract number. L/C advised by BANK OF CHINA, GUANGZHOU BRANCH. TLX: 444U4K GZBC CN. All banking Charges outside China (the mainland of China) are for account of the Drawee.

（11）Insurance:

To be effected by Sellers for 110% of full invoice value covering FPA up to HELSINKI.

~~To be effected by the buyers~~

（12）Arbitration:

All dispute arising from the execution of or in connection with this contract shall be settled amicably by negotiation. In case of settlement can be reached through negotiation the case shall then be submit China International Economic & Trade Arbitration Commision. In Shenzhen (or in Beijing) for arbitration in act with its sure of procedures. The arbitral award is final and binding upon both parties for setting the Disputes. The fee, for arbitration shall be borne by the losing party unless otherwise awarded.

The Seller 张三 The Buyer PAUL

Issue of Documentary Credit

Issuing Bank	:	METITA BANK LTD. , FINLAND
Doc. Credit No.	:	REVOCABLE
Credit Number	:	LRT9802457
Date of Issue	:	980428
Expiry	:	Date 980416 Place FINLAND
Applicant	:	ABC CO. AKEKSANTERINK AUTO P. O. BOX 9, FINLAND
Beneficiary	:	GUANGDONG LIGHT ELECTRICAL APPLANCES CO. , LTD. 52 DEZHENG ROAD SOUTH, GUANGZHOU,CHINA
Amount	:	USD 3,648.00 (SAY US DOLLARS THIRTY SIX THOUSAND FOUR HUNDRED AND EIGHT ONLY)
Pos. / Neg. Tol. (%)	:	5/5
Available with/by	:	ANY BANK IN ADVISING COUNTRY BY NEGOTIATION
Draft at...	:	DRAFTS AT 20 DAYS' SIGHT FOR FULL INVOICE VALUE
Partial Shipments	:	NOT ALLOWED
Transshipment	:	Allowed
Loading in Charge	:	Guangzhou
For Transport to	:	HELSINKI
Shipment Period	:	AT THE LATEST MAY 30, 1998
Descript. of Goods	:	960PCS OF HALOGEN FITTING W500, USD6.80 PER PC AS PER SALES CONTRACT 98SG468001 DD 22, 04, 98 CIF HESINKI
Documents Required	:	* COMMERCIAL INVOICE 1 SIGNED ORIGINAL AND 5 COPIES * PACKING LIST 1 SIGNED ORIGINAL AND 5 COPIES * FULL SET OF CLEAN ON BOARD MARINE BILLS OF LADING, MADE OUT TO ORDER , MARKED "FREIGHT PREPAID" AND NOTIFY APPLICANT (AS INDICATE ABOVE) * GSP CERTIFICATE OF ORIGIN FORM A, CERTIFYING GOODS OF ORIGIN IN CHINA, ISSUED BY COMPETENT AUTHORITIES * INSURANCE POLICY/CERTIFICATE COVERING ALL RISKS AND WAR RISKS OF PICC. INCLUDING WAREHOUSE TO WAREHOUSE CLAUSE UP TO FINAL DESTINATION AT HELSINKI, FOR AT LEAST 120 PCT OF CIF-VALUE. * SHIPPING ADVICES MUST BE SENT TO APPLICANT WITHIN 2 DAYS AFTER SHIPMENT, ADVISING NUMBER OF PACKAGES, GROSS & NET WEIGHT, VESSEL NAME, B/L NO. AND DATE, CONTRACT NO., VALUE.
Presentation Period	:	3 DAYS AFTER ISSUANCE DATE OF SHIPPING DOCUMENT
Confirmation	:	WITHOUT
INSTRUCTIONS	:	THE NEGOTIATION BANK MUST FORWARD THE DRAFTS AND ALL DOCUMENTS BY REGISTERED AIRMAIL DIRECT TO US IN TWO CONSECUTIVE LOTS, UPON RECEIPT OF THE DRAFTS AND DOCUMENTS IN ORDER, WE WILL REMIT THE PROCEEDS AS INSTRUCTED BY THE NEGOTIATING BANK.

2. 信用证审核二

根据下面的销货确认书审核信用证：

卖 方
SICHUAN CHANGHONG
ELECTRIC CO., LTD.
35 EAST MIANXING ROAD,
HIGH - TECH PARK,
MIANYANG, SICHUAN,
CHINA

销 货 确 认 书
SALES CONFIRMATION

号码：
No. 800678
日期：
Date: 13 - 02 - 2005
签约地点：
Signed at: MIANYANG, CHINA
电报挂号：
Cable:
TELEX:
FAX: 86 - 760 - 3138616

买 方
Buyers: ABC CORP. ORATION LIMITED
地 址
Address:

电报挂号：
Cable Address:
TELEX:
FAX:

兹经买卖双方同意按下列条款成交：

The undersigned Sellers and Buyers have agreed to close the following transactions according to the terms and conditions stipulated below:

1.

货 号 Art. No.	品名及规格 Description	数 量 Quantity	单 价 Unit Price	金 额 Amount
80230019	AIR CONDITIONER KFR - 35GW/NL, MODEL, R407C, 220V	10,000SETS	CIF VALENCIA @ USD160.00	USD1,600,000.00

数量及总值均有 5 %的增减，由卖方决定。

With 5 % more or less both in amount and quantity allowed at the Sellers' option.

2. 总 值

Total Value: USD1, 600, 000.00 (US Dollars ONE MILLION SIX HUNDRED THOUSAND ONLY.)

3. 包 装

Packing: ONE SET IN TOW CARTONS, TOTAL 20, 000 CARTONS

4. 装运期

Time of Shipment: 3,000 STES BY 31ST, MARCH 2005, 7,000 SETS BY 15TH, APRIL 2005

5. 装运口岸和目的地

Loading port & Destination: FROM SHENZHENG TO VALENCIA SPAIN

6. 保 险 由卖方按发票全部金额110%投保至______为止的______险。

Insurance: To be effected by Sellers for 110% of full invoice value covering FPA up to VALENCIA SPAIN only.

7. 付款条件： 买方须于 年 月 日将不可撤销的见票30天付款的信用证开到卖方，议付有效期延至上列装运期后15天在中国到期，该信用证中必须注明允许分运及转运。

Terms of payment:

By Irrevocable Letter of Credit to be available by 30 DAYS' AFTER sight draft to reach the Sellers before MAR. 13, 2005 and to remain valid for negotiation in China until the 15th day after the aforesaid Time of Shipment. The L/C must specify that transshipment and partial shipments are allowed.

8. 装船标记

Shipping Mark: N/M

9. 开立信用证时请注明我成交确认书号码。

When opening L/C, Please mention our S/C number.

10. 备 注

Remarks:

卖 方
THE SELLERS
张明华

买 方
THE BUYERS
MARRY

希将本确认书一份签署后寄回本公司

Please sign and one copy of this sales confirmation to us at your earliest convenience.

2005FEB20 Logical Terminal GDPF

MT S700 **Issue of a Documentary Credit** Page 00001

Func JSRVP

User Header	Service Code	103:		
	Bank Priority	113:		
	Msg User Ref.	108:		
	Info. From CI	115:		
Sequence of Total	*27		:	1 / 1
Form of Doc. Credit	*40	A	:	IRREVOCABLE
Doc. Credit Number	*20		:	C20050226
Date of Issue	31	C	:	050220
Expiry	*31	D	:	050430
Applicant	*50		:	ABC CORPORATION LTD. , SPAIN
Beneficiary	*59		:	SICHUAN CHANGHONG ELECTRIC CO. , LTD. 35 EST MIANXING ROAD, HIGH-TECH PARK MIANYANG, SICHUAN, CHINA
Amount	*32	B	:	Currency Amount 1,600,000.00
Pos. / Neg. Tol. (%)	39	A	:	05/05
Available with/by	*41	D	:	ANY BANK BY NEGOTIATION
Draft at ...	42	C	:	30 DAYS' AFTER SIGHT
Drawee	42	D	:	OURSELVES
Partial Shipments	43	P	:	ALLOWED
Transshipment	43	T	:	ALLOWED
Loading in Charge	44	A	:	ANY CHINESE PORTS
For Transport to...	44	B	:	VALENCIA PORT
Shipment Period	44	C	:	LATEST MAR. 30, 2005
Descript. of Goods	45	A	:	

AIR CONDITIONER

KFR-35GW/NL, MODEL, R407C, 220V, 10,000SETS, @USD160.00, CIF VALENCIA 3,000SETS SHIPMENT BY 31ST, MARCH 2005, 7,000SETS SHIPMENT BY 15TH, APRIL 2005, OTHER DETAILES AS PER S/C

Documents required 46 A :

+ COMMERCIAL INVOICE IN 3 COPIES

+ PACKING LIST IN 3 COPIES

+ 2/3 ORIGINAL CLEAN SHIPPED ON BOARD B/L, MADE OUT TO ORDER, MARKED "FREIGHT PREPAID" AND NOTIFY APPLICANT

+ GSP CERTIFICATE OF ORIGIN FORM A, CERTIFYING GOODS OF ORIGIN IN CHINA, ISSUED BY COMPETENT AUTHORITIES

+ INSURANCE POLICY/CERTIFICATE COVERING RISKS FPA OF PICC. INCLUDING WAREHOUSE TO WAREHOUSE CLAUSE, FOR AT LEAST 110 PCT OF CIF-VALUE.

+ SHIPPING ADVICES MUST BE SENT TO APPLICANT WITHIN 2 DAYS AFTER-SHIPMENT ADVISING NUMBER OF PACKAGES, GROSS & NET WEIGHT, VESSEL NAME, BILL OF LADING NO. AND DATE, CONTRACT NO. , VALUE.

2005FEB20　　Logical Terminal GDPF

MT S700　　**Issue of a Documentary Credit**　　Page 00001

Func JSRVP

Addition Cond.　47 A :

1. 1/3 ORIGINAL B/L MUST BE SENT DIRECTRY TO APPLICANT IN 3 DAYS AFTER B/L DATE AND SENT BY FAX.
2. QUANTITY 3PCT MORE OR LESS ALLOWED.
3. ALL DOCUMENTS MUST BE MADE OUT IN ENGLISH LANGUAGE.
4. ALL DOCUMENTS MUST BEAR OUR LETTER OF CREDIT NUMBER.
5. DISCREPANCY FEE OF USD 80.00(OR EQUIVALENT)WILL BE DEDUCTED FROM THE PROCEEDS OF ANY DRAWING IF DOCUMENTS ARE PRESENTED WITH DISCREPANCY (IES) UNDER THIS DOCUMENTARY CREDIT. NOT WITH STANDING ANY INSTRUCTIONS TO THE CONTRARY, THIS CHARGE SHALL BE FOR THE ACCOUNT OF BENEFICIARY.

Details of Charges　71 B :　ALL BANK CHARGES EXCLUDING ISSUING BANKS ARE FOR ACCOUNT OF BENEFICIARY.

Presentation Period　48 :　DOCUMENTS TO BE PRESENTED WITHIN 15 DAYS FROM SHIPMENT DATE.

Confirmation　*49 :　WITHOUT

Instructions　78 :

DISCREPANT DOCUMENTS, IF ACCEPTABLE, WILL BE SUBJECT TO A DISCREPANCY HANDLING FEE OF USD50.00 OR EQUIVALENT WHICH WILL BE FOR ACCOUNT OF BENEFICIARY. ON RECEIPT OF COMPLETE SET OF DOCUMENTS IN CONFORMITY WITH THE TERMS OF THIS CREDIT, WE WILL BE DULY HONOURED ON PRESENTATION IF THE DRAFT(S) ACCEPTED BY APPLICNT.

Send To Rec. Info.　72 :　THIS CREDIT IS ISSUED SUBJECT TO 1993 REVISION, I.C.C. PUBLICATIONS NO. 500

Trailer　　Order is <MAC:><PAC:><ENC:><CHK:><THG:><PDE:>

MAC: AD9A4F07

CHK: E2069EEF189A

二、练习题参考答案

（一）中英文术语、短语互译

1. 中译英

（1）Irrevocable L/C
（2）Date of Issue
（3）T/T Reimbursement
（4）All banking charges
（5）Commission
（6）Drawn under
（7）Original documents
（8）Advising Bank
（9）account
（10）Confirming Bank

2. 英译中

（1）开证人
（2）受益人
（3）议付行
（4）付款行
（5）有效期
（6）跟单信用证
（7）需要的单据
（8）特别条款
（9）总金额不超过
（10）开证人的详细姓名、地址

（二）单项选择题

1. D。理由：根据《UCP600》的规定，不可撤销信用证在信用证的有效期内，未经受益人、开证人以及有关银行的同意，开证行或开证人不得撤销或修改。

2. A。理由：根据《UCP600》的规定，若信用证没有注明“Confirmed”字样，都认为该信用证为不保兑信用证。

3. D。理由：对此类进料加工采用对开信用证，第一张信用证的受益人为外商，我方为开证人，该证用于购买生产加工成品的原材料或配件；第二张信用证的受益人为我方，提供原材料或配件的外商为开证人，用于外商购买我方的产品。

4. C。理由：该选项要求信用证在2002年10月1日止在中国议付有效。其他选项的时间都属于相对固定的时间，必须根据交单日期或装运日期才能确定具体的日期。

5. B。理由：根据《UCP600》第3条的规定，如使用“于或约于（on or about）”之类词语限定装运日期，银行将视为在所述日期前后各5天内装运，起讫日包括在内。

6. A。理由：permitted 和 allowed 都是允许的意思，each item 是指每个品种。

7. A。理由：该选项的中文意思为“一切银行费用由卖方负担”。

8. B。理由：该选项的中文意思为“凡按本信用证所列条款开具并提示的汇票，我行保证承兑”。

9. C。理由：Negotiation Bank 的中文意思为“议付行”。Confirming Bank 为“保兑行”，Opening Bank 为“开证行”，Advising Bank 为“通知行”。

10. C。理由：根据《UCP600》的规定，若信用证没有特别说明，信用证未注明“Confirmed”字样，即为不保兑信用证。

（三）多项选择题

1. ABCDE。理由：在信用证中，Principal、Opener、Applicant、account of ...、Accountee 都表示开证人的意思。

2. ABD。理由：在信用证中，Beneficiary、in favour of ...、in your favour 都表示受益人的意思，Opener 是开证人的意思。

3. CD。理由：在信用证付款方式下，开证行承担第一性的付款责任，保兑行与开证行一样也承担第一性的付款责任。

4. BCD。理由：A 选项中文意思为“装运时如有港口拥挤附加费，应由开证人负担”。

5. ABCDE。理由：本题 5 个选项都是 SWIFT 信用证具有的特点。

（四）判断题

1. 错误。理由：SWIFT 电文的日期表示为 YYMMDD（年月日）。2005 年 6 月 18 日应表示为 050618。

2. 正确。理由：在 SWIFT 电文中，数字不使用分格号，小数点用逗号“,”来表示。

3. 错误。理由：根据《UCP600》第 30 条的规定，信用证不准分批，又没有数量增减条款，则实际装运数量不得增减。只有对于未以包装单位件数或货物自身件数的方式规定货物数量时，货物数量允许有 5% 的增减幅度，只要总支取金额不超过信用证金额。

4. 错误。理由：CHINA PORTS 允许在多个港口装货，即使来证禁止分批，也允许同一条船、同一航次的不同港口装货；但 CHINA PORT 只能在一个中国港口装货。

5. 错误。理由：信用证必须规定有效期，没有有效期的信用证为无效信用证。但信用证可不规定装运期，若没有规定装运期，根据《UCP600》的规定，可理解为双到期。即装运期与信用证的有效期相同。

6. 错误。理由：根据《UCP600》规定，一份信用证的修改通知书的内容要么全部接受，要么全部拒绝，不能接受其中一部分拒绝另一部分。

7. 正确。理由：信用证修改通知书必须由原通知行转递或通知，如由开证人或开证行直接寄给出口商的应提请原证通知行证实。

8. 错误。理由：信用证的性质是银行信用，但信用证项下使用的汇票可以是银行汇票，也可以是商业汇票。实务中，跟单信用证项下使用的汇票多数是商业汇票。

9. 错误。理由：背对背信用证是指转口商收到进口商开来的信用证后，要求该证的通知行或其他银行以该证作为保证，另外开立一张除价格和交货期外，其他条件基本相同的信用证给他的供货人，这张另开的信用证称为背对背信用证。

10. 错误。理由：根据《UCP600》的规定，除非得到信用证所有当事人的一致同意，任何当事人都不得以任何方式改变开证行对该信用证的义务。

（五）案例分析

1. 答：开证行拒绝有理。因为我方要求开证行拒付，实质为撤销信用证，不可撤销信用证未经有关当事人同意不得撤销。开证行在单证相符时必须付款，不管货物是否与合同相符。有关品质与合同不符，进口方应直接向出口方索赔。

2. 答：(1) 保兑行的做法是不正确的。本案是以不可撤销保兑信用证方式结汇的一宗业务。在保兑信用证下，保兑银行与开证银行一样承担第一性的付款责任，其付款依据是只要出口商在信用证有效期内提交符合信用证条款规定的合格单据，保兑行就必须履行付款义务，而不是在开证行不能履行付款义务时才付款，因此，只要我方提交的单据符合信用证的规定，保兑行就应履行付款义务。

(2) 在此情况下，我方应责成保兑行履行付款义务，以确保我方的利益不受损害。

（六）阅读理解

1. 阅读理解一

(1) 开证人：METCH THAI CHEMICAL COMPANY LIMITED
45 -7 MAITRICHITR RD., BANGKOK, THAILAND

(2) 受益人：SINOCHEM GUANGDONG IMPORT AND
EXPORT CORPORATION,
58 ZHANQIAN ROAD, GUANGZHOU, CHINA

(3) 信用证号码：BL 120197

(4) 开证日期：010123

(5) 信用证有效期及到期地点：010422, CHINA

(6) 装运港：GUANGZHOU, CHINA

(7) 目的港：BANGKOK, THAILAND

(8) 装运期限：010412

(9) 分批和转船的要求：允许转船，不允许分批

(10) 商品数量及名称：42.80MT LITHOPONE 30PCT ARROW BRAND

(11) 要求单据：①商业发票；②清洁已装船提单；③保险单或保险凭证；④装箱单；⑤产品分析证明；⑥受益人证明书（证明装运后3天内已发装运通知）；⑦受益人证明书（证明装运后3天内已传真有关单据）。

(12) 交单期限：根据《UCP500》，提单日后21天内，但须在信用证的有效期内。

(13) 信用证金额：USD16,264.00

(14) 信用证数量和金额增减百分比：5%

(15) 信用证特殊条款：①ALL DOCUMENTS MENTIONING THIS L/C NO.; ②THE NAME, ADDRESS, TELEPHONE NUMBER OF SHIPPING AGENT IN BANGKOK MUST BE MENTIONED ON B/L。

(16) 单据不符点扣费额：USD50.00

(17) 形式发票号码及日期：01TH44GD176A3 -032 DATED JAN. 22, 2001

(18) 贸易术语：CIF BANGKOK, THAILAND

2. 阅读理解二

(1) 开证人：SUMITOMO CORPORATION

(2) 受益人：GUANGDONG YUEFENG TRADING CO.
NO. 31 ZHEN'AN ROAD GUANGZHOU, CHINA

(3) 信用证号码：LC -410 -046405

（4）开证日期：981022

（5）信用证有效期及到期地点：990115，CHINA

（6）装运港：CHINESE MAIN PORT

（7）目的港：OSAKA，JAPAN

（8）装运期限：981231

（9）分批和转船的要求：ALLOWED

（10）商品数量及名称：4,200　CASE HALF FRIED PRUNE 1998 CROP

（11）要求单据：①清洁已装船提单；②商业发票；③装箱单；④原产地证；⑤受益人证明书；⑥重量及数量证明书。

（12）交单期限：提单日后 15 天，但须在信用证的有效期内。

（13）信用证金额：USD 98,000.00

（14）信用证数量和金额增减百分比：5%

（15）信用证特殊条款：①1/3 ORIGINAL B/L AND OTHER SHIPPING DOCUMENTS MUST BE SENT DIRECTRY TO APPLICANT SUMITOMO CORP ESCLZ SECTION IN 3 DAYS AFTER B/L DATE,AND SENT BY FAX；②THIS COMMODITY FREE FROM RESIN。

（七）信用证审核

1. 信用证审核一

（1）信用证为可撤销信用证不符合同的要求，应将“REVOCABLE”改为“IRREVOCABLE”。

（2）到期日早于开证日不妥，一般应为开证日后 45 天至 90 天为宜。根据合同，原证应将 4 月 16 日改为 6 月 15 日。

（3）议付信用证的到期地点在国外不妥，应改为中国。

（4）开证人名称错误，应为 ABC CORP. ,而不是 ABC CO. 。

（5）货款金额大小写均与合同不符，应为 USD36,480.00（SAY US DOLLARS THIRTY SIX THOUSAND FOUR HUNDRED AND EIGHTY ONLY.）。

（6）金额增减幅度 5% 与合同不符，应改为允许增减 10% 。

（7）汇票的付款期限为见票 20 天，与合同不符，应删除“20 DAYS’”，改为即期。

（8）信用证不允许分批运输的规定与合同不符，应将“NOT ALLOWED”改为“ALLOWED”。

（9）信用证中的合同号码“98SG468001”写错，应改为 98SGQ468001。

（10）信用证中的投保险别为“ALL RISKS AND WAR RISKS ”与合同条款不符，应改为 F. P. A. 。

（11）信用证中的商品数量为“960PCS”与合同不符，应改为 9,600PCS。

（12）信用证中的商品单价为“USD6.80”与合同不符，应改为 USD3.80。

（13）信用证中的投保加成为“120%”与合同不符，应改为发票金额的“110%”。

（14）信用证中的“CIF HESINKI”目的港拼写错误，应改为“CIF HELSINKI”。

（15）信用证中的交单时间太紧，应把 3 天改为 15 天。

（16）不保兑与合同要求不符，应改为保兑。

（17）信用证没有说明采用 SWIFT 开证，因此，信用证应说明适用的惯例，如 SUBJECT TO “UCP500”。

2. 信用证审核二

（1）信用证金额缺货币单位，应改为“Currency USD Amount 1, 600, 000. 00”。

（2）信用证的装运期限为 3 月 30 日错误，因第二批货物的装运期在 4 月，应改为“LATEST APR. 30, 2005”。

（3）因不是近洋运输，信用证要求三份正本提单中的一份直接寄给开证人，增加受益人的收汇风险，应删除该条款，改为三份正本交银行议付。

（4）信用证数量只有 3% 的增减，与合同条款不符，应改为 5% 。

（5）信用证条款“ON RECEIPT OF COMPLETE SET OF DOCUMENTS IN CONFORMITY WITH THE TERMS OF THIS CREDIT, WE WILL BE DULY HONOURED ON PRESENTATION IF THE DRAFT(S) ACCEPTED BY APPLICANT”说明，银行付款需以开证人在汇票上的承兑为前提，属于软条款，应删除该条款。

（6）货物指定某月某日装运，对受益人不利，因实际中很难做到，船公司或货代一般不接受指定装运日的托运。应改为不迟于某日装运较妥，即：“3，000 SETS SHIPMENT NOT LATER THAN 31ST, MARCH 2005，7，000 SETS SHIPMENT NOT LATER THAN 15TH，APRIL 2005。”

第二章 常用结汇单证

第一节 发 票

一、练习题

（一）中英文术语、短语互译

1. 中译英

（1）商业发票　（2）海关发票

（3）运费　（4）保险费

（5）佣金　（6）折扣

（7）付款方式　（8）生产国别

（9）运输方式　（10）一式三份

2. 英译中

（1）Invoice No.　（2）Date

（3）Marks & Nos　（4）Contract No.

（5）Shipped from... to...　（6）Description of Goods

（7）Quantity　（8）Unit Price

（9）Amount Total　（10）Currency of Settlement

（二）单项选择题

1. 信用证的货物名称错把 BLACK TEA（红茶）写作 BLACK TEE，审证时没留意到这个问题，那么制作单据时应（　　）。

A. 改作“BLACK TEA”

B. 按原文写作“BLACK TEE”

C. 按原文写作“BLACK TEE”，然后在后面加上（BLACK TEA）

D. 把“信用证”改成“托收”收款

2. 根据《UCP600》的规定，商业发票中货物的描述（　　）。

A. 可以使用统称，不得与信用证中有关货物的描述有抵触

B. 可以使用统称，并可与信用证中有关货物的描述有所不同

C. 必须完全符合信用证中的描述

D. 必须与合同的描述完全一致

3. 一般情况下，发票金额应与（　　）一致。

A. 合同金额　　B. 信用证金额

C. 保险金额　　D. 汇票金额

4. 来证规定："COMMERCIAL INVOICE IN TRIPLICATE CERTIFYING THAT THE GOODS HEREIN ARE IN ACCORDANCE WITH THOSE SPECIFIED IN THE S/C NO. 9857"，制作发票时应（　　）。

A. 商业发票一式两份，然后在发票上注明"COMMERCIAL INVOICE IN TRIPLICATE CERTIFYING THAT THE GOODS HEREIN ARE IN ACCORDANCE WITH THOSE SPECIFIED IN THE S/C NO. 9857"

B. 商业发票一式三份，然后在发票上注明"COMMERCIAL INVOICE IN TRIPLICATE CERTIFYING THAT THE GOODS HEREIN ARE IN ACCORDANCE WITH THOSE SPECIFIED IN THE S/C NO. 9857"

C. 商业发票一式三份，然后在发票上注明"WE CERTIFY THAT THE GOODS HEREIN ARE IN ACCORDANCE WITH THOSE SPECIFIED IN THE S/C NO. 9857"

D. 商业发票一式两份，然后在发票上注明"WE CERTIFY THAT THE GOODS HEREIN ARE IN ACCORDANCE WITH THOSE SPECIFIED IN THE S/C NO. 9857"

5. 如来证没有申请人（或付款人）一栏，而是直接指明汇票付款人时，如"WE OPEN CREDIT NO. PS8803 AVAILABLE BY DRAFTS DRAWN ON EEC CO., LTD."，那么发票的抬头人应做成（　　）。

A. 不填　　B. 开证行

C. DRAWN ON EEC CO., LTD.　　D. EEC CO., LTD.

6. 合同规定按 CIF 价成交，已知总 CIF 价为 USD17,200，运费为 USD2,528，保险费为 3%，来证要求分别注明 FOB 价、运费、保险费，那么制作发票时填写正确的是(　　)。

A. TOTAL FOB VALUE　USD14,156.00
　FREIGHT　USD2,528.00
　INSURANCE　USD516.00
　TOTAL CIF VALUE　USD17,200.00

B. TOTAL CIF VALUE　USD17,200.00

C. TOTAL FOB VALUE　USD13,956.00
　FREIGHT　USD2,528.00
　INSURANCE　USD716.00
　TOTAL CIF VALUE　USD17,200.00

D. TOTAL FOB VALUE　USD13,956.00
　FREIGHT　USD2,528.00
　INSURANCE　USD716.00

7. 假如信用证的价格条款规定，商品的价格为 STG4.00，CIFC5 London，且商品数量为 6,145PCS，信用证的金额为扣除佣金的净值，那么在发票总值栏中的金额应填写（　　）。

A. CIFC5 London	STG24,580.00
－C5	STG1,229.00
CIF London	STG23,351.00
B. CIFC5 London	STG24,580.00
－C5	STG2,229.00
CIF London	STG22,351.00
C. CIFC5 London	STG24,580.00
－C5	STG1,299.00
CIF London	STG23,281.00
D. CIFC5 London	STG24,580.00
－C5	STG1,339.00
CIF London	STG23,241.00

8. 海关发票是由（　　）制定的一种特殊发票格式。

A. 出口方　　B. 进口方

C. 出口国海关　　D. 进口国海关

9. 根据《UCP600》的规定，信用证金额前有"大约"、"大概"或类似的词语，交货时允许总值有（　　）的增减幅度。

A. 5%　　B. 3%

C. 10%　　D. 20%

10. 海关发票的抬头一般应该是（　　）。

A. 开证申请人　　B. 受益人

C. 进口国海关　　D. 进口地的收货人

（三）多项选择题

1. 商业发票的作用主要有（　　）。

A. 进出口报关完税必不可少的单据　　B. 是全套单据的中心

C. 是结算货款的依据　　D. 是物权凭证

2. 发票的抬头人应是（　　）。

A. 托收项下的卖方　　B. 托收项下的买方

C. 信用证项下的受益人　　D. 信用证项下的开证申请人

3. 某来证规定："ABOUT 20 MT CITRIC ACID MONO BP80 AT USD1,180.00/MT CFR HAIFA PORT"，"PCT credit amount tolerance：10/10"，"CURRENCY CODE AMOUNT：USD23,600.00"，那么以下发票的数量和金额可以符合规定的是（　　）。

A. 20 MT，USD23,600.00　　B. 25 MT，USD29,500.00

C. 22 MT，USD25,960.00　　D. 18 MT，USD21,240.00

4. 海关发票的主要内容包括（　　）。

A. 商品数量　　B. 商品成本价值
C. 商品的生产国家　　D. 商品的品质

5. 海关发票的主要作用是（　　）。
A. 作为进口货物估价完税的依据　　B. 是买卖双方收付货款的依据
C. 核定货物原产地的依据　　D. 进口国海关统计资料的依据

（四）判断题

1. 商业发票日期应早于提单日期。（　　）
2. 商业发票是由买方开给卖方的价目清单，是出口交易中最重要的单据之一。（　）
3. 信用证规定：FROM CHINA PORT TO LONDON 发票上应严格按照信用证要求填上“FROM CHINA PORT TO LONDON”。（　　）
4. 按照《UCP600》规定，无论信用证有无规定，商业发票必须签章才能生效。（　　）
5. 除非信用证另有规定，银行将不接受出单日期早于信用证开立日期的单据。（　　）
6. 除非信用证另有规定，商业发票必须由信用证的受益人开立。（　　）
7. 商业发票的主要内容包括货物名称、数量、单价、总价等。（　　）
8. 海关发票是由进口国海关制定并由进口方填制的一种特殊发票格式的书面单据。（　　）
9. 海关发票中“出口国国内价格”一栏，应以出口国货币填写 CIF 价格，同时应注意价格不得低于该出口商品在国内的价格，否则将被进口国视为低价倾销。（　　）
10. 有的来证要求在发票上加注“证明所列内容真实无误”，我们为避免麻烦应一律拒绝。（　　）

（五）案例分析

1. 有一份信用证对货物的描述如下：7,000PCS OF 100% COTTON SHIRTS AT USD9.60 PER PCS AS PER CONTRACT NO. 02AB120 FOB QINGDAO。开证行收到单据后经审核发现商业发票未注明 FOB QINGDAO，因此认为单证不符而拒绝付款。而受益人认为价格术语并不是货物描述的一部分，而且其已经在提单中注明了“FREIGHT COLLECT”，表明价格术语就是 FOB 价，因此单证是相符的。请问哪一方有理？

2. 某轻工业品进出口公司出口一批商品，于 3 月 4 日收到信用证，信用证中条款规定：“... Amount: USD616,000.00... Quantity: 400M/T (quantity 5% more or less allowed), Price: @USD1,540.00 per M/T net, CIF Hamburg. Shipments to Hamburg immediately. Partial shipments are not allowed.”（……总金额 616,000.00 美元。……某商品 400 公吨，数量允许增减 5%。价格：每公吨净重 1,540.00 美元，CIF 汉堡。立即装运至汉堡。不许分批装运。）轻工业品进出口公司根据信用证条款，在接到信用证后立即安排装运出口。轻工业品进出口公司于 4 月 7 日将货装运出口，取得 4 月 7 日签发的已装船的提单，并备妥信用证项下所需的其他单据向议付行交单办理议付。议付行经审单发现单证不符，不同意议付，因信用证规定总金额为 USD616,000.00，而发票和汇票金额却为

USD634, 480. 00，议付金额比信用证规定总金额超出 USD18, 480. 00。轻工业品进出口公司认为其不符点不成立，即向议付行申述：信用证规定 400 公吨货物的数量，又规定装运数量可允许增减 5%。按 400 公吨的增减 5% 计算，即最高可以装 420 公吨，最低可以装 380 公吨。我们实际只装了 412 公吨，仅增装 3%，不超出信用证规定的 5% 范围。信用证规定每公吨单价 USD1, 540. 00，按 412 公吨计算，其总金额即 USD634, 480. 00，是信用证允许的，所以说其单证不符是不成立的。你认为轻工业品进出口公司的理由是否充分？其能否顺利收取货款？最后应如何处理为妥？

（六）阅读理解

1. 阅读理解一

HUIZOU TEA IMPORT & EXPORT CORPORATION

6 NANTAN EAST ROAD, HUIZHOU, GUANGDONG, CHINA

INVOICE

TO MESSRS.:
YAKAHUCHI CO., LTD.
NO. 689 NADA - KU, KOBE,
JAPAN

INVOICE NO.: SHE01/7203
DATE: MAY 27, 2002
L/C NO.: COM 8722732
CONTRACT NO.: HZT(02)003

TRANSPORT DETAILS:
FROM SHENZHEN TO KOBE VIA HONGKONG
BY VESSEL

TERMS OF PAYMENT:
BY SIGHT L/C

MARKS & NOS.	DESCRIPTION	QUANTITY	UNIT PRICE (USD)	AMOUNT (USD)
R. AND D.	AS PER S/C NO.:HZT(02)003			
RIO HAINA	APPLICANT'S REF NO. 3 - 1190			
R. 10.990 D.				
	BLACK TEA	6,000KGS	1.22/KG	USD7,320.00
		TOTAL: 6,000KGS	CIF KOBE	USD7,320.00

FOB VALUE:
USD6,620.00
FREIGHT CHARGES:
USD600.00
INSURANCE PRMIUM:
USD100.00

WE CERTIFY THAT THE ABOVE GOODS ARE OF CHINESE ORIGIN.

根据上面单据找出下列内容：

（1）出口商名称：

（2）发票抬头人：

（3）发票号码：

（4）发票日期：

（5）合同号码：

（6）付款方式：

（7）装运港：

（8）目的港：

（9）转运港：

（10）运输方式：

（11）货物描述：

（12）价格术语：

（13）商品单价：

（14）总值：

（15）唛头：

（16）运费：

（17）保险费：

（18）证明文句：

2. 阅读理解二

根据下面单据找出下列内容：

（1）出票人名称：

（2）发票抬头人：

（3）发票号码：

（4）发票日期：

（5）合同号码：

（6）信用证号码：

（7）付款方式：

（8）装运港：

（9）目的港：

（10）转运港：

（11）运输方式：

（12）运输工具名称：

（13）货物名称：

（14）商品编码：

（15）价格术语：

（16）数量：

（17）总值：

（18）唛头：

（19）原产国：

（20）证明文句：

Issuer GAWEN COMPANY LIMITED, AUSTRALIA	**COMMERCIAL INVOICE**	
To JIANGXI JIANGHAI GARMENTS IMPORT AND EXPORT CO. ,LTD. NO. 25 CHANGDAI ROAD, NANCHANG CITY, JIANGXI, CHINA	No. GA289	Date 20/05/2004
Transport details FROM: SYDNEY, AUSTRALIA W/T: TO: FUZHOU, CHINA VESSEL: Northern WIND	S/C No. J0254	L/C No. ZJJ04LC0300135
	Terms of payment D/P At Sight	

Marks and Numbers	Number and kind of packages; Description of goods	Quantity	Unit price	Amount
	LEATHER GARMENTS H. S. CODE:62011210			
GAWEN	ART 1212/100	200 PCS	USD52. 20	USD10,440. 00
SYDNEY	ART 1212/32	500 PCS	USD54. 20	USD27,100. 00
NO. 1 – 160	ART 1213/00	400 PCS	USD56. 40	USD22,560. 00
	ART 1214/00	350 PCS	USD58. 20	USD20,370. 00
	ART 1215/00	500 PCS	USD62. 00	USD31,000. 00
	ART 1216/00	400 PCS	USD65. 20	USD26,000. 00
	TOTAL:	2,350 PCS	CFR FUZHOU	USD137,470. 00

TOTAL: US DOLLARS ONE HUNDRED THIRTY SEVEN THOUSAND FOUR HUNDRED AND SEVENTY ONLY.

WE CERTIFY THAT THE GOODS ARE IN ACCORDANCE WITH PURCHASE ORDER NUMBER 8803.

（七）单据填制

1. 单据填制一

根据有关信用证条款和参考资料缮制发票。（空白发票见本书 248 页）

A. 信用证有关条款。

Issuing bank: THE SAKURA BANK, LIMITED
56, NANIWA - CHO, CHUO - KU, KOBE, JAPAN

20 /documentary credit number: KUW25847

31c /date of issue: May 15, 2004

31d /date and place of expiry: June 30, 2004 beneficiaries' country

50 /applicant: MOMO CO., LTD.
NO. 215 NADA - KU, KOBE, JAPAN

59 /beneficiary: HUNAN TEA IMPORT & EXPORT CORPORATION
WUYI ROAD, CHANGSHA, HUNAN, CHINA

32 /currency code amount: USD26, 640. 00

39a /percent credit amt tolerance: 05 / 05

41d /available with... by...: Any bank in china by negotiation

45a /descript. of goods and/or services:

As per S/C No. HNT (04) 021
Applicant's Ref No. 3 - 1190
12, 000 kgs Pu-erh tea at USD2. 22 per kg. CIF Kobe
Packed : in 50 kgs per cartons

46a /documents required:

+ commercial invoice in one original plus 6 copies, showing that the goods exported are of Chinese Origin, all of which must be manually signed.

47a/ additional conditions:

+ all documents required under this credit must mention this L/C number and the issuing bank name.

B. 参考资料。

2004 年 6 月 12 日装 "FENGQING V. 25" 从广州出运。

唛头自行设计。

发票号码：HT - 04 - 28931

2. 单据填制二

根据有关信用证条款和参考资料缮制发票。（空白发票见本书 249 页）

A. 信用证有关条款。

We hereby establish our Irrevocable Documentary Credit No. MNL030850 dated AUG. 25, 2003 by order and for account of MRISSINA GARMENTS INC (8/F EXECUTIVE BLDG. CENTER GIL PUYAT COR MAKATI AVE. MAKATI CITY PHILIPPINES) in favor of CHINA TEXTILES IMPORT AND EXPORT CORP. (8 DONG' AN ROAD, BEIJING, CHINA) for the amount of USD179, 700. 00 available by your manually signed Drafts drawn on us at sight for full invoice value. Covering the following goods:

CIF MANILA, DISCOUNT OF 5% DEDUCTED

54, 000 YARDS 100PCT COTTON DARK NAVY DENIM, 12 OZ. CTW0945 USD2. 75 PER YARD

12, 000 YARDS 100PCT COTTON INDIGO BLACK DENIM, 11 OZ. CTW0939 USD2. 60 PER YARD

AS PER PROFORMA INVOICE NOS. PI－187/2003 DATED 08AUG2003

ACCOMPANIED BY THE FOLLOWING DOCUMENTS：

＋SINGED COMMERCIAL INVOICE IN QUADRUPLICATE INDICATING L/C NUMBER AND TOTAL NUMBER OF PACKAGES.

B．参考资料。

INVOICE NO. MM024

DATED SEP. 10，2003

SHIPPING MARKS：

M. G. I

MANITA

NO. 1－795

TOTAL PACKAGES：　DARK NAVY DENIM 466 ROLLS

INDIGO BLACK DENIM 329 ROLLS

TOTAL 795 ROLLS

SHIPPED PER S. S. “MAYOR” V. 36 FROM DALIAN TO MANILA ON SEP. 8，2003

3．单据填制三

根据有关信用证条款和参考资料缮制发票。（空白发票见本书 250 页）

A．信用证有关条款。

Type of Documentary Credit：IRREVOCABLE

Letter of Credit Number：LC84E0081/99

Date of Issue：990916

Date and Place of Expiry：991015 CHINA

Applicant Bank：FIRST SEOUL CITY BANK，LTD.

Applicant：SANGYONG CORPORATION

CPO BOX 110

SEOUL，KOREA

Beneficiary：DALIAN WEIDA TRADING CO.，LTD.

Currency Code Amount：about USD12，400，less 5% commission and 5% allowance（dis.）

Available with... by...：ANY BANK BY NEGOTIATION

Drafts at...：45 DAYS AFTER SIGHT

Drawee：US

Partial Shipments：NOT ALLOWED

Transshipment：NOT ALLOWED

Shipping on Board/Dispatch/Packing in Charge at/ from：DALIAN PORT，P. R. CHINA

Transportation to：RUSSIAN SEA

Latest Date of Shipment：991013

Description of Goods or Services：

RORCELAIN POT AS PER SALES CONTRACT NO. TH99/1689 DATED 13 JUN. 1999

6－1/2 “DAI×6－1/2” H PORCELAIN FLOWER WHITE POT 4，000PCS

W/PINK/PURPLE FLOWER PATTERN

EACH/BUBBLE WRAPPED

4PCS/3－LAYER STRONG INNER

16PCS/5－LAYER STRONG CARTON

AT USD3. 10 PER PC. CIF RUSSIAN SEA

Documents Required:

1. BENEFICIARY'S MANUALLY SIGNED ORIGINAL COMMERCIAL INVOICES IN DUPLICATE CERTIFYING MERCHANDISE OF CHINESE ORIGIN AND SHOWING HAMERNISED CODE 6913. 9000.

B. 其他资料自拟。

（八）单据改错

1. 单据改错一

广东省华联贸易有限公司与加拿大的 EEN 公司成交了一笔出口交易，EEN 公司按期开来信用证，华联贸易有限公司备货出运后收妥提单，立即制作好全套单证并准备交单议付，请根据以下信用证提供的内容审核并修改其中的商业发票。

DOC. CREDIT NUMBER:	044/307587
APPLICANT:	EEN CO. , Vancouver, CANADA
BENEFICIARY:	GUANGDONG HUALIAN TRADING CORPORATION 60 HUHAI ROAD GUANGZHOU, CHINA
AMOUNT CURRENCY:	USD5, 256. 00
AVAILABLE WITH/BY:	FREELY NEGOTIABLE AT ANY BANK BY NEGOTIATION
LOADING IN CHARGE:	CHINA
FOR TRANSPORT TO:	Vancouver VIA HONGKONG
LATEST DATE OF SHIPMENT:	020131

DESCRIPTION OF GOODS:

2, 920YDS OF 100PCT COTTON DENIM - 8 OZ - ROPE DYED INDIGO (CT - 121)

DOUBLE P/SHRUNK RESIDUAL AHRINKAGE NOT MORE THAN 3 - 4PCT 82 × 50/14S × 14S - WIDTH: 58/59'

AT USD1. 80/YD AS PER PURCHASE ORDER NO. FAB10 - 20030087/01 - 02, CIF Vancouver

DOCUMENTS REQUIRED: + SIGNED COMMERCIAL INVOICE IN TRIPLICATE.

GUANGDONG HUALIA TRADING CORPORATION
60 **HUHAI ROAD, GUANGZHOU, CHINA**

INVOICE

TO MESSRS.: EEN CO.,
VANCOUVER, CANADA

INVOICE NO.: SHE01/7203
DATE: JAN. 28, 2002
L/C NO.: 044/387587
P. O. No.: FAB10-20030087/01-02

SHIPPED FROM GUANGZHOU TO VANCOUVER

MARKS & NOS.	DESCRIPTION	QUANTITY	UNIT PRICE	AMOUNT
GOLDTRON GARMENTS SDN BHD PO NO. FAB10-20030087/01-02 COLOR: INDIGO R/NO.: 1-4, 6-36				
		2, 928 YARDS	USD1.80/YARD	USD5, 256.00

100PCT COTTON DENIM-8 OZ-ROPE DYED INDIGO (CT-121)
DOUBLE P/SHRUNK RESIDUAL AHRINKAGE NOT MORE THAN
3-4PCT 82×50/14S×14S-WIDTH: 58/59'
AS PER PURCHASE ORDER NO. FAB10-20030087/01-02

TOTAL: US DOLLARS FIVE THOUSAND TWO HUNDRED FITY SIX ONLY.

2. 单据改错二

天津体育用品进出口公司向日本的 Tokyo Keyboard Distributer 出口一批足球，该公司在货物出运后立即着手制单结汇，请根据以下的信用证内容审核并修改其制作的商业发票。

Name of Issuing Bank : The Mitsui Bank Ltd. , Tokyo, 15 Marunouche 3 – Chome

Place and date of issue : 3 March, 1999, Tokyo, Japan

To: Tianjin Sporting Goods Imp. & Exp. Corp.

68 Yentai Street, Tianjin, China

This Credit is advised through Bank of China, 50 Yentai Street, Tianjin, China.

Dear Sirs,

By order and for account of Tokyo Keyboard Distributer, 12 – 14 Monmachi 3 – Chome, Tokyo, Japan. We hereby issue an Irrevocable Documentary Credit No. 901026 for USD5,600. 00 (say US dollars five thousand six hundred only) to expire on 30 June, 1999 in China available with any bank in China by negotiation against beneficiary's draft(s) at sight drawn on us and the documents detailed herein, marked with " × ";

[×] Commercial Invoice in triplicate visaed by the chamber of commerce certifying goods origin.

[×] Full set 2/2 originals clean on board marine Bills of Lading made out to order and blank endorsed marked freight prepaid notifying Tokyo Keyboard Distributer, 12 – 14 Monmachi 3 – Chome, Tokyo, Japan.

[×] Packing List in triplicate.

[×] Certificate of Origin in China.

[×] Insurance Policy or Certificate covering All Risks and War Risk for 110% of the invoice value stipulating claim, if any, to be payable in currency of the draft.

[×] Certificate of Weight in triplicate.

[×] Certificate of Analysis in triplicate Evidencing shipment of 1, 600PCS GBW32P Football USD3. 5/PC CIF Tokyo AS PER S/C NO. TSG0215.

Shipping Marks: TTK/TOKYO/NO. 1 – 520

Shipment from Tianjin port to Tokyo not later than 16 June, 1999.

Partial shipment: allowed

Transshipment: not allowed

Documents to be presented within 15 days after the date of the transport documents but within the validity of the credit.

We hereby engage with drawers and /or bona fide holders that drafts drawn and negotiated in conformity with the terms of Credit will be fully honored on presentation.

Instructions to the advising bank:

Please advise the Credit to the beneficiary:

The number and the date of the Credit must be quoted on all documents required.

Please acknowledge receipt.

Reimbursement: The negotiating bank is authorized to claim reimbursement on The Mitsui Bank Ltd. , New York by telex. All drafts and documents must be sent to us by airmail.

Yours faithfully,
The Mitsui Bank Ltd. , Tokyo
Signature(s)

Tianjin Sporting Goods Imp. & Exp. Corp.
68 **Yentai Street, Tianjin, China**

TO MESSRS.: Tokyo Keyboard Distributer,
12 – 14 Monmachi 3 – Chome,
Tokyo, Japan

INVOICE NO.: TS99012
INVOICE DATE: JUNE 12, 1999
L/C NO.: 901026
S/C NO.: TSG0205

TRANSPORT DETAILS:
From Tianjin port to Tokyo by Vessel

MARKS & NOS.	DESCRIPTION	QUANTITY	UNIT PRICE	AMOUNT
TK TOKYO NO. 1 – 520	GBW32P Football	1, 600PCS	USD3.5/PC	USD5, 600.00

TOTAL: US DOLLARS FIVE THOUSAND SIX HUNDRED ONLY.

受益人签章

二、练习题参考答案

（一）中英文术语、短语互译

1. 中译英

(1) Commercial Invoice (2) Customs Invoice
(3) Freight Charge (4) Insurance Premium
(5) Commission (6) Discount
(7) Terms of Payment (8) Country of Origin of Goods
(9) Means of Transportation (10) In Triplicate

2. 英译中

(1) 发票号码 (2) 日期
(3) 唛头及件号 (4) 合同号
(5) 装运从……至…… (6) 货物内容
(7) 数量 (8) 单价
(9) 总价 (10) 货币名称

（二）单项选择题

1. C。理由：商品名称和规格，原则上保持与信用证完全一致。如有个别字母笔误，可以在错误品名后另注正确词句并加括号。

2. C。理由：《UCP600》第 18 条 c 款的规定：商业发票中货物的描述必须与信用证中的描述相一致。在一切其他单据中，货物描述可使用与信用证中对货物的描述无矛盾的统称。

3. D。理由：因为汇票是按照发票制作的，所以除非信用证另有规定，一般情况下，发票金额须与汇票金额保持一致。

4. C。理由："IN TRIPLICATE" 为一式三份，证明文句前应加主语 "WE"，并非全部照抄。

5. D。理由：如来证没有申请人（或付款人）一栏，而是直接指明汇票付款人时，那么汇票付款人就是发票抬头人。

6. A。理由：FOB 与 CIF 的价格转换公式是 FOB = CIF ×（1 - 保险费率）- 运费，应严格按信用证要求分别填写 FOB 价、运费、保险费。

7. A。理由：含佣价和佣金的计算公式为：含佣价 = 净价/（1 - 佣金率）；佣金 = 含佣价 × 佣金率。

8. D。理由：海关发票是由进口国海关制定的一种专用于向该国出口的一种特别的发票格式。

9. C。理由：根据《UCP600》第 30 条 a 款的规定，信用证金额前有"大约"、"大概"或类似的词语，交货时允许总值有不超过 10% 的增减幅度。

10. D。理由：海关发票的抬头不同于商业发票，一般是货物在进口地的收货人，也就是提单的被通知人。

（三）多项选择题

1. ABC。理由：发票是所有单据中的中心单据，作用很大，但本身没有价值，不能代表货物所有权，不能转让。

2. BD。理由：发票的抬头人如属托收方式，一般为合同的买方；如属信用证方式，按信用证规定填，一般为开证申请人。

3. ACD。理由：《UCP600》第 30 条 a 款的规定，信用证数量有"大约"等字样的，交货数量允许有不超过 10% 的增减幅度。

4. BC。理由：海关发票的主要内容是证明商品的成本价值和商品的原产国别。

5. ACD。理由：商业发票才是买卖双方收付货款的依据。

（四）判断题

1. 正确。

2. 错误。理由：商业发票应是由卖方开给买方的注有品名、数量、价格、支付条件及装运内容的清单。

3. 错误。理由：发票上应注明实际装运港口，而不能笼统地写中国港口。

4. 错误。理由：《UCP600》第 18 条规定，除非信用证另有规定，商业发票不需要签名。

5. 错误。理由：《UCP600》第 14 条 I 款规定，除非信用证另有规定，银行将接受出单日期早于信用证开立日期的单据，但不得晚于交单日期。

6. 正确。

7. 正确。

8. 错误。理由：海关发票由进口国海关制定格式，但须由出口方填写内容。

9. 错误。理由：海关发票中“出口国国内价格”一栏，应以出口国货币填写 FOB 价格。

10. 错误。理由：遇到这种情况，我们应在不违背我国方针、政策和法令的情况下，酌情办理，办理时应将发票下端通常印有的“有错当查（E. &O. E.)”字样删去。

（五）案例分析

1. 开证行有理。理由是《UCP600》第 18 条 c 款规定，商业发票的货物描述必须与信用证中的描述一致。FOB QINGDAO 的文字放在货物描述这一部分，因此被视为货物描述的一部分。因此，需要在商业发票上说明来满足这个要求。由于提交的商业发票中未注明贸易术语 FOB QINGDAO，银行有权把单据看做不符而拒绝接受。

2. 分析：轻工业品进出口公司的主要缺点就是在审证时未发现信用证只在数量上规定允许增减装 5%，而信用证金额并没有所增加的幅度。轻工业品进出口公司没有严格审查和注意这个问题，误认为信用证既然允许数量可以增减装 5%，所以就增装了 3%，结果造成信用证金额不够。一般以重量为计量单位的货物，如果允许有增减装的幅度要求，条款应作类似这样的规定：“Amount of credit and quantity of merchandise 5% more or less acceptable”（信用证的金额及货物的数量均可允许 5% 增减），该条款就明确指出金额及货量均可增减 5%。像本案例的信用证只在数量上允许增减 5%，而金额既没有增减的条款，也未在信用证总金额的数额中含有 5%，这样的信用证在实际装运数量上只能掌握减装 5%，不能增装。如果要增装，只有向买方提出修改信用证，以增加金额的增减条款。

（六）阅读理解

1. 阅读理解一

（1）出口商名称：HUIZOU TEA IMPORT & EXPORT CORPORATION

（2）发票抬头人：YAKAHUCHI CO. , LTD.

（3）发票号码：SHE01/7203

（4）发票日期：MAY 27, 2002

（5）合同号码：HZT（02）003

（6）付款方式：BY SIGHT L/C

（7）装运港：SHENZHEN

（8）目的港：KOBE

（9）转运港：HONGKONG

（10）运输方式：BY VESSEL

（11）货物描述：BLACK TEA

（12）价格术语：CIF KOBE

（13）商品单价：USD1. 22/KG

（14）总值：USD7,320. 00

（15）唛头：R. AND D.
RIO HAINA
R. 10. 990 D.

（16）运费：USD600. 00

（17）保险费：USD100. 00

（18）证明文句：WE CERTIFY THAT THE ABOVE GOODS ARE OF CHINESE ORIGIN.

2. 阅读理解二

（1）出票人名称：GAWEN COMPANY LIMITED，AUSTRALIA

（2）发票抬头人：JIANGXI JIANGHAI GARMENTS IMPORT AND EXPORT CO.，LTD.

（3）发票号码：NO. GA289

（4）发票日期：20/05/2004

（5）合同号码：J0254

（6）信用证号码：ZJJ04LC0300135

（7）付款方式：D/P At Sight

（8）装运港：SYDNEY

（9）目的港：FUZHOU

（10）转运港：无转运

（11）运输方式：BY VESSEL

（12）运输工具名称：Northern WIND

（13）货物名称：LEATHER GARMENTS

（14）商品编码：62011210

（15）价格术语：CFR FUZHOU

（16）数量：2,350 PCS

（17）总值：USD137,470. 00

（18）唛头：GAWEN
SYDNEY
NO. 1－160

（19）原产国：AUSTRALIA

（20）证明文句：WE CERTIFY THAT THE GOODS ARE IN ACCORDANCE WITH PURCHASE ORDER NUMBER 8803.

（七）单据填制

1. 单据填制一

简要提示：本题是考核按照 SWIFT 标准格式信用证制作商业发票，注意要点：

—读懂本证英文内容，找出制单资料。

—发票内须注明信用证的证明文句。

—按信用证的附加条款要求注明信用证号码和开证行名称。

—唛头可由卖方自行设计，标准唛头的设计由 4 行组成，每行不超过 17 个英文字母，第一栏为收货人简称，第二栏为目的港，第三栏为参考号（例如合同号等），第四栏为件号。

—商业发票的号码由出口企业按习惯编排，一般以企业开头大写字母加年份加序列号编排。

2. 单据填制二

简要提示：本题是考核按照非标准格式信用证制作商业发票，注意要点：

—读懂本证英文内容，找出制单资料。

—折扣的计算和扣除方法。

—发票内应注明信用证号码和总件数。

3. 单据填制三

简要提示：本题是考核信用证金额既有佣金又有折扣时，应如何制作商业发票金额，注意要点：

—读懂本证英文内容，找出制单资料。

—发票内须注明货物原产地和商品编码6913.9000。

—需按照信用证内列出的一系列时间，合理填写发票制作时间，按习惯方法自拟发票号码和唛头。

—发票金额的制作方法：应在总金额（单价×数量）中先扣除5%优惠（折扣），得出一个毛净价，然后在此基础上再扣除5%佣金，得出净价。在既有折扣又有佣金的交易中，我们应掌握先扣除折扣，然后再计扣佣金，因为折扣部分是不应支付佣金的。具体金额制作如下：

4,000 PCS @ USD 3.10	USD12,400.00
Less 5% allowance:	USD620.00
	USD11,780.00
Less 5% commission:	USD589.00
CIF RUSSIAN SEA net:	USD11,191.00

（八）单据改错

1. 单据改错一

—受益人名称漏打“N”，应为“GUANGDONG HUALIAN TRADING CORPORATION”；

—信用证号码错了，应为“044/307587”；

—运输路线应注明经香港转船到温哥华；

—数量应为2,920 YARDS；

—单价漏打价格术语：CIF Vancouver；

—总价应为US DOLLARS FIVE THOUSAND TWO HUNDRED FIFTY SIX ONLY.；

—最后应按信用证要求签章。

正确单据如下：

GUANGDONG HUALIAN TRADING CORPORATION

60 **HUHAI ROAD, GUANGZHOU, CHINA**

INVOICE

TO MESSRS.: EEN CO.,
VANCOUVER, CANADA

INVOICE NO.: SHE01/7203
DATE: JAN. 28, 2002
L/C NO.: 044/307587
P. O. NO.: FAB10 - 20030087/01 - 02

SHIPPED FROM GUANGZHOU TO VANCOUVER VIA HONGKONG

MARKS & NOS.	DESCRIPTION	QUANTITY	UNIT PRICE	AMOUNT
GOLDTRON GARMENTS SDN BHD PO NO. FAB10 - 20030087/01 - 02 COLOR: INDIGO R/NO.: 1 - 4, 6 - 36		2, 920 YARDS	USD1.80/YARD	USD5, 256.00

100PCT COTTON DENIM - 8 OZ - ROPE DYED INDIGO (CT - 121)
DOUBLE P/SHRUNK RESIDUAL AHRINKAGE NOT MORE THAN
3 - 4PCT 82 × 50/14S × 14S - WIDTH: 58/59'
AS PER PURCHASE ORDER NO. FAB10 - 20030087/01 - 02
CIF Vancouver

TOTAL: US DOLLARS FIVE THOUSAND TWO HUNDRED FIFTY SIX ONLY.

GUANGDONG HUALIAN TRADING CORPORATION
60 HUHAI ROAD, GUANGZHOU, CHINA
（受益人签章）

2. 单据改错二

—漏打单据名称“COMMERCIAL INVOICE”；
—漏打开证日期，DATE OF L/C：March 3, 1999；
—成交确认书号码错，应为 TSG0215；
—唛头错；
—单价漏价格术语；
—漏货物原产地；
—漏商会签章。

正确单据如下：

Tianjin Sporting Goods Imp. & Exp. Corp.
68 **Yentai Street**, **Tianjin**, **China**

COMMERCIAL INVOICE

TO MESSRS.: Tokyo Keyboard Distributer,
12－14 Monmachi 3－Chome,
Tokyo, Japan

INVOICE NO.: TS99012
INVOICE DATE: JUNE 12, 1999
L/C NO.: 901026
S/C NO.: TSG0215

TRANSPORT DETAILS:
From Tianjin port to Yokyo by Vessel

MARKS & NOS.	DESCRIPTION	QUANTITY	UNIT PRICE	AMOUNT
TTK	GBW32P Football	1, 600PCS	USD3. 5/PC	USD5, 600. 00
TOKYO			CIF Tokyo	
NO. 1－520				

TOTAL: US DOLLARS FIVE THOUSAND SIX HUNDRED ONLY.
DATE OF L/C: March 3, 1999
GOODS ORIGIN: CHINA

Tianjin Sporting Goods Imp. & Exp. Corp.
68 Yentai Street, Tianjin, China
（受益人签章）
商会签章

第二节　汇　票

一、练习题

（一）中英文术语、短语互译

1. 中译英

（1）商业汇票　　（2）银行汇票

（3）即期汇票　　（4）远期汇票

（5）提示　　（6）承兑

（7）背书　　（8）拒付

（9）付款　　（10）跟单汇票

2. 英译中

（1）Drawer　　（2）Drawee

（3）Payee　　（4）Protect

（5）Without Recourse　　（6）Drawn on

（7）Drawn Under　　（8）Pay ××× Company Only

（9）Payment at 60 Days after Sight　　（10）Available by Your Drafts on Us at Sight

（二）单项选择题

1. 一张汇票的收款人抬头注明："PAY TO THE ORDER OF ABC CO." 即表示(　　)。

A. 该汇票只能由 ABC 公司收取货款

B. 该汇票不能转让

C. 该汇票可以转让，但只能转让一次

D. 该汇票可以转让，而且可一直转让下去

2. 信用证上关于汇票的条款规定：AVAILABLE BY YOUR DRAFT AT 30 DAYS SIGHT DRAWN ON OPPENING BANK，那么汇票应填写为（　　）。

A. 付款期限为 AT 30 DAYS SIGHT，付款人为开证申请人

B. 付款期限为 AT 30 DAYS SIGHT，付款人为开证行

C. 付款期限为 AT ××× SIGHT，付款人为开证行

D. 付款期限为 AT 30 DAYS SIGHT，付款人为 "APPLICANT"

3. 如信用证未作规定，则按《UCP600》的规定，汇票的付款人是（　　）。

A. 开证申请人　　B. 受益人

C. 开证行　　D. 议付行

4. 汇票的号码一般填写（　　）。

A. 合同号码　　B. 商业发票号码

C. 提单号码　　D. 装箱单号码

5. 汇票的抬头人是汇票的（　　）。

A. 出票人　B. 受票人
C. 付款人　D. 受款人

6. 商业汇票是指汇票的（　　）为商业企业的汇票。
A. 受票人　B. 受款人
C. 付款人　D. 出票人

7. 托收汇票一般应在出票条款栏内加注（　　）。
A. COLLECTNG　B. FOR COLLECTION
C. COLLECTION　D. ON COLLECTION

8. 当信用证规定“DRAWN ON US”，那么汇票应该（　　）。
A. 在付款人栏目处填写“US”
B. 在受款人栏目处填写“US”
C. 在付款人栏目处填写“开证行名称及地址”
D. 在付款人栏目处填写“开证申请人名称及地址”

9. 汇票的抬头做成指示样式，说明（　　）。
A. 汇票不能通过背书转让　B. 汇票无须通过背书即可转让
C. 仅能由银行转让　D. 须经过背书方能转让

10. 信用证规定：DRAFTS AT 90 DAYS SIGHT DRAWN ON SAKULA BANK LTD. USANCE DRAFTS DRAWN UNDER THIS L/C ARE TO BE NEGOTIATED AT SIGHT BASIS. DISCOUNT CHARGES AND ACCEPTANCE COMMISSION ARE FOR ACCOUNT OF ACCOUNTEE，汇票的付款期限和付款人应分别填写为（　　）。
A. AT 90 DAYS SIGHT 和 SAKULA BANK LTD.
B. AT 90 DAYS SIGHT 和开证申请人名称
C. AT 90 DAYS SIGHT AND NEGOTIABLE AT SIGHT DAYS 和 SAKULA BANK LTD.
D. AT ××× SIGHT 和开证申请人名称

（三）多项选择题

1. 以下情况属于拒付的是（　　）。
A. 付款人破产
B. 付款人虽不拒绝付款，但承诺延缓一个月付款
C. 付款人拒绝付款
D. 付款人虽不拒绝付款，但承诺到期付款，并办理了承兑手续

2. 汇票的抬头限定“PAY TO ABC CO. ONLY”，表明（　　）。
A. 限付给 ABC CO.　B. 凭 ABC CO. 公司指示
C. 可以转让　D. 不能转让

3. 如果信用证没有规定出票依据，那么一般要填写的内容有（　　）。
A. 开证行名称　B. 开证申请人名称
C. 信用证号码　D. 开证日期

4. 汇票小写金额为 58,673.56 港元，那么汇票大写正确的是（　　）。

A. HONGKONG DOLLARS FIFTY EIGHT THOUSAND SIX HUNDRED AND SEVENTY THREE CENTS FIFTY SIX ONLY.

B. HONGKONG DOLLARS FIFTY EIGHT THOUSAND SIX HUNDRED AND SEVENTY THREE 56/100 ONLY.

C. HONGKONG DOLLARS FIFTY EIGHT THOUSAND SIX HUNDRED AND SEVENTY THREE POINT FIFTY SIX ONLY.

D. HONGKONG DOLLARS FIFTY EIGHT THOUSAND SIX HUNDRED AND SEVENTY THREE 56% ONLY.

5. 当来证规定：“INVOICE MUST SHOW CIF VALUE INCLUDING 5% COMMISSION AT THE TIME OF NEGOTIATION, 5% COMMISSION MUST BE DEDUCTED FROM DRAWINGS UNDER THIS CREDIT.”那么汇票金额应该（　　）。

A. 小于发票金额　　B. 大于发票金额

C. 是不含佣的 CIF 价　　D. 是含佣的 CIF 价

（四）判断题

1. 汇票是出票人承诺在见票时或在未来某一规定的或可以确定的时间，对持票人或其指定人支付一定金额的书面文件。（　　）

2. 承兑是指持票人将汇票提交付款人要求承兑的行为。（　　）

3. A 公司因资金吃紧，把手头上的一张 6 个月期汇票经背书后转让给 B 公司，B 公司后来又转让给 C 公司，C 公司于汇票到期之日到银行收款，被告之汇票原付款人已破产，无力支付款项，C 公司转向 B 公司要求其付款，B 公司认为自己只是中间者，而要求 C 公司直接向 A 公司索款。B 公司的做法合理。（　　）

4. 商业汇票和银行汇票的主要区别在于前者的付款人是商业企业，后者的付款人是银行。（　　）

5. 出口人开具的汇票，如开证行付款后向开证人提示遭拒付时，开证行有权行使追索权。（　　）

6. L/C 条款规定：THIS L/C IS AVAILABLE WITH US BY PAYMENT AT 30 DAYS AFTER RECEIPT OF FULL SET OF DOCUMENTS AT OUR COUNTER，那么制单时应在汇票付款期限栏目填上：30 DAYS AFTER RECEIPT OF FULL SET OF DOCUMENTS AT OUR COUNTER。（　　）

7. 一般汇票有两张正本，根据票据法规定，两张正本汇票具有同等效力，都可以同时收取款项。（　　）

8. 汇票出票人应该是信用证指定的受益人。（　　）

9. 假远期信用证项下汇票，其利息由卖方负担。（　　）

10. 远期汇票只有经过承兑才能转让。（　　）

（五）案例分析

1. 2004 年 TW 进出口公司向 PU 有限公司出口一批大麻籽。对方开来信用证有关条款规定：“... Credit available by the beneficiary's draft(s) at sight, pay to The Standard

Bank, Ltd. only..."（……由受益人开具的即期汇票，只限付给标准银行……）TW 进出口公司在装运后，于 9 月 13 日将信用证所要求的单据向议付行交单议付。9 月 29 日开证行却提出如下单证不符：我信用证规定："... The beneficiary's draft(s) at sight, pay to The Standard Bank, Ltd. only..."（只限付给标准银行），你方提交的汇票收款人却只表示："pay to The Standard Bank, Ltd."（付给标准银行），漏"only"，违背了信用证规定。TW 进出口公司对开证行所提的不符点，经研究认为对方是无理挑剔。于 10 月 4 日即作出如下反驳意见：汇票收款人名称有三种惯例填法，即记名式抬头、指示式抬头和来人式抬头。记名式抬头即直接指定某某人为收款人。你信用证所规定和我提交的汇票均属于记名式标准银行，有无"only"，其作用没有很大的差别，均以标准银行为该汇票的收款人。我们认为我汇票的收款人缮制方法已符合你信用证要求，应认为单证一致。你认为哪方有理呢？

2. 2001 年 3 月 1 日，广州甲公司以广州乙公司为收款人，签发商业汇票一张，汇票金额为 50 万元人民币，汇票到期日为 2002 年 7 月 31 日。乙公司在接到该商业汇票后将该汇票背书转让给江门丙公司。江门丙公司在接到该商业汇票后将该汇票背书转让给佛山丁公司，同年 8 月 1 日，佛山丁公司持该商业汇票向银行提示付款。银行在接到该商业汇票后经查实，确认广州甲公司在银行的存款不足以支付票据款而将商业汇票退回给佛山丁公司。之后，佛山丁公司依法向其前手江门丙公司进行票据追索，江门丙公司在支付款项后又向其前手广州乙公司追偿，但广州乙公司拒绝偿付票据款项。

为此，江门丙公司向人民法院提起诉讼，诉称：被告广州乙公司背书转让给原告（丙公司）商业承兑汇票，被告广州乙公司系汇票出票人和付款人。在丙公司将汇票背书转让给后手后，当最后持票人在汇票到期日提示付款时，因广州甲公司银行存款不足被退票。要求判令广州乙公司支付票据款项及利息，并由广州甲公司承担连带清偿责任。广州乙公司辩称广州甲公司系商业汇票的出票人，应当由广州甲公司独立承担汇票款项的偿付责任。广州甲公司未答辩。请讨论该案例谁将会胜诉。

（六）阅读理解

1. 阅读理解一

BILL OF EXCHANGE

NO. SHE01/7203 DATE JUNE 5, 2002

EXCHANGE FOR USD7,320.00

AT ××× DAYS AFTER SIGHT OF THIS FIRST OF EXCHANGE (SECOND OF EXCHANGE BEING UNPAID)

PAY TO THE ORDER OF CONSTRUCTION BANK OF CHINA

THE SUM OF US DOLLARS SEVEN THOUSAND THREE HUNDRED AND TWENTY ONLY.

DRAWN UNDER L/C NO. COM 8722732 DATED MAY 15, 2002

ISSUED BY THE SAKURA BANK, LIMITED

TO THE SAKURA BANK, LIMITED

56 NANIWA - CHO, CHUO - KU, KOBE,

JAPAN

HUIZHOU TEA IMPORT & EXPORT CORPORATION

根据上列汇票，找出以下所列内容：

（1）开证行名称：

（2）信用证号码：

（3）开证日期：

（4）出票人：

（5）付款人：

（6）受款人：

（7）付款期限：

（8）汇票大写金额：

（9）议付时间：

（10）汇票号码：

2. 阅读理解二

F11

凭 Drawn under　NATIONAL COMMERCIAL BANK, THE JEDDAH (HEAD OFFICE)

信用证 L/C　第 No.　号　613M9732808

日期 dated　年 月 日　Oct.02,1997

1

按 息 付款
Payable with interest @ ...... % per annum

号码 No. ......　汇票金额 Exchange for USD37,800.00　中国．广州 Guangzhou,China　年 月 日　19 ......

见票 At　PAYABLE AFTER 60 DAYS FROM THE DATE OF RECEIPT OF ORIGINAL DOCTS BY NCB JEDDAH LC DEPT.　sight of this FIRST of Exchange (Second of exchange being unpaid) 付

pay to the order of　BANK OF CHINA ,GUANG DONG ,BRANCH　或其指定人

金额 the sum of　US DOLLARS THIRTY SEVEN THOUSAND EIGHT HUNDRED ONLY

此致 To　NATIONAL COMMERCIAL BANK, THE JEDDAH (JEDDAH, MAIN BRANCH)

广东省纺织品进出口针织品有限公司
GUANGDONG TEXTILES IMPORT & EXPORT KNITWEARS COMPANY LIMITED
林樹宗

根据上列汇票，找出以下所列内容：

(1) 开证行名称：

(2) 信用证号码：

(3) 开证日期：

(4) 出票人：

(5) 付款人：

(6) 受款人：

(7) 付款期限：

(8) 汇票大写金额：

（七）单据改错

1. 单据改错一

广东省华达食品有限公司按期收到香港 ABC 公司的信用证，请根据以下信用证内容审核并修改汇票。

FROM: KWANGTUNG PROVINCIAL BANK, HK
TO: BANK OF CHINA, GUANGZHOU BRANCH
DATE AND PLACE OF ISSUE: NOV. 13, 1994, CHINA
IRREVOCABLE DOCUMENTARY CREDIT NO. : 002 - 10358

ADVISING BANK:	BANK OF CHINA, GUANGZHOU BRANCH
BENEFICIARY:	GUANGDONG HUADA FOOD CO. , LTD. 58 BEIJING ROAD, GUANGZHOU, CHINA
APPLICANT:	HONGKONG ABC CO. 3/F GUANGTEX BUILDING TAIKOKTSUI KOWLOON, HONGKONG
AMOUNT:	USD14, 200.00
EXPIRY DATE:	JAN. 15, 1995

DEAR SIRS,

WE HEREBY ISSUE AN IRREVOCABLE DOCUMENT CREDIT IN YOUR FAVOUR WHICH IS AVAILABLE BY NEGOTIATION OF YOUR DRAFTS AT SIGHT DRAWN ON US, FOR 100% INVOICE VALUE MARKED AS DRAWN UNDER THIS CREDIT ACCOMPANIED BY THE FOLLOWING DOCUMENTS:

SPECIAL CONDITIONS: ALL DOCUMENTS MENTIONING THIS CREDIT NUMBER. DOCUMENTS TO BE PRESENTED WITHIN 15 DAYS AFTER DATE OF ISSUANCE OF TRANSPORT DOCUMENTS BUT WITHIN VALIDITY OF CREDIT.

...

BILL OF EXCHANGE

NO. 002 - 10358 DATE JAN. 10, 1995

EXCHANGE FOR USD14, 200.00

AT 15 DAYS AFTER SIGHT OF THIS FIRST OF EXCHANGE (SECOND OF EXCHANGE BEING UNPAID)

PAY TO THE ORDER OF KWANGTUNG PROVINCIAL BANK, HK

THE SUM OF US DOLLARS FOURTEEN THOUSAND TWO HUNDRED.

DRAWN UNDER THIS CREDIT

TO HONGKONG ABC CO.
3/F GUANGTEX BUILDING TAIKOKTSUI
KOWLOON, HONGKONG

HONGKONG ABC CO.
（签名）

2. 单据改错二

广东省五矿进出口公司收到沙特阿拉伯的 MIGHWLLI STEEL PRODUCTS CO. 的信用证后，如期交货，请按其开来的信用证内容审核并修改该公司制单员制作的一份汇票。

TO: BANK OF CHINA, GUANGDONG
FM: ARAB NATIONAL BANK
P. O. BOX 18745 JEDDAH SAUDI ARABIA
DEAR SIRS,
KINDLY ADVISE BENEFICIARY'S M/S GUANGDONG METALS AND MINERALS I/E CORP. 5 TIANHE ROAD, GUANGZHOU, CHINA
OF OUR OPENING WITH YOU AN IRREVOCABLE DOCUMENTARY CREDIT DATED 10 MARCH, 2002 IN THEIR FAVOUR ON BEHALF OF M/S MIGHWLLI STEEL PRODUCTS CO. P. O. BOX 18741 JEDDAH SAUDI ARABIA FOR AMOUNT ABOUT USD75, 683.00 VALID IN CHINA UNTIL 20 MAY 2002, AVAILABLE WITH YOU BY PAYMENT AGAINST PRESENTATION OF BENEFICIARYS' DRAFT(S) AT 30 DAYS AFTER B/L DATE DRAWN ON OURSELVES AND MARKED "DRAWN UNDER ARAB NATIONAL BANK CREDIT NO. 254LK254".
5% COMMISSION MUST BE DEDUCTED FROM DRAWINGS UNDER THIS CREDIT.

F14

1

凭
Drawn under ARAB NATIONAL BANK
信用证 第 号
L/C *No.*
日期 年 月 日
dated 10 MARCH, 2002
按 息 付 款
Payable with interest @ *% per annum*
号码 汇票金额 中国 广州 年 月 日
No. **Exchange** *for* USD75, 683.00 *Guangzhou, China* 20
见票 日 后（本 汇 票 之 副 本 未 付）付
At 30 DAYS *sight of this* **FIRST** *of Exchange (second of exchange being unpaid)*
pay to the order of BANK OF CHINA, GUANGDONG 或其指定人
金 额
the sum of US DOLLARS SEVENTY FIVE THOUSAND SIX HUNDRED AND EIGHTY THREE

此致
To: MIGHWLLI STEEL PRODUCTS CO.
P.O.BOX 18741 JEDDAH
SAUDI ARABIA

GUANGDONG METALS AND MINERALS I/E CORP.
（签名）

（八）单据填制

1. 单据填制一

根据以下内容，填写一份汇票。

INVOICE NO.：TU231

ISSUING BANK：KUWAIT REAL ESTATE BANK

L/C NO.：SP00256　　DATED MARCH 21，2002

INVOICE AMOUNT：USD9,785.00

BENEFICIARY：BEIJING NATIONAL NATIVE PRODUCE IMP. & EXP. CORPORATION

APPLICANT：HAMEED ALI AL TUHOO CO.，KUWAIT

NEGOTIATING BANK：THE INDUSTRIAL & COMMERCIAL BANK OF CHINA

DATE OF NEGOTIATION：APRIL 18，2002

... AVAILABLE WITH YOUR DRAFT AT SIGHT DRAWN ON US FOR THE FULL INVOICE VALUE. ALL DRAFTS MUST BE MARKED "DRAWN UNDER KUWAIT REAL ESTATE BANK".

BILL OF EXCHANGE

NO. ____________________　　DATE ______________________________

EXCHANGE FOR ______________________________

AT ________ DAYS AFTER SIGHT OF THIS FIRST OF EXCHANGE（SECOND OF EXCHANGE BEING UNPAID）

PAY TO THE ORDER OF ____

THE SUM OF ____

DRAWN UNDER ____

____

TO ______________________________

____

　　　　　　　　　　　　　　　　______________________________

　　　　　　　　　　　　　　　　______________________________

2. 单据填制二

根据以下内容，填写一份汇票。

WE HEREBY ISSUE OUR IRREVOCABLE DOCUMENTARY LETTER OF CREDIT NO. 45BC123 DATED JAN. 02, 2003 AVAILABLE WITH US BY PAYMENT AT 30 DAYS AFTER RECEIPT OF FULL SET OF DOCUMENTS AT OUR COUNTERS FOR ACCOUNT OF STG99, 012. 52.

INVOICE NO.: NL0321

ISSUING BANK: THE CHARTERED BANK LONDON, ENGLAND

BENEFICIARY: CHINA NATIONAL LIGHT INDUSTRIAL PRODUCTS IMP. & EXP. CORP.
GUANGDONG BRANCH, NO. 87 THE BUND, GUANGHZOU, CHINA

APPLICANT: LONDON EXPORT CO., LTD.
P. O. BOX 56387 LONDON, ENGLAND

NEGOTIATING BANK: BANK OF CHINA

DATE OF NEGOTIATION: FEB. 23, 2003

F14

凭
Drawn under ....

信用证 第 号
L/C *No.* ....

日期 年 月 日
dated ....

1

按 息 付款
Payable with interest @ .... *% per annum*

号码 汇票金额 中国 广州 年 月 日
No. .... **Exchange** *for* .... *Guangzhou, China* .... 19 ....

见票 日后（本汇票之副本未付）付
At .... *sight of this* **FIRST** *of Exchange (second of exchange being unpaid)*

pay to the order of .... 或其指定人

金额
the sum of ....

此致
To: ....

3. 单据填制三

根据以下内容，制作一份托收项下汇票：

COVERING 3,000 DOZ OF GARMENTS AT JPY20.2 PER DOZ. UNDER CONTRACT NO.: 02PT744. THE BUYERS SHALL DULY ACCEPT THE DOCUMENTARY DRAFT DRAWN BY THE SELLERS AT 90 DAYS SIGHT UPON FIRST PRESENTATION AND MAKE PAYMENT ON ITS MATURITY. THE SHIPPING DOCUMENTS ARE TO BE DELIVERED AGAINST PAYMENT ONLY.

COLLECTING BANK: THE BANK OF TOKYO, LTD.
P. O. BOX 240, NAGOYA - NAKA, NAGOYA, 460 - 91 JAPAN

PRINCIPAL: SHANGHAI FENGHUA TEXTILES I/E CORP.
25 GUANGDONG ROAD, SHANGHAI, CHINA

PAYER: TOYOHANM AND CO., LTD.
58 NISHIKI 6 - CHOME, NAKAKU

INVOICE NO.: YU25868

DATE OF NEGOTIATION: APR. 14, 2002

BILL OF EXCHANGE

NO. ______________________ DATE ______________________

EXCHANGE FOR ______________________

AT ________ DAYS AFTER SIGHT OF THIS FIRST OF EXCHANGE (SECOND OF EXCHANGE BEING UNPAID)

PAY TO THE ORDER OF ______________________

THE SUM OF ______________________

____

DRAWN UNDER ______________________

TO ______________________

____

____

　　　　　　　　　　______________________

二、练习题参考答案

（一）中英文术语、短语互译

1. 英译中

(1) Commercial Bill　(2) Bankers' Bill

(3) Sight Bill　(4) Time Bill (Usance Draft)

(5) Presentation　(6) Acceptance

(7) Endorsement　(8) Dishonor

(9) Payment　(10) Documentary Bill

2. 中译英

(1) 出票人　(2) 受票人

(3) 受款人　(4) 拒付证书

(5) 不受追索　(6) 以……为付款人

(7) 出票依据　(8) 仅付×××公司

(9) 见票60天后付款　(10) 凭你方即期汇票付款

（二）单项选择题

1. D。理由：此属于指示式抬头，经ABC公司背书后，可由ABC公司收款，也可一直转让下去。

2. B。理由：此条款意思为"以开证行为付款人，凭你方30天期汇票议付"，所以B为正确选项。

3. C。理由：按规定，如信用证未作规定，则汇票的付款人就是开证行，在信用证支付条件下，开证行付第一性付款责任。

4. B。理由：为了核对方便，汇票的号码一般填写商业发票号码，也可空白不填。

5. D。理由：汇票的抬头是指汇票的受款人，即PAY TO THE ORDER OF栏目所填的内容。

6. D。理由：汇票的出票人是商业企业的汇票就是商业汇票。

7. B。理由：以区别于信用证项下的汇票。

8. C。理由：此句翻译为"以我行为付款人"。填写"US"不能反映出开证行的具体名称，应填写开证行的名称及地址。

9. D。理由：指示汇票必须通过背书才能转让。

10. C。理由：此条款为假远期信用证，对受益人来说是即期收款，因此付款期限填写远期，但受益人可即期收款，付款人应按照DRAWN ON后面规定的银行名称填写。

（三）多项选择题

1. ABC。理由：付款人承诺到期付款，证明汇票尚没到期，不属于拒付。

2. AD。理由：该条款属于限制性抬头，仅限付给ABC CO.，不能转让。

3. ACD。理由：出票依据一般要具备开证行名称、信用证号码、开证日期三项内容。

4. ABCD。理由：四种表达方式都可以。

5. AC。理由：此句意思为：议付时发票表明 CIF 价包含 5% 佣金，而在填写汇票时，应扣除 5% 的佣金。

（四）判断题

1. 错误。理由：汇票是无条件的支付命令，而不是承诺。

2. 错误。理由：此行为是提示，承诺是指付款人对远期汇票表示承担到期付款责任的行为。

3. 错误。理由：汇票经背书后可不断转让下去，但对受让人来说，所有他之前的背书人都是他的前手，负有担保汇票付款的责任，所以此案件中 B 公司应接受 C 公司的索款要求，然后再向 A 公司索款。

4. 错误。理由：商业汇票和银行汇票是根据出票人的不同进行分类的，因此，应该把题目中的付款人改为出票人。

5. 错误。理由：议付银行在议付后，因单证不符等原因遭开证行拒付时，可向受益人行使追索权。但开证行付款后，即使单证不符，也不能向受益人行使追索权。

6. 错误。理由：应该填为：30 DAYS AFTER RECEIPT OF FULL SET OF DOCUMENTS AT YOUR COUNTER。

7. 错误。理由：两张汇票付一不付二，先到先付，后到无效。

8. 正确。

9. 错误。理由：假远期信用证项下的汇票必须做成远期汇票，但受益人可即期收回票款，其利息由买方承担。

10. 错误。理由：远期汇票不一定要经过承兑才能转让。

（五）案例分析

1. 分析：开证行有理，本案例的信用证规定受益人开具汇票的收款人做成“只限（only）付给标准银行（Pay to ××× Co. only）”应该是限制记名式，这样记名式限制付款人只能将票款付给该抬头人，不得转让。这种方式是由于出票人不想使该单据流给第三者，限制该债权关系落在其他收款人手里，这是本抬头方式的主要目的。所以“Pay to ×××Co. only”就等于“Pay to ××× Co. not transferable”（付给×××公司，不得转让）。不能做成“Pay to ××× Co.”。

2. 分析：本案系一起汇票到期后，因出票人原因致银行拒绝付款而引起的票据法律纠纷，是涉及连续背书的汇票如何行使追索权的问题。追索权，是指持票人行使付款请求权遭到拒绝或有其他法定原因时，向其前手请求偿还票据金额及其他法定款项的权利。通过背书转让的汇票，汇票的收款权利便转移给受让人，对于受让人来说，所有在他以前的背书人以及原出票人都属他的前手，对于出让人来说，所有在他让与以后的受让人都是他的后手，前手对后手负有担保汇票必然被承兑或付款的责任。在本案中丙公司在支付完毕全部款项后，依法取得了对票据权利中的追偿权，即有权向其前手甲公司和乙公司行使偿付票据款项的权利。在丙公司取得追偿权后，其权利范围应是请求汇票债务人支付自己已经清偿的全部金额和该项金额自清偿日至再追索清偿日按照中国人民银行规定的利率计算的利息。由于背书的连续性，其汇票追偿权利的行使直至丙公司向其前手请求追偿为止。

因此，甲、乙两公司依法享有票据权利。甲公司系汇票的出票人，为票据的主债务人，在完成票据行为后，即承担保证该汇票承兑和付款的责任。乙公司系汇票的背书人，在以背书方式转让汇票后，即承担保证其后手所持汇票承兑和付款的责任。因此，在丙公司依法履行其偿付款项的义务后，有权向其前手的乙公司行使追偿权，而乙公司也负有向丙公司支付款项的义务。由于甲公司系汇票的出票人也对乙公司的偿付款项的义务承担连带清偿责任，结果是丙公司会胜诉。

（六）阅读理解

1. 阅读理解一

（1）开证行名称：THE SAKURA BANK, LIMITED

（2）信用证号码：COM 8722732

（3）开证日期：MAY 15, 2002

（4）出票人：HUIZHOU TEA IMPORT & EXPORT CORPORATION

（5）付款人：THE SAKURA BANK, LIMITED
56, NANIWA - CHO, CHUO - KU, KOBE, JAPAN

（6）受款人：TO THE ORDER OF CONSTRUCTION BANK OF CHINA

（7）付款期限：见票即付

（8）汇票大写金额：US DOLLARS SEVEN THOUSAND THREE HUNDRED AND TWENTY ONLY.

（9）议付时间：JUNE 5, 2002

（10）汇票号码：SHE01/7203

2. 阅读理解二

（1）开证行名称：NATIONAL COMMERCIAL BANK, THE JEDDAH（HEAD OFFICE）

（2）信用证号码：613M9732808

（3）开证日期：Oct. 02, 1997

（4）出票人：GUANGDONG TEXTILES IMPORT & EXPORT KNITWEARS COMPANY LIMITED

（5）付款人：NATIONAL COMMERCIAL BANK, THE JEDDAH（JEDDAH, MAIN BRANCH）

（6）受款人：BANK OF CHINA, GUANG DONG, BRANCH

（7）付款期限：PAYABLE AFTER 60 DAYS FROM THE DATE OF RECEIPT OF ORIGINAL DOCTS BY MCB JEDDAH LC DEPT.

（8）汇票大写金额：US DOLLARS THIRTY THOUSAND EIGHT HUNDRED ONLY.

（七）单据改错

1. 单据改错一

—汇票号码错，不是填信用证号码，应该填写商业发票号码或空白不填；

—汇票期限错，信用证规定“YOUR DRAFTS AT SIGHT”，应是即期汇票，填写×××；

—受款人抬头错，不是开证行，应是议付行或通知行“BANK OF CHINA，GUANGZHOU BRANCH”；

—汇票大写金额错，后面应加“ONLY”；

—出票依据错，应填信用证号码、开证日期和开证行名称；

—付款人错，按照信用证规定，“DRAWN ON US，应填开证行的名称；

—出票人错，应填受益人名。

正确汇票如下：

BILL OF EXCHANGE

NO. ________　　　　DATE JAN. 10, 1995

EXCHANGE FOR USD14, 200.00

AT ××× DAYS AFTER SIGHT OF THIS FIRST OF EXCHANGE (SECOND OF EXCHANGE BEING UNPAID)

PAY TO THE ORDER OF BANK OF CHINA, GUANGZHOU BRANCH

THE SUM OF US DOLLARS FOURTEEN THOUSAND TWO HUNDRED ONLY.

DRAWN UNDER THIS CREDIT NO. 002 - 10358　　DATED NOV. 13, 1994

ISSUED BY KWANGTUNG PROVINCIAL BANK, HK

TO KWANGTUNG PROVINCIAL BANK, HK

GUANGDONG HUADA FOOD CO., LTD.

（签名）

2. 单据改错二

—出票条款漏了信用证号码；

—小写金额错，应扣除5%的佣金；

—汇票期限错，应为提单日后30天，而不是见票后30天；

—大写金额错，应该与小写金额一致；

—付款人填写错，应为开证行。

正确答案如下：

F14

凭
Drawn under ARAB NATIONAL BANK
信用证 第 号
L/C No. 254LK254
日期 年 月 日
dated 10 MARCH, 2002
按 息 付 款
Payable with interest @ % per annum
号码 汇票金额 中国 广州 年 月 日
No. **Exchange** for USD71, 898.85 Guangzhou, China 19
见票 日 后（本 汇 票 之 副 本 未 付）付
At 30 DAYS AFTER B/L DATE sight of this **FIRST** of Exchange (second of exchange being unpaid)
pay to the order of BANK OF CHINA, GUANGDONG 或其指定人
金 额
the sum of US DOLLARS SEVENTY ONE THOUSAND EIGHTY HUNDRED AND NINETY EIGHT CENTS EIGHTY FIVE ONLY.
此致
To: ARAB NATIONAL BANK
P.O.BOX 18745 JEDDAH
SAUDI ARABIA

GUANGDONG METALS AND MINERALS I/E CORP.
（签名）

（八）单据填制

1. 单据填制一

BILL OF EXCHANGE

NO. TU231　　　DATE APRIL 18, 2002

EXCHANGE FOR USD9, 785.00
AT ×××DAYS AFTER SIGHT OF THIS FIRST OF EXCHANGE (SECOND OF EXCHANGE BEING UNPAID)
PAY TO THE ORDER OF THE INDUSTRIAL & COMMERCIAL BANK OF CHINA
THE SUM OF US DOLLARS NINE THOUSAND SEVEN HUNDRED EIGHTY FIVE NOLY.
DRAWN UNDER L/C NO.: SP00256 DATEDMARCH 21, 2002 ISSUED BY KUWAIT REAL ESTATE BANK
TO KUWAIT REAL ESTATE BANK

BEIJING NATIONAL NATIVE PRODUCE
IMP. & EXP. CORPORATION
（签名）

2. 单据填制二

F14

1

凭
Drawn under THE CHARTERED BANK LONDON, ENGLAND

信用证 第 号
L/C No. 45BC123

日期 年 月 日
dated JAN. 02, 2003

按 息 付 款
Payable with interest @ % per annum

号码 汇票金额 中国. 广州 年 月 日
No. NL0321 **Exchange** for STG99,012.52 Guangzhou, China FEB. 23, 2003

见票 日后(本汇票之副本未付)付
At 30 DAYS AFTER RECEIPT OF FULL SET OF DOCUMENTS AT YOUR COUNTERS sight of this FIRST of Exchange (Second of exchange being unpaid)

pay to the order of BANK OF CHINA 或其指定人

金额
the sum of STG NINETY NINE THOUSAND AND TWELVE POINT FIFTY TWO ONLY.

此致
To: THE CHARTERED BANK
LONDON, ENGLAND

CHNA NATIONAL LIGHT INDUSTRIAL
PRODUCTS IMP. & EXP. CORP. GUANGDONG BRANCH
(签名)

3. 单据填制三

BILL OF EXCHANGE

NO. YU25868 DATE APR. 14, 2002

EXCHANGE FOR JPY60, 600.00
AT D/P 90 DAYS SIGHT OF THIS FIRST OF EXCHANGE (SECOND OF EXCHANGE BEING UNPAID)
PAY TO THE ORDER OF THE BANK OF TOKYO, LTD.
THE SUM OF JAPAN YUAN SIXTY THOUSAND SIX HUNDRED ONLY.
DRAWN UNDER COVERING 3, 000 DOZ OF GARMENTS UNDER CONTRACT NO.: 02PT744 FOR COLLECTION
TO TOYOHANM AND CO., LTD.
58 NISHIKI 6-CHOME, NAKAKU

SHANGHAI FENGHUA TEXTILES I/E CORP.
(签名)

第三节　海运提单

一、练习题

(一) 中英文术语、短语互译

1. 中译英

(1) 全套清洁已装船提单　(2) 指示提单
(3) 多式联运提单　(4) 托运人
(5) 装运港　(6) 收货人
(7) 卸货港　(8) 交货地点
(9) 集装箱货运站　(10) 集装箱堆场

2. 英译中

(1) Freight Prepaid　(2) Freight Collect
(3) THC　(4) ORC
(5) GP　(6) S. T. C.
(7) Consignor　(8) Shipper's Load and Count
(9) Made Out to Order　(10) Blank Endorsed

(二) 单项选择题

1. 海运提单的签发日期是指（　　）。
A. 货物实际装船完毕的日期　B. 托运人填写托运单的日期
C. 货物开始装船的日期　D. 托运人办理报关的日期

2. 下列提单中，只有经过背书才能转让的提单是（　　）。
A. 指示提单　B. 不记名提单
C. 记名提单　D. 清洁提单

3. 我某公司与外商签订一份 CIF 出口合同，以 L/C 为支付方式。国外银行开来的信用证中规定："信用证有效期为 8 月 8 日，最迟装运期为 7 月 31 日。"我方加紧备货出运，于 7 月 21 日取得大副收据，并换回正本已装船清洁提单，我方应不迟于（　　）向银行提交单据。
A. 7 月 21 日　B. 7 月 31 日
C. 8 月 8 日　D. 8 月 11 日

4. 信用证的到期日为 12 月 31 日，最迟装运期为 12 月 16 日，最迟交单日期为运输单据出单后 15 天，出口人备妥货物安排出运的时间是 12 月 10 日，则出口人最迟应于（　　）向银行交单议付。
A. 12 月 16 日　B. 12 月 25 日
C. 12 月 28 日　D. 12 月 31 日

5. 按《UCP600》解释，若信用证条款中未明确规定是否"允许分批装运"、"允许转运”，则应视为（　　）。

A. 可允许分批装运，但不允许转运　B. 可允许分批装运和转运

C. 可允许转运，但不允许分批装运　D. 不允许分批装运和转运

6. 信用证条款：

DOCUMENTS REQUIRED：FULL SET OF CLEAN ON BOARD OCEAN B/L MADE OUT TO THE ORDER OF SHIPPER，MARKED FREIGHT PREPAID，NOTIFY APPLICANT.

假定：货物的承运人为 COSCO，船长为 MARK TOE，承运人的代理人为 ABC SHIPPING CO.，提单由承运人的代理签发，签发人为张三，如果提单表面未表明承运人的身份，则提单的签发应为（　　）。

A. ABC SHIPPING CO.
MARK TOE AS THE CARRIER

B. ABC SHIPPING CO.
张三 AS AGENT FOR THE CARRIER：COSCO

C. COSCO
张三 AS CARRIER

D. COSCO
MARK TOE AS MASTER

7. 信用证条款：

APPLICANT：ABC CO.

BENEFICIARY：GD TRADING CO.，LTD.

DOCUMENTS REQUIRED：FULL SET OF CLEAN ON BOARD BILL OF LADING CONSIGNED TO THE ORDER OF APPLICANT，MARKED FREIGHT PREPAID，NOTIFY APPLICANT.

信用证未对提单作任何其他规定，则提单的收货人应为（　　）。

A. TO THE ORDER OF APPLICANT

B. TO ORDER

C. TO THE ORDER OF ABC CO.

D. CONSIGNED TO THE ORDER OF APPLICANT

8. 信用证条款：

FROM：VOLKSBANK SCHORNDORF，GERMANY

TO：DG－BANK，HONGKONG/HONGKONG

APPLICANT：ABC CO.

BENEFICIARY：GD TRADING CO.，LTD.

DOCUMENTS REQUIRED：FULL SET OF CLEAN ON BOARD OCEAN BILL OF LADING MADE OUT TO OUR ORDER，MARKED FREIGHT PREPAID，NOTIFY APPLICANT.

信用证未对提单作任何其他规定，则提单的收货人应为（　　）。

A. TO OUR ORDER

B. TO ORDER OF VOLKSBANK SCHORNDORF，GERMANY

C. TO ORDER OF ABC CO.

D. TO ORDER OF GD TRADING CO.，LTD.

9. 信用证条款：

FROM：VOLKSBANK SCHORNDORF，GERMANY
TO：DG－BANK，HONGKONG/HONGKONG
APPLICANT：ABC CO.
BENEFICIARY：GD TRADING CO.，LTD.
PARTIAL SHIPMENTS：ALLOWED
TRANSSHIPMENT：ALLOWED
LOADING IN CHARGE：CHINA PORTS
FOR TRANSPORT TO：ROTTERDAM PORT BY SEAFREIGHT
LATEST DATE OF SHIPMENT：JANUARY 3，1998
DOCUMENTS REQUIRED：FULL SET OF CLEAN ON BOARD MARINE BILL OF LADING，MADE OUT TO ORDER OF WIM BOSMAN BV，P. O. BOX 54064，NL－3008 JB ROTTERDAM，NETHERLANDS.

信用证未对提单作任何其他规定，提单签发日期为 JANUARY 2，1998，实际装船日期为 JANUARY 3，1998，则收妥备运提单的装船批注应为（　　）。

A. JANUARY 2，1998

B. JANUARY 3，1998

C. ON BOARD DATE：JANUARY 2，1998

D. ON BOARD DATE：JANUARY 3，1998

10. 信用证条款：

DOCUMENTS REQUIRED：FULL SET OF CLEAN ON BOARD CHARTER PARTY BILL OF LADING MADE OUT TO ORDER，MARKED FREIGHT PAYABLE AS PER CHARTER PARTY.

假定：船东为 XYZ SHIPPING CO.，货运代理人 ABC SHIPPING CO. 作为船东的代理人签发租船提单，签发人为张三，如果租船提单表面未表明船东及货运代理人的名称和身份，则提单的签发应为（　　）。

A. ABC SHIPPING CO.
张三 AS THE CARRIER

B. ABC SHIPPING CO.
张三 AS AGENT FOR THE CARRIER：XYZ SHIPPING CO.

C. ABC SHIPPING CO.
张三 AS AGENT FOR THE OWNER：XYZ SHIPPING CO.

D. XYZ SHIPPING CO.
张三 AS THE OWNER

（三）多项选择题

1. 下列应向提单持有人交付货物的提单有（　　）。

A. Blank B/L　　B. Open B/L

C. Straight B/L　　D. Bearer B/L

2. 海运提单的作用主要有（　　）。

A. Receipt for the goods　　B. Documents of title

C. Evidence of Contract of Carrier　　D. Commercial Bill

3. 已知货物承运人为 XYZ SHIPPING CO.，承运人提单签发人为张三，承运人的代理人为 ABC SHIPPING CO.，承运人的代理人提单签发人为李四，如果提单表面未表明承运人及代理人的名称和身份，则提单的签发应为（　　）。

A. ABC SHIPPING CO.
李四 AS THE CARRIER

B. ABC SHIPPING CO.
张三 AS AGENT FOR THE CARRIER：XYZ SHIPPING CO.

C. ABC SHIPPING CO.
李四 AS AGENT FOR THE CARRIER：XYZ SHIPPING CO.

D. XYZ SHIPPING CO.
张三 AS THE CARRIER

4. 信用证有关条款：

ISSUING BANK：XYZ BANK

APPLICANT：ABC CO.

BENEFICIARY：GD TRADING CO.，LTD.

DOCUMENTS REQUIRED：FULL SET OF CLEAN ON BOARD BILL OF LADING MADE OUT TO ORDER OR TO OUR ORDER，MARKED FREIGHT PREPAID NOTIFY APPLICANT.

信用证未对提单作任何其他规定，则提单的收货人应为（　　）。

A. TO ORDER　　B. TO ORDER OF XYZ BANK

C. TO ORDER OF ABC CO.　　D. TO ORDER OF GD TRADING CO.，LTD.

5. 信用证有关提单条款：

DOCUMENTS REQUIRED：FULL SET OF CLEAN ON BOARD MARINE BILL OF LADING，MADE OUT TO ORDER OF WIM BOSMAN BV，P. O. BOX 54064，NL－3008 JB ROTTERDAM，NETHERLANDS.

信用证未对提单作任何其他规定，提单正本的签发份数（NO. OF ORIGINAL B(S)/L）应为（　　）。

A. 1 份　　B. 2 份

C. 3 份　　D. 选项 A 和 B 错误

6. 如果货物运输的装运港为 GUANGZHOU，目的港为 LONDON，转运港为 HONGKONG，且合同和信用证没有对提单中的转运港有特别要求，那么，海运提单对转运港的标示方式可采用（　　）。

A. 在装运港栏目填写 GUANGZHOU/HONGKONG

B. 在目的港栏目填写 LONDON W/T HONGKONG

C. 在目的港栏目填写 LONDON VIA HONGKONG

D. 在海运提单上注明 FROM GUANGZHOU TO LONDON VIA HONGKONG

7. 对集装箱运输，由托运人装箱的整箱货，只要海关已对集装箱封箱，承运人对箱内的内容和数量不负责，因此，提单在填写装运数量时应加注（　　）。

A. SHIPPER'S LOAD AND COUNT　　B. SAID TO CONTAIN

C. SHIPPER'S LOAD AND COUNT AND SEAL　　D. SAID BY SHIPPER

8. 海运提单中运费缴付方式填写为“FREIGHT PREPAID”，如果信用证没有特别要求，那么此缴付方式一般适用于（　　）。

A. FOB　　B. CFR　　C. CIP　　D. CIF

（四）判断题

1. 海运提单只有签发日期而没有已装船日期，按惯例，提单的签发日期可视为装船日期。如果海运提单上批注有已装船日期，则该批注的日期不得早于海运提单的签发日期。（　　）

2. 信用证的有关条款表明："FULL SET OF CLEAN ON BOARD BILL OF LADING MADE OUT TO OUR ORDER, MARKED FREIGHT PREPAID NOTIFY APPLICANT." 则出具的正本提单托运人必须空白背书。（　　）

3. 来证对提单没有特殊要求，正本提单上有如下批注："FREIGHT CHARGES: USD2,700.00; ORC: USD500.00; DOCUMENTATION FEE: USD100.00"，银行将接受该提单。（　　）

4. 来证对提单没有特殊要求，有关提单的信用证条款如下："FULL SET OF CLEAN ON BOARD BILL OF LADING MADE OUT TO OUR ORDER, MARKED FREIGHT PREPAID NOTIFY APPLICANT." 如果正本提单上没有特别标明开证人的名称和地址，则正本提单的被通知人应填写为"APPLICANT"。（　　）

5. TEU 是标准吨的缩语。（　　）

6. 对于托运人托运整箱货，海运提单上常批注有 CFS/CFS。（　　）

7. 海运提单上装运港栏目填写："INTENDED: DONGFANGHONG V. 001"，如果实际装运船只也是 DONGFANGHONG V. 001，则海运提单不必另行批注。（　　）

8. 国外开来信用证规定的装运期限为"after 12th May 2001"，则正本提单的装运日期应理解为在 2001 年 5 月 12 日或以后。（　　）

9. 正本海运提单上批注有："TOTAL FIVE HUNDRED CARTONS ONLY. BUT TEN BROKEN CARTONS." 若来证对提单没有特别要求，银行将不接受该提单。（　　）

10. 在规定装运期条文时，如使用了"迅速"、"立即"、"尽速"或类似词句者，按《UCP600》规定，银行将不予置理。（　　）

（五）案例分析

1. 某农产品进出口公司向国外某贸易公司出口一批花生仁，国外客户在合同规定的开证时间内开来一份不可撤销信用证，证中的装运条款规定："Shipment from Chinese Ports to Singapore in May, Partial shipment prohibited." 农产品进出口公司按证中规定，于 5 月 15 日将 200 公吨花生仁在福州港装上"嘉陵"号轮，又由同轮在厦门港续装 300 公吨花生仁，5 月 20 日农产品进出口公司同时取得了福州港和厦门港签发的两套提单。该农产品公司在信用证有效期内到银行交单议付，却遭到银行以单证不符为由拒付货款。问：银行的拒付是否有理？为什么？

2. 国外开来不可撤销信用证，证中规定最迟装运期为 2000 年 12 月 31 日，议付有效期为 2001 年 1 月 15 日。我方按证中规定的装运期完成装运，并取得签发日为 2000 年 12 月 10 日的提单，当我方备齐议付单据于 2001 年 1 月 4 日向银行议付交单时，银行以我方单据已过期为由拒付货款。问：银行的拒付是否有理？为什么？

（六）阅读理解

1. 阅读理解一

Shipper GUANGDONG TEXTILES IMP. AND WOOLEN KNITWEAR CO., LTD.
13/F.,GUANGDONG TEX. MANSION ,NO.168
XIAOBEI RD.GUANGZHOU,CHINA

BL No. KRL030523

COMBINED TRANSPORT
BILL OF LADING

KINGROAD LOGISTICS LTD.

Consignee
CONSIGNED TO CANADIAN IMPERIAL BANK OF COMMERCE,QUEEN AND SIMCOE, TORONTO,ONTARIO,CANADA

Notify
A. B C CO.

RECEIVED in apparent good order and condition except as otherwise noted the total number of Containers or other packages or units enumerated below (*) for transportation from the place of receipt to the place of delivery subject to the terms hereof.
One of the original Bills of Lading must be surrendered duly endorsed in exchange for the Goods or Delivery Order.
MINTRANS
On presentation of this document (duly endorsed) to the Carrier by or on behalf of the Holder, the rights and liabilities arising in accordance with the terms hereof shall (without prejudice to any rule of common law or statute rendering them binding on the Merchant) become binding in all respects between the Carrier and the Holder as though the contract evidenced hereby had been made between them. IN WITNESS whereof the number of original Bills of Lading stated have been signed, one of which being accomplished, the other(s) to be void.

Place of Receipt	GUANGZHOU, CHINA
Ocean Vessel: REPULSE BAY V.48E21	Port of loading: GUANGZHOU CHINA
Port of discharge: VANCOUVER,CANADA	Place of delivery: VANCOUVER,CANADA

(Terms of Bill of Lading continued on the back hereof)

Marks and numbers	Number and kind of packages	Description of goods	Gross weight	Measurement
P.O.# STYLE#: QUANTITY PRE-PACK MADE IN CHINA CARTON #	30CTNS	LADIES 95 PERCENT COTTON, 5 PERCENT (SPANDEX) KNITTED TOP. GOODS HAVE BEEN LOADED ON BOARD VESSEL NAME : REPULSE BAY V.48E21 DATE: 2003/5/21 THE ESTIMIATED ARRIVAL DATE : 2003.6.20 THE L/C NO.: P/O NO.06674 STYLE NO.05-168 SHIPPED QUANTITY OF EACH ORDER.: 1,260 PCS	285 KGS	1.85 CBM
	CFS-CFS	FREIGHT PREPAID & DDC COLLECT		

SAY: TOTAL THIRTY (30) CARTONS ONLY.

According to the declaration of the merchant

For delivery of goods please apply to:
THE FORWARDER AGENT IN CANADA:
WSA LINE INT'L (VANCOUVER) INC
#213-3889 HENNING DRIVE
BURNAY.BC V5C 5N5 CANADA
TEL: 804-2986448 FAX: 804-2928834
ATTN: MR. KEVIM MOK

Freight amount	Freight payable at GUANGZHOU	Place and date of issue GUANGZHOU MAY 15,2003
Cargo Insurance through the undersigned ☐ not covered ☐ Covered according to attached Policy	Number of Original BL's THREE	For and on behalf of KINGROAD LOGISTICS LTD. KINGROAD LOGISTICS LIMITED
Laden on board the vessel Date: MAY 15,2003 By:	BO SHI JI 282 V.0227S KINGROAD LOGISTICS LTD.	AS CARRIER Authorized Signature

根据上面单据回答问题：

（1）托运人：

（2）收货人：

（3）被通知人：

（4）提单号码：

（5）船名：

（6）装货港：

（7）目的港：

（8）唛头：

（9）件数和包装：

（10）总毛重：

（11）总尺码：

（12）货物名称：

（13）运费缴付方式：

（14）“DDC COLLECT”的中文意思为：

（15）正本提单件数：

（16）提单日期及签发地点：

（17）货物的装运日期：

2. 阅读理解二

根据下面单据回答问题：

（1）提单的承运人是哪个公司？

（2）按运输过程中是否转船分类，提单属于何种提单？

（3）按提单收货人抬头分类，提单属于何种提单？

（4）提单是承运人签发还是代理人签发？

（5）提单是否需要托运人背书？

（6）提单为何有两个船名？

（7）提单中批注有“SHIPPER'S LOAD & SEAL S. T. C.”，该批注是何意思？

（8）提单中批注有“CY/CY FCL”，该批注是何意思？

（9）提单中批注的特殊条款有“THIS IS TO CERTIFY THAT THE CARRYING VESSEL IS NOT OVER 15 YEARS OF AGE AT THE TIME OF LOADING. THE AGE IS 8 YEARS. L/C NO. IS 613R9846106”，该批注是何意思？

（10）提单是否有运输标志？如果有，是什么？

（11）提单标明的运费缴付方式是什么？

（12）提单标明承运船只在卸货港的代理人的名称、地址和电话号码，请找出来。

Carrier Hapag-Lloyd Container Linie GmbH, Hamburg **Bill of Lading** Multimodal Transport or Port to Port Shipment

Hapag-Lloyd

Shipper
WENZHOU E.T.D.Z. GENERAL ECONOMIC AND
TECHNICAL DEVELOPMENT CORP.
ROOM 906 BLOCK C. 30 LUCHENG ROAD WENZHOU CHINA
TEL 86-577-8236094 FAX NO. 86-577-8236091

Carrier's Reference:
B/L-No.: KCT-9808181
Page:
Export References: (PG831005)

Consignee or Order:
TO ORDER OF N. C. B JEDDAH

Forwarding Agent:

Notify Address (Carrier not responsible for failure to notify; see clause 20 (1) hereof):
AL-KHAIRAT CORP.
P.O.BOX 42369 JEDDAH 21541 SAUDI ARABIA
TEL 6515536 FAX NO.6520532

Consignee's Reference:

Place of Receipt:

Precarrying Vessel: SUI YUE NO.1 **Voyage-No.:**

Ocean Vessel(s): KITANO V.50WE35 **Voyage-No.:**

Place of Delivery: JEDDAH

Port of Loading: GUANGZHOU **Port of Discharge:** JEDDAH

Port(s) of Transhipment: SHEKOU

Container Nos., Seal Nos., Marks and Nos.	Number and Kind of Packages, Description of Goods	Gross Weight	Measurement
	SHIPPER'S LOAD & COUNT & SEAL S.T.C.		
A.K.C - jeddah	310 CTNS STATIONERY GOODS	6,780KGS	29.048CBM
	FREIGHT PAYABLE AT DESTINATION		
1×20' CY/CY FCL HLCU2044684			
	THIS IS TO CERTIFY THAT THE CARRYING VESSEL IS NOT OVER 15 YEARS OF AGE AT THE TIME OF LOADING. THE AGE IS 8 YEARS. L/C NO. IS 613R9846106		

NAME ,ADDRESS AND TEL NO. OF THE CARRYING VESSELS' AGENT
AT THE PORT OF DISCHARGE:
HAJI ABDULLAH ALIREZA & CO., LTD.
P.O.BOX 7158, KIMG ABDUL AZIZ STREET,
JEDDAH 21462, PHONE(2)6472233,
TELEX 601037 REZASJ, FAX(2)6484644
CABLE ZAINAL - REZASHIP

ORIGINAL

Shipper's declared Value [see clause 7(1) and 7(2)]

Above Particulars as declared by shipper. Without responsibility or warranty as to correctness by carrier [see clause 11(1) and (2)]

Total No. of Containers received by the Carrier:	Packages received by the Carrier:
ONE (20') CONTAINER ONLY	

Movement:	Currency:
CY/CY	

Charge	Rate	Basis	Wt/Vol/Val	P/C	Amount

RECEIVED by the Carrier from the Shipper in apparent good order and condition (unless otherwise noted herein) the total number or quantity of Containers or other packages or units indicated in the box opposite entitled "Total No. of Containers/Packages received by the Carrier" for Carriage subject to all the terms and conditions hereof (INCLUDING THE TERMS AND CONDITIONS ON THE REVERSE HEREOF AND THE TERMS AND CONDITIONS OF THE CARRIER'S APPLICABLE TARIFF) from the Place of Receipt or the Port of Loading, whichever is applicable, to the Port of Discharge or the Place of Delivery, whichever is applicable. One original Bill of Lading, duly endorsed, must be surrendered by the Merchant to the Carrier in exchange for the Goods or a delivery order. In accepting this Bill of Lading the Merchant expressly accepts and agrees to all its terms and conditions whether printed, stamped or written, or otherwise incorporated, notwithstanding the non-signing of this Bill of Lading by the Merchant.

IN WITNESS WHEREOF the number of original Bills of Lading stated below all of this tenor and date has been signed, one of which being accomplished the others to stand void.

Place and date of issue: GUANGZHOU, AUG.24,1998

Freight payable at:

Number of original Bs/L: THREE

SHIPPED ON BOARD

Total Freight Prepaid	Total Freight Collect	Total Freight

For Hapag-Lloyd Container Linie GmbH, Hamburg (as Carrier)

AS AGENT FOR THE CARRIER: HAPAG-LLOYD

CHINA OCEAN SHIPPING AGENCY GUANGZHOU
AS AGENTS (8)

90116745

（七）单据改错

1. 单据改错一

广东省荣华贸易有限公司与芬兰 ABC 公司成交一笔出口交易。ABC 公司按期开来信用证，荣华公司按期出运，并填制好海运提单，请根据下面信用证提供的内容审核海运提单编号①至⑧的内容，对单证不符的内容进行修改。

ISSUING BANK:	METITA BANK LTD. FIN－00020 METITA, FINLAND
Term of Doc. Credit:	IRREVOCABLE
Credit Number:	LRT9802457
Date of Issue:	020505
Expiry:	Date 020716 Place CHINA
Applicant:	ABC CORP. AKEKSANTERINK AUTO P. O. BOX 9, FINLAND
Beneficiary:	GUANGDONG RONGHUA TRADE CO., LTD. 168 DEZHENG ROAD SOUTH, GUANGZHOU, CHINA
Amount:	Currency USD Amount 36,480.00 (SAY US DOLLARS THIRTY SIX THOUSAND FOUR HUNDRED AND EIGHTY ONLY.)
Pos. /Neg. Tol. (%):	5/5
Available with/by:	ANY BANK IN ADVISING COUNTRY BY NEGOTIATION
Partial Shipments:	Not Allowed
Transshipment:	Allowed
Loading in Charge:	GUANGZHOU
For Transport to:	HELSINKI
Shipment Period:	AT THE LATEST JULY 16, 2002
Descript. of Goods:	9,600PCS OF WOMEN'S SWEATERS UNIT PRICE: USD3.80/PC PACKING: 12PCS/CTN TOTAL 800CTNS OTHER DETAILS AS PER S/C NO. 98SGQ468001 CFR HELSINKI
Documents Required:	FULL SET OF CLEAN ON BOARD MARINE BILLS OF LADING, MADE OUT TO ORDER OF METITA BANK LTD., FINLAND, MARKED "FREIGHT PREPAID" AND NOTIFY APPLICANT (AS INDICATE ABOVE)
Additional Cond.:	1. T. T. REIMBURSEMENT IS PROHIBITED. 2. ALL DOCUMENTS MUST BE MARKED THE S/C NO.. 3. SHIPPING MARKS: ABC/HELSINKI/ NO. 1－800.

BILL OF LADING

Shipper GUANGDONG RONGHUA TRADE CO. ,LTD. 168 DEZHENG ROAD SOUTH, GUANGZHOU,CHINA ①	B/L No. KFT2582588 Combined Transport BILL OF LADING RECEIVED in apparent good order and condition except as otherwise noted the total number of containers or other packages or units enumerated below for transportation from the place of receipt to the place of delivery subject to the terms and conditions hereof. One of the Bills of Lading must be surrendered duly endorsed to the Carrier by or on behalf of the Holder of the Bill of Lading, the rights and liabilities arising in accordance with the terms and conditions hereof shall, without prejudice to any rule of common law or statute rendering them binding on the Merchant, become binding in all respects between the Carrier and the Holder of the Bill of Lading as though the contract evidenced hereby had been made between them. IN WITNESS whereof the number of original Bills of Lading stated under have been signed. All of this tenor and date,one of which being accomplished, the other(s) to be void.
Consignee ABC CORP. AKEKSANTERINK AUTO P. O. BOX 9,FINLAND ②	
Notify Address METITA BANK LTD. , FIN -00020 METITA,FINLAND ③	For delivery of goods please apply to:

Pre-carriage by DONGFANGHONG	Place of Receipt	
Ocean Vessel Voy. No. SUISUN 103	Port of Loading GUANGZHOU	
Port of Discharge HELSINKI VIA HONGKONG	Place of Delivery	Final Destination for the Merchant's Reference only

Container, Seal No. & Marks & Nos.	No. of Package & Description of Goods	Gross Weight Kgs	Measurement m^3
N/M ④	9,600PCS WOMEN'S SWEATERS ⑤ TOTAL:EIGHT HUNDRED CARTONS ONLY. ⑥ S/C NO. :LRT9802457 ⑦	13,600.00KGS FREIGHT COLLECT ⑧	25CBM

FREIGHT & CHARGES	Revenue Tons.	Rate Per	Prepaid	Collect

	Prepaid at	Payable at	Place and Date of Issue GUANGZHOU MAY 20,2002
	Total Prepaid	No. of Original B(s)/L THREE(3)	Stamp & Signature ABC SHIPPING CO. 刘五 AS MASTER

LADEN ON BOARD THE VESSEL
Date

By..................................
(TERMS CONTINUED ON BACK HEREOF)

2. 单据改错二

广东省荣华贸易有限公司与芬兰 ABC 公司成交一笔出口交易。ABC 公司按期开来信用证，荣华公司按期出运，并填制好海运提单，请根据下面信用证提供的内容审核海运提单编号①至⑧的内容，对单证不符的内容在单据上进行修改。

ISSUING BANK:	METITA BANK LTD. FIN－00020 METITA, FINLAND
Term of Doc. Credit:	IRREVOCABLE
Credit Number:	LRT9802457
Date of Issue:	020505
Expiry:	Date 020716 Place CHINA
Applicant:	ABC CORP.　AKEKSANTERINK AUTO P. O.　BOX 9, FINLAND
Beneficiary:	GUANGDONG RONGHUA TRADE CO., LTD. 168 DEZHENG ROAD SOUTH, GUANGZHOU, CHINA
Amount:	Currency USD Amount 36,480.00 (SAY US DOLLARS THIRTY SIX THOUSAND FOUR HUNDRED AND EIGHTY ONLY.)
Pos. / Neg. Tol. (%):	5/5
Available with/by:	ANY BANK IN ADVISING COUNTRY BY NEGOTIATION
Partial Shipments:	Not Allowed
Transshipment:	Allowed
Loading in Charge:	GUANGZHOU
For Transport to:	HELSINKI
Shipment Period:	AT THE LATEST JULY 16, 2002
Descript. of Goods:	9,600PCS OF WOMEN'S SWEATERS UNIT PRICE: USD3.80/PC PACKING: 12PCS/CTN OTHER DETAILS AS PER S/C NO. 98SGQ468001 CFR HELSINKI
Documents Required:	FULL SET OF CLEAN ON BOARD MARINE BILLS OF LADING, MADE OUT TO THE ORDER OF ISSUING BANK, MARKED "FREIGHT PREPAID" AND NOTIFY APPLICANT (AS INDICATE ABOVE)
Additional Cond.:	1. T. T. REIMBURSEMENT IS PROHIBITED. 2. ALL DOCUMENTS MUST BE MARKED THE S/C NO. AND THE L/C NO. 3. SHIPPING MARKS: ABC/HELSINKI/NO. I－UP.

BILL OF LADING

Shipper GUANGDONG RONGHUA TRADE CO. ,LTD. 168 DEZHENG ROAD SOUTH, GUANGZHOU,CHINA	B/L No. KEN –98 –25401
Consignee TO THE ORDER OF ISSUING BANK ①	Combined Transport BILL OF LADING RECEIVED in apparent good order and condition except as otherwise noted the total number of containers or other packages or units enumerated below for transportation from the place of receipt to the place of delivery subject to the terms and conditions hereof. One of the Bills of Lading must be surrendered duly endorsed to the Carrier by or on behalf of the Holder of the Bill of Lading, the rights and liabilities arising in accordance with the terms and conditions hereof shall, without prejudice to any rule of common law or statute rendering them binding on the Merchant, become binding in all respects between the Carrier and the Holder of the Bill of Lading as though the contract evidenced hereby had been made between them. IN WITNESS whereof the number of original Bills of Lading stated under have been signed. All of this tenor and date, one of which being accomplished, the other(s) to be void.
Notify Address ABC CORP. AKEKSANTERINK AUTO P. O. BOX 9, FINLAND	For delivery of goods please apply to :

Pre-carriage by	Place of Receipt	
Ocean Vessel Voy. No. DONGFANGHONG/SUISUN 103 ②	Port of Loading HELSINKI VIA HONGKONG ③	
Port of Discharge GUANGZHOU ④	Place of Delivery	Final Destination for the Merchant's Reference only

Container, Seal No. & Marks & Nos.	No. of Package & Description of Goods	Gross Weight Kgs	Measurement m^3
ABC/HELSINKI/NO. I – UP 1 ×20'DHSU3654872 SEAL NO. 123456 CY/CY FCL	SHIPPER'S LOAD & COUNT & SEAL S. T. C. 9,720PCS WOMEN'S SWEATERS ⑤ TOTAL:EIGHT HUNDRED AND TEN CARTONS ONLY. ⑥ SHIPPED ON BOARD DATE:MAY 22,2002 ⑦ L/C NO. :LRT9802457	13,600.00KGS	25CBM

FREIGHT & CHARGES	Revenue Tons.	Rate Per	Prepaid	Collect
FREIGHT PREPAID				

Prepaid at	Payable at	Place and Date of Issue
GUANGZHOU		GUANGZHOU MAY 20,2002
Total Prepaid	No. of Original B(s)/L THREE(3)	Stamp & Signature XYZ SHIPPING CO. 刘五 ⑧ AS AGENT FOR THE CARRIER: ABC SHIPPING CO.

LADEN ON BOARD THE VESSEL
Date

By................................
(TERMS CONTINUED ON BACK HEREOF)

（八）单据填制

1. 单据填制一

根据给出的信用证条款和其他资料缮制提单。

A. 信用证条款。

Issuing Bank:	METITA BANK LTD. FIN - 00020 METITA, FINLAND
Term of Doc. Credit:	IRREVOCABLE
Credit Number:	KHL02 - 22457
Date of Issue:	020505
Expiry:	Date 020716 Place CHINA
Applicant:	FFK CORP. AKEKSANTERINK AUTO P. O. BOX 9, FINLAND
Beneficiary:	GUANGDONG RONGHUA TRADE CO., LTD. 168 DEZHENG ROAD SOUTH, GUANGZHOU, CHINA
Amount:	Currency USD Amount 38,400.00
Pos. / Neg. Tol. (%):	5/5
Available with/by:	ANY BANK IN ADVISING COUNTRY BY NEGOTIATION
Partial Shipments:	Not Allowed
Transshipment:	Allowed
Loading in Charge:	GUANGZHOU
For Transport to:	HELSINKI
Shipment Period:	AT THE LATEST JULY 16, 2002
Description of Goods:	9,600PCS OF WOMEN'S SWEATERS Unit Price: USD4.00/PC, CFR HELSINKI Packing: 12PCS/CTN
Documents Required:	FULL SET OF CLEAN ON BOARD MARINE BILLS OF LADING, MADE OUT TO ORDER OF METITA BANK LTD., FINLAND, MARKED "FREIGHT PREPAID" AND NOTIFY APPLICANT

B. 其他资料。

提单号码：KTT0245678

货物总毛重：6,500KGS

货物总尺码：25CBMS

船名：MAKIS V. 002

唛头：ABC/ HELSINKI/ NO. 1 - 800

集装箱号码：SIHU365487 - 1 (20') SEAL NO. 123456 CY/CY

提单签发日期：2002 年 7 月 10 日

提单签发地点：广州

承运人：ABC SHIPPING CO.

提单签发人：张三

货物由托运人负责装箱及计数。

BILL OF LADING

Shipper

B/L No.

Combined Transport BILL OF LADING

RECEIVED in apparent good order and condition except as otherwise noted the total number of containers or other packages or units enumerated below for transportation from the place of receipt to the place of delivery subject to the terms and conditions hereof. One of the Bills of Lading must be surrendered duly endorsed to the Carrier by or on behalf of the Holder of the Bill of Lading, the rights and liabilities arising in accordance with the terms and conditions hereof shall, without prejudice to any rule of common law or statute rendering them binding on the Merchant, become binding in all respects between the Carrier and the Holder of the Bill of Lading as though the contract evidenced hereby had been made between them. IN WITNESS whereof the number of original Bills of Lading stated under have been signed. All of this tenor and date, one of which being accomplished, the other(s) to be void.

Consignee

Notify Address

For delivery of goods please apply to:

Pre-carriage by | Place of Receipt

Ocean Vessel Voy. No. | Port of Loading

Port of Discharge | Place of Delivery | Final Destination for the Merchant's Reference only

Container, Seal No. & Marks & Nos.	No. of Package & Description of Goods	Gross Weight Kgs	Measurement m^3

FREIGHT & CHARGES	Revenue Tons.	Rate Per	Prepaid	Collect

Prepaid at	Payable at	Place and Date of Issue
Total Prepaid	No. of Original B(s)/L	Stamp & Signature

LADEN ON BOARD THE VESSEL
Date

By................................
(TERMS CONTINUED ON BACK HEREOF)

2. 单据填制二

根据给出的信用证条款和其他资料缮制提单。

A. 信用证条款。

Issuing Bank:	METITA BANK LTD., FIN－00020 METITA, FINLAND
Term of Doc. Credit:	IRREVOCABLE
Credit Number:	KHL02－22457
Date of Issue:	020505
Expiry:	Date 020716 Place CHINA
Applicant:	FFK CORP. AKEKSANTERINK AUTO P. O. BOX 9, FINLAND
Beneficiary:	GUANGDONG RONGHUA TRADE CO., LTD. 168 DEZHENG ROAD SOUTH, GUANGZHOU, CHINA
Amount:	Currency USD Amount 38,400.00
Pos. / Neg. Tol. (%):	5/5
Available with/by:	ANY BANK IN ADVISING COUNTRY BY NEGOTIATION
Partial Shipments:	Not Allowed
Transshipment:	Allowed
Loading in Charge:	GUANGZHOU
For Transport to:	HELSINKI
Shipment Period:	AT THE LATEST JULY 16, 2002
Description of Goods:	9, 600PCS OF WOMEN'S SWEATERS UNIT PRICE: USD4.00/PC, CFR HELSINKI (INCOTERMS 2000) OTHER DETAILS AS PER S/C NO. 98SGQ468001 PACKING: 12PCS/CTN
Documents required:	FULL SET OF CLEAN ON BOARD MARINE BILLS OF LADING, MADE OUT TO ORDER OF ISSUING BANK, MARKED FREIGHT PREPAID AND DDC COLLECT, SHOWING INSURANCE PREMIUM, SURCHARGE AND TRADE TERMS NOTIFY APPLICANT
Additional Cond.:	1. T. T. REIMBURSEMENT IS PROHIBITED. 2. ALL DOCUMENTS MUST BE MARKED THE S/C NO. AND L/C NO.

B. 其他资料。

提单号码：KTT0245678	货物总毛重：6,500KGS
货物总尺码：25CBMS	唛头：ABC/ HELSINKI/ NO. 1－800
转运港：香港	船名：第一程 DONGFANG 第二程 MAKIS V. 002
集装箱号码：SIHU365487－1 (20')	SEAL NO. 123456
保险费：USD100.00	附加费：USD300.00
提单签发地点：广州	提单签发日期：2002 年 7 月 10 日
承运人：ABC SHIPPING CO.	承运人代理人：XYZ SHIPPING CO.
提单签发人：李四	提单装船批注日期：2002 年 7 月 11 日

货物由托运人负责装箱、计数和封箱，整箱装，由集装箱堆场至集装箱堆场。

BILL OF LADING

<table>
<tr><td colspan="2">Shipper</td><td colspan="2">B/L No.</td></tr>
<tr><td colspan="2">Consignee</td><td colspan="2" rowspan="1">Combined Transport BILL OF LADING
RECEIVED in apparent good order and condition except as otherwise noted the total number of containers or other packages or units enumerated below for transportation from the place of receipt to the place of delivery subject to the terms and conditions hereof. One of the Bills of Lading must be surrendered duly endorsed to the Carrier by or on behalf of the Holder of the Bill of Lading, the rights and liabilities arising in accordance with the terms and conditions hereof shall, without prejudice to any rule of common law or statute rendering them binding on the Merchant, become binding in all respects between the Carrier and the Holder of the Bill of Lading as though the contract evidenced hereby had been made between them. IN WITNESS whereof the number of original Bills of Lading stated under have been signed. All of this tenor and date, one of which being accomplished, the other (s) to be void. Consignee</td></tr>
<tr><td colspan="2">Notify Address</td><td colspan="2" rowspan="2">For delivery of goods please apply to:</td></tr>
<tr><td>Pre-carriage by</td><td>Place of Receipt</td></tr>
<tr><td>Ocean Vessel Voy. No.</td><td>Port of Loading</td><td colspan="2"></td></tr>
<tr><td>Port of Discharge</td><td>Place of Delivery</td><td colspan="2">Final Destination for the Merchant's Reference only</td></tr>
<tr><td>Container, Seal No. & Marks & Nos.</td><td>No. of Package & Description of Goods</td><td>Gross Weight Kgs</td><td>Measurement m^3</td></tr>
</table>

FREIGHT & CHARGES	Revenue Tons.	Rate Per	Prepaid	Collect

	Prepaid at	Payable at	Place and Date of Issue
	Total Prepaid	No. of Original B(s) /L	Stamp & Signature

LADEN ON BOARD THE VESSEL
Date

By.................................
(TERMS CONTINUED ON BACK HEREOF)

二、练习题参考答案

（一）中英文术语、短语互译

1. 中译英

(1) Full Sets of Clean Shipping B/L
(2) Order B/L
(3) Combined Transport B/L
(4) Shipper
(5) Port of Loading
(6) Consignee
(7) Port of Discharge
(8) Place of Delivery
(9) Container Freight Station
(10) Container Yard

2. 英译中

(1) 运费预付
(2) 运费待付
(3) 码头作业费（Terminal Handling Charge）
(4) 原产地接货费（Original Receiving Charge）
(5) 通用集装箱（General Propose Container）
(6) 据称包括（Said to Contain）
(7) 托运人
(8) 托运人装货并计数
(9) 做成空白抬头
(10) 空白背书

（二）单项选择题

1. A。理由：海运提单的签发日期是指货物实际装船完毕的日期或已经接受船方或船代理监管的日期。选项 BCD 与提单签发日期的规定不符。

2. A。理由：提单根据收货人抬头不同可分为记名提单、不记名提单和指示提单三种。其中记名提单只能由提单上指定的收货人提货，不能背书转让；不记名提单在收货人栏内没有指明具体的收货人，该提单不必背书就可以转让，谁取得提单，谁就可以提货；指示提单必须经过背书才能转让，在国际贸易中被广泛使用。清洁提单既可以是记名提单、不记名提单，也可以是指示提单。

3. C。理由：信用证中未规定具体的交单期，根据《UCP600》第 14 条 c 款的规定，凡要求提交运输单据的信用证，尚需规定一个在装运日后按信用证规定必须交单的特定期限。如未规定该期限，银行将不予接受迟于装运日期后 21 天提交的单据。但无论如何，提交单据不得迟于信用证的到期日。依题意，卖方应考虑在信用证规定的有效期内交单，即最迟在 8 月 8 日交单。

4. B。理由：信用证中规定了交单期，则卖方应根据信用证的规定，最迟在 12 月 25 日交单。

5. B。理由：根据《UCP600》第 31 条规定，除非信用证另有规定，允许分批装运。因而，若信用证条款中未明确规定是否“允许分批”、“允许转运”，则应视为允许分批装运和转运。

6. B。理由：依题目提示，该提单的签发人是承运人的代理张三签发，而不是由承运人或由船长签发，必须选 B。

7. C。理由：提单中 APPLICANT 不明确，应列明具体的开证人名称，应选 C 项，其他与信用证的要求不符。

8. B。理由：信用证中的 OUR 意指开证行本身，而不是开证人或受益人，选项 A 中的 OUR 不明确，应选择 B 项。

9. D。理由：提单为收妥备运提单，而信用证要求已装船提单，本提单必须进行装船批注，方符合信用证的要求，且批注的日期应为实际装船的日期。选项 B 虽是实际装船的日期，但没有表明“ON BOARD”，正确选项应为 D。

10. C。理由：选项 A 错把货运代理人 ABC SHIPPING CO. 当成承运人，选项 B 错把货运代理人 ABC SHIPPING CO. 当成承运人的代理人，选项 D 错把张三当成船东的提单签发人，正确选项应为 C，货运代理人 ABC SHIPPING CO. 作为船东的代理人，由张三签发提单。

（三）多项选择题

1. ABD。理由：选项 C 为记名提单，只有提单上填明的收货人方可向船公司提货，选项 ABD 均为不记名提单，提单的持有人可凭该提单向船公司提货。

2. ABC。理由：海运提单的作用主要有货物收据（Receipt for the goods），货物所有权的凭证（Documents of title）和运输契约的证明（Evidence of Contract of Carrier）。选项 D 的内容 Commercial Bill 是商业汇票的意思。

3. CD。理由：根据《UCP600》第 20 条 a 款的规定，如信用证要求港至港运输提单，除非信用证另有规定，银行将接受下述单据，不论其称谓如何：表面注明承运人的名称，并由下列人员签字或以其他方式证实：——承运人或作为承运人的具名代理或代表，或——船长或作为部长的具名代理或代表。承运人或船长的任何签字或证实，必须表明“承运人”或“船长”的身份。代理人代表承运人或船长签字或证实时，也必须表明所代表的委托人的名称和身份，即注明代理人是代表承运人或船长签字或证实的。

选项 A 把李四作为承运人的提单签发人错误，选项 B 把张三作为代理人的提单签发人错误，选项 C、D 分别以代理人和承运人签发提单。

4. AB。理由：选项 AB 符合信用证的要求，选项 C 和 D 分别做成开证人指示和受益人指示，不符合信用证的要求，造成单证不符。

5. ABC。理由：按惯例，承运人通常签发两份或三份正本提单，但根据《UCP600》第 20 条Ⅳ的规定，开立全套正本提单可以是仅有一份正本提单或者是一份以上正本提单，因此，承运人签发一份正本提单也行。

6. ABCD。理由：四个选项都符合海运提单对转运港的标示规范。

7. ABCD。理由：“SHIPPER'S LOAD AND COUNT”意思是“托运人装货和计数”，常缩写为“SLAC”；“SAID TO CONTAIN”意思是“据称包括”，常缩写为“STC”；“SHIPPER'S LOAD AND COUNT AND SEAL”意思是“托运人装货、计数和加封”，常缩写为“SLACS”；“SAID BY SHIPPER”意思是“托运人申报”，常缩写为“SBS”。

8. BCD。理由：根据《2000年通则》的规定，选项BCD的卖方负责签订运输合同并支付运费，如信用证没特别规定，一般采用运费预付（FREIGHT PREPAID）的缴费方式；选项A由买方负责租船订舱，支付运费，如信用证没有特别规定，一般采用运费待付（FREIGHT COLLECT）的缴费方式。

（四）判断题

1. 错误。理由：前一句的表述正确，但后一句的表述错误，根据惯例，如果海运提单上批注有已装船日期，则该批注的日期可以早于或迟于海运提单的签发日期，且该批注的装船日期被视为装运日期。

2. 错误。理由：依信用证的规定，在正本提单背书的应该是信用证的开证银行，而非托运人。

3. 正确。理由：根据《UCP600》第26条c款的规定，银行将接受以戳记或其他方式提及运费以外的附加费用，诸如有关装卸或其他类似作业所引起的费用或开支的运输单据，除非信用证条款明确禁止接受此类运输单据。本题因信用证对提单没有特殊规定，故正本提单上批注有运费、ORC费用和单证费等内容银行也可接受。

4. 错误。理由：正本海运提单的被通知人应填写具体的开证申请人的名称和地址，不能只填写："APPLICANT"，除非提单上已标明开证人的名称和地址。

5. 错误。理由：TEU的全称为"twenty-foot equivalent unit"，中文意思为20英尺标准集装箱。

6. 错误。理由：对于托运人托运整箱货，一般采用堆场（CY）到堆场的交接方式，海运提单上常批注为CY/CY；对于托运人托运散货，一般采用货运站到货运站的交接方式，海运提单上常批注为CFS/CFS。

7. 错误。理由：根据《UCP600》第20条a款Ⅲ的规定，当提单含有"预期船"字样或类似有关限定船只的词语时，装上具名船只必须由提单上的装船批注来证实。该项装船批注除批注货物已装船的日期外，还应包括实际装货的船名，即使实际装货船只的名称为"预期船"，亦是如此。

8. 错误。理由：根据《UCP600》第3条的规定，诸如"止"、"至"、"直到"、"从"及类似意义的词语用于限定信用证中有关装运的日期或期限时，应理解为包括所述日期。而"after"应理解为"在……之后装运"，即不包括所述日2001年5月12日。

9. 正确。理由：该批注使提单变成不清洁提单，不清洁提单是指承运人加注了货物包装不良或存在缺陷等批语的提单。对于不清洁提单，银行将不予接受。

10. 正确。理由：《UCP600》第3条规定，除非要求在单据中使用，否则，诸如"迅速"、"立即"、"尽可能快"或类似词语，银行将不予置理。

（五）案例分析

1. 答：银行的拒付是无理的。信用证中的装运条款规定："Shipment from Chinese Ports to Singapore in May，Partial shipment prohibited."即规定不允许分批装运。而我方的500公吨货物分别在福州和厦门装运，且同为"嘉陵"号，因此，本案的主要问题是要确定运往同一目的地的货物在不同的时间和地点分别装上同一航次、同一艘载货船只，属不属于分批装运的问题。根据《UCP600》第 31 条 b 款的规定，运输单据表面注明货物系使用同一运输工具并经同一路线运输的，即使每套运输单据注明的装运日期不同及/或装货港、接受监管地、发运地不同，只要运输单据注明的目的地相同，也不视为分批装运。由此可见，本案中我方的做法是不属于分批装运的，所以，银行拒绝付款无理。

2. 答：银行的拒付是有理的。因为，本案中，我方取得了签发日期为 2000 年 12 月 10 日的提单，于 2001 年 1 月 4 日到银行交单议付。尽管我方未超过信用证规定的有效期到银行议付，但我方提交的提单已构成了过期提单。根据《UCP600》第 14 条 c 款的规定，除规定一个交单到期日外，凡要求提交运输单据的信用证，还须规定一个装运日后按信用证规定必须交单的特定期限。如未规定该期限，银行将不予接受迟于装运日期后 21 天提交的单据。因此，我方提交的过期提单银行是有权拒付的。

（六）阅读理解

1. 阅读理解一

（1）托运人：	GUANGDONG TEXTILES IMP. AND WOOLEN KNITWEAR CO. , LTD. 13/F. , GUANGDONG TEX. MANSION NO. 168 XIAOBEI RD. GUANGZHOU, CHINA
（2）收货人：	CONSIGNED TO CANADIAN IMPERIAL BANK OF COMMERCE QUEEN AND SIMCOE, TORONTO, ONTARIO, CANADA
（3）被通知人：	ABC CO.
（4）提单号码：	KRL030523
（5）船名：	REPULSE BAY V. 48E21
（6）装货港：	GUANGZHOU, CHINA
（7）目的港：	VANCOUVER, CANADA
（8）唛头：	P. O. # STYLE# QUANTITY PRE-PACK MADE IN CHINA CARTON#
（9）件数和包装：	30CTNS
（10）总毛重：	285KGS
（11）总尺码：	1. 85CBM
（12）货物名称：	LADIES 95 PERCENT COTTON 5 PERCENT（SPANDEX）KNITTED TOP
（13）运费缴付方式：	FREIGHT PREPAID & DDC COLLECT

（14）“DDC COLLECT”的中文意思为：目的地交货费待付

（15）正本提单件数：	THREE

（16）提单日期及签发地点： GUANGZHOU MAY 15，2003

（17）货物的装运日期： 2003/5/21

2. 阅读理解二

（1）提单的承运人为 Hapag - Lloyd Container Line GmbH，Hamburg。

（2）按运输过程中是否转船分类，提单属于转船提单。

（3）按提单收货人抬头分类，提单属于指示提单。

（4）提单是承运人的代理人签发的。

（5）提单的抬头为“TO ORDER OF N. C. B JEDDAH”，不需要托运人背书，应该由“N. C. B JEDDAH”背书。

（6）因提单属于转船提单，装运港为 GUANGZHOU，转运港为 SHEKOU，目的港为 JEDDAH，第一程船名及航次为 SUI YUE NO. 1，第二程船名及航次为 KITANO V. 50WE35。

（7）提单中批注有“SHIPPER'S LOAD & SEAL S. T. C.”，该批注的意思是“托运人装货和封箱，据称包括”。

（8）提单中批注有“CY/CY FCL”，其意思是整箱货，由集装箱堆场至集装箱堆场。

（9）提单中批注的特殊条款的意思是“兹证明承运船只的船龄在装运时不超过 15 年，其船龄为 8 年，信用证号码为 613R9846106”。

（10）提单有运输标志，具体是“A. K. C - jeddah”。

（11）运费缴付方式是“FREIGHT PAYABLE AT DESTINATION（运费到付）”。

（12）提单标明承运船只在卸货港的代理人的名称、地址和电话号码为：

HAJI ABDULLAH ALIREZA & CO. , LTD.

P. O. BOX 7158, KIMG ABDUL AZIZ STREET,

JEDDAH 21462, PHONE（2）6472233,

TELEX 601037 REZASJ, FAX（2）6484644

CABLE ZAINAL - REZASHIP

（七）单据改错

1. 单据改错一

依据信用证审核，提单存在如下主要问题：

（1）编号②收货人“ABC CORP. AKEKSANTERINK AUTO P. O. BOX 9, FINLAND”与信用证条款“FULL SET OF CLEAN ON BOARD MARINE BILLS OF LADING, MADE OUT TO ORDER OF METITA BANK LTD. , FINLAND”要求不符，应改为“TO ORDER OF METITA BANK LTD. , FINLAND”；

（2）编号③通知人“METITA BANK LTD. , FIN - 00020 METITA, FINLAND”与信用证条款“NOTIFY APPLICANT（AS INDICATE ABOVE）”要求不符，应改为“ABC CORP. AKEKSANTERINK AUTO P. O. BOX 9, FINLAND”；

（3）编号④唛头“N/M”应改为“ABC/ HELSINKI/NO. 1 - 800”；

（4）编号⑤“9,600PCS WOMEN'S SWEATERS”错误，应改为“800CTNS WOMEN'S SWEATERS”；

（5）编号⑦“S/C NO. : LRT9802457”错误，应改为“S/C NO. : 98SGQ468001”；

（6）编号⑧运费支付方式“FREIGHT COLLECT”与信用证条款“MARKED FREIGHT PREPAID”不符，应改为“FREIGHT PREPAID”。

2. 单据改错二

依据信用证审核，提单存在如下主要问题：

（1）编号①收货人“TO THE ORDER OF ISSUING BANK”不明确，应改为“TO ORDER OF METITA BANK LTD.，FIN－00020 METITA，FINLAND”；

（2）编号③装运港“HELSINKI VIA HONGKONG ”错误，应改为“GUANGZHOU”；

（3）编号④目的港“GUANGZHOU”错误，应改为“HELSINKI VIA HONGKONG”；

（4）编号⑤“9,720PCS WOMEN'S SWEATERS”错误，应改为“800CTNS WOMEN'S SWEATERS”。

（八）单据填制

1．单据填制一

BILL OF LADING

Shipper
GUANGDONG RONGHUA TRADE CO., LTD.
168 DEZHENG ROAD SOUTH, GUANGZHOU, CHINA

B/L No.

Combined Transport BILL OF LADING
RECEIVED in apparent good order and condition except as otherwise noted the total number of containers or other packages or units enumerated below for transportation from the place of receipt to the place of delivery subject to the terms and conditions hereof. One of the Bills of Lading must be surrendered duly endorsed to the Carrier by or on behalf of the Holder of the Bill of Lading, the rights and liabilities arising in accordance with the terms and conditions hereof shall, without prejudice to any rule of common law or statute rendering them binding on the Merchant, become binding in all respects between the Carrier and the Holder of the Bill of Lading as though the contract evidenced hereby had been made between them. IN WITNESS whereof the number of original Bills of Lading stated under have been signed. All of this tenor and date, one of which being accomplished, the other (s) to be void. Consignee

Consignee
TO ORDER OF METITA BANK LTD., FINLAND

Notify Address
FFK CORP. AKEKSANTERINK AUTO
P. O. BOX 9, FINLAND

For delivery of goods please apply to:

Pre-carriage by	Place of Receipt
Ocean Vessel Voy. No. MAKIS V. 002	Port of Loading GUANGZHOU
Port of Discharge HELSINKI	Place of Delivery

Final Destination for the Merchant's Reference only

Container, Seal No. & Marks & Nos.	No. of Package & Description of Goods	Gross Weight KGS	Measurement m^3
ABC HELSINKI NO. 1－800 SIHU365487－1 (20') SEAL NO. 123456CY/ CY FCL	SHIPPER'S LOAD & COUNT & SEAL S. T. C 800CARTONS WOMEN'S SWEATERS TOTAL: EIGHT HUNDRED CARTONS ONLY. SHIPPED ON BOARD DATE: JULY 10, 2002 "FREIGHT PREPAID"	6,500KGS	25CBM

FREIGHT & CHARGES	Revenue Tons.	Rate Per	Prepaid	Collect

Prepaid at	Payable at	Place and Date of Issue GUANGZHOU JULY 10, 2002
Total Prepaid	No. of Original B(s)/L THREE (3)	Stamp & Signature ABC SHIPPING CO. 张三　AS THE CARRIER

LADEN ON BOARD THE VESSEL
Date

By
(TERMS CONTINUED ON BACK HEREOF)

2. 单据填制二

BILL OF LADING

Shipper GUANGDONG RONGHUA TRADE CO., LTD. 168 DEZHENG ROAD SOUTH, GUANGZHOU, CHINA	B/L No. KTT0245678
Consignee TO ORDER OF METITA BANK LTD., FINLAND., FIN-00020 METITA, FINLAND	Combined Transport BILL OF LADING RECEIVED in apparent good order and condition except as otherwise noted the total number of containers or other packages or units enumerated below for transportation from the place of receipt to the place of delivery subject to the terms and conditions hereof. One of the Bills of Lading must be surrendered duly endorsed to the Carrier by or on behalf of the Holder of the Bill of Lading, the rights and liabilities arising in accordance with the terms and conditions hereof shall, without prejudice to any rule of common law or statute rendering them binding on the Merchant, become binding in all respects between the Carrier and the Holder of the Bill of Lading as though the contract evidenced hereby had been made between them. IN WITNESS whereof the number of original Bills of Lading stated under have been signed. All of this tenor and date, one of which being accomplished, the other (s) to be void. Consignee
Notify Address FFK CORP. AKEKSANTERINK AUTO P. O. BOX 9, FINLAND	For delivery of goods please apply to:

Pre-carriage by DONGFANG	Place of Receipt	
Ocean Vessel Voy. No. MAKIS V. 002	Port of Loading GUANGZHOU	
Port of Discharge HELSINKI VIA HONGKONG	Place of Delivery	Final Destination for the Merchant's Reference only

Container, Seal No. & Marks & Nos.	No. of Package & Description of Goods	Gross Weight KGS	Measurement m^3
	SHIPPER'S LOAD & COUNT & SEAL S. T. C		
ABC HELSINKI NO. 1-800	800CARTONS WOMEN'S SWEATERS TOTAL: EIGHT HUNDRED CARTONS ONLY.	6,500KGS	25CBM
SIHU365487-1 (20') SEAL NO. 123456CY/ CY FCL	FREIGHT PREPAID AND DDC COLLECT SHIPPED ON BOARD DATE: 2002/7/11 INSURANCE PREMIUM: USD100.00 SURC HARGE: USD300.00 TRADE TERMS: CFR HELSINKI (INCOTERMS 2000) S/C NO.: 98SGQ468001 L/C NO.: KHL02-22457		

FREIGHT & CHARGES	Revenue Tons.	Rate Per	Prepaid	Collect

Prepaid at	Payable at	Place and Date of Issue GUANGZHOU JULY 10, 2002
Total Prepaid	No. of Original B(s)/L THREE (3)	Stamp & Signature XYZ SHIPPING CO. 李四 AS AGENT FOR THE CARRIER: ABC SHIPPING CO.

LADEN ON BOARD THE VESSEL
Date

By
(TERMS CONTINUED ON BACK HEREOF)

第四节　保险单

一、练习题

（一）中英文术语、短语互译

1. 中译英

（1）保险单

（2）预约保险单

（3）航空运输险

（4）仓至仓条款

（5）平安险

（6）罢工险

（7）单独海损

（8）淡水雨淋险

（9）中国人民保险公司海洋运输货物保险条款

（10）保费

2. 英译中

（1）Insurance Certificate

（2）Combined Insurance Certificate

（3）Covering All Risks and War Risks

（4）Amount Insured

（5）Institute Cargo Clauses

（6）Made out to Order

（7）Theft Pilferage & Non-delivery Risk

（8）Irrespective of Percentage

（9）General Average

（10）Insured

（二）单项选择题

1. 以 CIF 术语达成的交易，如信用证没有特别规定，保险单的被保险人一栏应填写（　　）。

A. 开证申请人的名称　　B. 受益人的名称

C. TO ORDER　　D. TO WHOM IT MAY CONCERN

2. 如信用证没有特别规定，按国际保险市场惯例，保险金额一般在发票金额的基础上（　　）填写。

A. 加一成　　B. 加两成

C. 加三成　　D. 加四成

3. 如信用证规定“COVERING MARINE RISKS OF THE PEOPLE’S INSURANCE COMPANY OF CHINA DD 1/1/1982”，则出口公司（　　）。

A. 只能投保平安险

B. 只能投保水渍险

C. 只能投保一切险

D. 可投保平安险、水渍险及一切险中的任一种

4. 信用证中规定“COVERING RISKS AS PER‘INSTITUTE CARGO CLAUSES（A）’, INCLUDING WAREHOUSE TO WAREHOUSE CLAUSE”，其中的“WAREHOUSE TO WAREHOUSE CLAUSE”是指（　　）。

A. 出口方负责的交货责任起讫的条款

B. 承运人负责的运输责任起讫的条款

C. 进口方负责的收货责任起讫的条款

D. 保险人负责的保险责任起讫的条款

5. 信用证中规定“ALL DOCUMENTS SHOULD INDICATE THE SHIPPING MARK”，出口公司在保单的“Marks & Nos.”一栏应填写（　　）。

A. 实际唛头

B. AS PER INVOICE NO. ×××

C. AS PER B/L NO. ×××

D. 既可按实际唛头填写，也可按“AS PER INVOICE NO. ×××”填写

6. 假设提单的签发日期为“MARCH 24，2005”，那么以下保单的开航日期中，（　　）的填写是错误的。

A. MARCH 24，2005　　B. AS PER B/L

C. MARCH 30，2005　　D. MARCH 23，2005

7. 保险的赔付地点一般填写（　　）。

A. 起运港（地）　　B. 目的港（地）

C. 投保人所在地　　D. 保险公司所在地

8. 预约保险是指根据预约保险合同，投保人以（　　）替代投保单，保险公司负自动承保的责任。

A. 大副收据　　B. 买卖合同

C. 海运提单　　D. 国外寄来的装运通知

9. 我方按 CIF 条件出口一批陶瓷制品，由于信用证中没有规定具体的投保险别，我方在办理投保手续时，一般可按（　　）投保。

A. 一切险 + 碰损破碎险　　B. 平安险 + 水渍险

C. 平安险 + 碰损破碎险　　D. 一切险 + 水渍险

10. 某公司以 CIF 条件出口一批货物，在广州港装上船只“DONGFENG”号运往香港，在香港装上第二程船“NATA”号后运往旧金山，该公司在保单的载运输工具栏（Per conveyance S. S.）应填写为（　　）。

A. DONGFENG　　B. NATA

C. DONGFENG/NATA　　D. DONGFENG/NATA W/T HONGKONG

（三）多项选择题

1. 根据伦敦保险协会制定的《协会货物条款》，以下险别能单独投保的有（　　）。

A. ICCA　　B. ICCB

C. 战争险　　D. 恶意损害险

2. 按照我国《海洋货物运输保险条款》的规定，以下险别属于特殊附加险的是(　　)。

A. 偷窃提货不着险　　B. 交货不到险

C. 甲板险　　D. 舱面险

3. 信用证中规定“MARINE INSURANCE POLICY OF CERTIFICATE IN DUPLICATE, COVERING FPA AS PER OCEAN MARINE CARGO CLAUSE OF THE PEOPLE'S COMPANY OF CHINA DATED 1/1/1981, INCLUDING T. P. N. D. LOSS AND DAMAGE CAUSED BY HEAT, SHIP'S SWEAT AND ODOUR, BREAKAGE OF PACKING”，按此规定，应投保的一般附加险有（　　）。

A. 偷窃不着提货险　　B. 受潮受热险

C. 串味险　　D. 破碎险

4. 按照我国《海洋货物运输保险条款》的规定，以下险别属于我国海洋运输货物保险中的基本险的是（　　）。

A. FPA　　B. ICCA

C. WPA　　D. WAR RISKS

5. 共同海损分摊时，涉及的受益方包括（　　）。

A. 船方　　B. 货方

C. 救助方　　D. 运费方

（四）判断题

1. 保险单俗称“大保单”，保险凭证俗称“小保单”，由于保险凭证背面没有列入保险条款，因而它们不具有同等的法律效力。(　　)

2. 保险单的签发日期应该不迟于海运提单的签发日期。(　　)

3. 我某外贸公司以 CIF 条件出口，代客户投保一切险，对于从装运港运往目的港途中由于任何外来原因所造成的损失，客户均可向保险公司索赔。(　　)

4. 我某公司以 CFR 术语进口钢材一批，我方在收到国外发来的装船通知后，按事先签订的预约保险合同，将该通知交保险公司，保险公司的承保责任起讫应该为“仓至仓”。(　　)

5. 如信用证规定按 ICC 条款投保，根据中国人民保险公司的现行做法是不能接受的，应要求对方修改信用证。(　　)

6. 当信用证要求提交的保险单份数为“IN TWO COPIES”时，我方应提交两份副本。(　　)

7. 按照我国现行的《海洋货物运输保险条款》的规定，保险公司对于海运战争险的保险责任起讫不采用仓至仓条款，而是仅负责水上风险。(　　)

8．某出口公司按 CIF 条件出口服装一批，我方按信用证要求投保水渍险，运输途中由于食用水管破裂，造成部分服装被浸泡，该损失保险公司将予以赔偿。(　　)

9．按照我国《海洋货物运输保险条款》的规定，战争险与罢工险均能单独投保。(　　)

10．保险公司按伦敦保险协会制定的《协会货物条款》中的 ICCA、ICCB 和 ICCC 三种险别承保的责任范围与按我国《海洋货物运输保险条款》中 ALL RISKS、WPA 和 FPA 承保的责任范围大致相同。(　　)

（五）案例分析

1．我某外贸公司以 CFR 条件出口货物一批，应买方要求，我方在装船前代为投保了一切险，保单的被保险人为买方。货物用驳船从广州乌冲码头运往盐田港装船时，由于触礁而全部灭失，卖方认为保险公司的保险责任范围为“仓至仓”，而该损失又在一切险的承保范围以内，因此持相关保险单向保险公司索赔。问保险公司对该损失应不应该赔偿？为什么？

2．我某公司以 CIF 条件出口一批羊肉到中东某国，信用证规定投保平安险加战争险、罢工险。货到目的港后由于码头工人罢工而致无人卸货，一个星期后由于无法补充燃料，货轮上的冷冻设备停止运转，等到罢工结束，该批羊肉已变质无法食用。问保险公司对于该损失是否赔偿？为什么？

（六）阅读理解

1．阅读理解一

中保财产保险有限公司
The people's Insurance (Property) Company of China, Ltd.
PICC PROPERTY

№ 0071897

发票号码 97-257-501367
Invoice No.

No.of Original: One
保险单号次
Policy No.
KC04 970 11505 104

海洋货物运输保险单
MARINE CARGO TRANSPORTATION INSURANCE POLICY

被保险人：
Insured: G M G HARDWARE & TOOLS IMP. & EXP. COMPANY LTD.

中保财产保险有限公司（以下简称本公司）根据被保险人的要求，及其所缴付约定的保险费，按照本保险单承保险别和背面所载条款与下列特别条款承保下述货物运输保险，特签发本保险单。

This policy of Insurance witnesses that The People's Insurance (Property) Company of China, Ltd.(hereinafter called "The Company"),at the request of the Insured and in consideration of the agreed premium paid by the Insured, undertakes to insure the undermentioned goods in transportation subject to the conditions of this Policy as per the Clauses printed overleaf and other special clauses attached hereon.

保险货物项目 Descriptions of Goods	包装 单位 数量 Packing Unit Quantity	保险金额 Amount Insured
HAND TOOLS TOTAL: 203 PACKAGES	203 PACKAGES	USD7,391.84

承保险别
Conditions

货物标记
Marks of Goods

Covering All Risks as per Ocean Marine Cargo Clauses (1/1/1981) (Warehouse to Warehouse Clause is included) of The People's Insurance Company of China.

GIATRAKIS

COPY

总保险金额：
Total Amount Insured: US Dollar SEVEN THOUSAND THREE HUNDRED & NINETY-ONE CENTS EIGHTY-FOUR ONLY.

保费
Premium as arranged

载运输工具
Per conveyance S.S. NING GLORY V.98/207W

开航日期
Slg. on or abt. DEC. 10, 1997

起运港
From GUANGZHOU

目的港
To PIRAEUS

所保货物，如发生本保险单项下可能引起索赔的损失或损坏，应立即通知本公司下述代理人查勘。如有索赔，应向本公司提交保险单正本（本保险单共有　份正本）及有关文件。如一份正本已用于索赔，其余正本则自动失效。

In the event of loss or damage which may result in a claim under this Policy, immediate notice must be given to the Company's Agent as mentioned hereunder. Claims, if any, one of the Original Policy which has been issued in　Original (s) together with the relevant documents shall be surrendered to the Company, If one of the Original Policy has been accomplished, the others to be void.

Macrymichalos Brothers S.A.
2, Gounari Street, Piraeus.

中保财产保险有限公司
THE PEOPLE'S INSURANCE (PROPERTY) COMPANY OF CHINA,LTD.

THE PEOPLE'S INSURANCE (PROPERTY) CO. OF CHINA, LTD.
GUANGDONG PROVINCIAL BRANCH
INTERNATIONAL DEPT.

赔款偿付地点
Claim payable at PIRAEUS

日期
Date DEC.10, 1997

在
at GUANGZHOU

地址：
Address: 2 Guangwei Road, Guangzhou,China
Fax:83324566 Tlx:440462 PICC CN

UNDERWRITING SIGNATORY (220)

如果该交易以 CIF 条件达成，请根据上面单据回答下列问题：

（1）该笔交易是进口贸易还是出口贸易？

（2）受益人到银行办理议付前，是否需要对该保单进行背书转让？

（3）保险金额为 USD7,391.84，该金额是否就是发票金额？

2. 阅读理解二

如果该交易以 CIF 条件达成，请根据下面单据回答下列问题：

（1）保险货物的名称是什么？

（2）该保单投保什么险别？采用什么保险条款？

（3）保险货物在运输过程中是否发生了转运？

PICC 中国人民保险公司
The People's Insurance Company of China

总公司设于北京 Head Office: BEIJING　　一九四九年创立 Established In 1949　　No. 0010951

发票号码 Invoice No. 2000057WBS-5　　保险单号次 Policy No. KC04 000110081000

海洋货物运输保险单
MARINE CARGO INSURANCE POLICY

被保险人：
Insured: GUANGDONG TEXTILES IE WOOLEN KNITWEARS CO. LTD. HELD TO ORDER OF (THE) A B C CO.

中国人民保险公司（以下简称本公司）根据被保险人的要求，及其所缴付约定的保险费，按照本保险单承保险别和背面所载条款与下列特别条款承保下述货物运输保险，特签发本保险单。
This policy of Insurance witnesses that The People's Insurance Company of China (hereinafter called "The Company"), at the request of the Insured and in consideration of the agreed premium paid by the insured, undertakes to insure the undermentioned goods in transportation subject to the conditions of this Policy as per the Clauses printed overleaf and other special clauses attached hereon.

保险货物项目 标记 数量及包装
Description, Marks, Numbers & Quantity of Goods:

PRATEX-TOR
P.O.#
STYLE#
COLOUR
QUANTITY
SIZE RATIO
LABEL
PREPACKS RATIO/

承保条件
Conditions:

COVERING ALL RISKS AS PER OCEAN MARINE CARGO CLAUSES (1/1/1981) (WAREHOUSE TO WAREHOUSE CLAUSE IS INCLUDED) OF THE PEOPLE'S INSURANCE COMPANY OF CHINA

MEN'S / WOMEN'S SWEATERS

2,297PCS (192CTNS)

COPY

Including Year 2000 Problem Exclusion Clause.

总保险金额
Total Amount Insured: US DOLLARS TWENTY TWO THOUSAND EIGHT HUNDRED AND SEVENTY TWO ONLY (USD22,872)

保费 Premium: as arranged　　装载运输工具 Per conveyance S. S: APL JAPAN V.043-2

开航日期 Slg. on or abt: July 30,2000　　自 from: (YANTIAN) GUANGDONG, CHINA　　至 TORONTO, CANADA

所保货物，如发生本保险单项下可能引起索赔的损失或损坏，应立即通知本公司下述代理人查勘。如有索赔，应向本公司提交保险单正本（本保险单共有 2 份正本）及有关文件。如一份正本已用于索赔，其余正本则自动失效。
In the event of loss or damage which may result in a claim under this Policy, immediate notice must be given to the Company's Agent as mentioned hereunder. Claims, if any, one of the Original Policy which has been issued in TWO Original(s) together with the relevant documents shall be surrendered to the Company, If one of the Original Policy has been accomplished, the others to be void.

NAME AND ADDRESS:
BOYD PHILLIPS & CO., LTD.
145 WELLINGTON ST.W., SUITE 310
TORONTO, ONT. CANADA M5J 1HB
TEL.:416-9719744 FAX.416-5917673
TELEX.06-218844"ADJUSTOR CABLE:"ADJUSTERS"

中国人民保险公司广东省分公司
THE PEOPLE'S INSURANCE CO. OF CHINA
GUANGDONG PROVINCIAL BRANCH

THE PEOPLE'S INSURANCE CO. OF CHINA
GUANGDONG PROVINCIAL BRANCH
INTERNATIONAL DEPT.
丘小山
AUTHORIZED SIGNATORY

赔款偿付地点
Claim payable at TORONTO, CANADA
日期 Date: July 29,2000　　广州 Guangzhou
地址：中国广州广卫路2号
Address: 2, Guangwei Road, Guangzhou China
Tlx: 44462 PICCG CN　Fax: 0086 20 83324566

（七）单据改错

1. 单据改错一

请根据以下材料修改一份保险单。

THE SAKURA BANK, LTD.
INT'L OPERATIONS CENTER
P. O. BOX 166, TOKYO, JAPAN

CREDIT NO.: 645 - 3000511
DATE OF ISSUE: OCTOBER 23, 1997　　EXPIRY DATE: DECEMBER 15, 1997

APPLICANT: SHITAYA KINSOKU CO., LTD. 6 - 11 7 - CHONE UENO TAITO - KU TOKYO, JAPAN	BENEFICIARY: GUANGDONG MACHINERY IMP. & EXP. CORP. (GROUP) 720 DONGFENG ROAD EAST GUANGZHOU, CHINA
ADVISING BANK: BANK OF CHINA, GUANGDONG BRANCH GUANGZHOU	AMOUNT: USD15,880.00 US DOLLARS FIFTEEN THOUSAND EIGHT HUNDRED AND EIGHTY ONLY.
PARTIAL SHIPMENTS ARE NOT ALLOWED TRANSSHIPMENT IS ALLOWED FROM: CHINESE PORTS TO: YOKOHAMA, JAPAN NOT LATER THAN NOVEMBER 30, 1997	CREDIT AVAILABLE WITH ANY BANK BY NEGOTIATION AGAINST PRESENTATION OF DOCUMENTS DETAILED HEREIN AND BENEFICIARY'S DRAFT(S) AT SIGHT DRAWN ON THE SAKURA BANK LTD., TOKYO FOR FULL INVOICE VALUE

LIST OF DOCUMENTS TO BE PRESENTED:
1) SIGNED COMMERCIAL INVOICES IN 2 COPIES.
2) FULL SET OF CLEAN ON BOARD OCEAN BILLS OF LADING MADE OUT TO ORDER OF SHIPPER AND BLANK ENDORSED, MARKED "FREIGHT PREPAID" AND NOTIFY APPLICANT.
3) INSURANCE POLICY OR CERTIFICATE IN DUPLICATE, ENDORSED IN BLANK FOR 110% OF THE CIF INVOICE VALUE COVERING OCEAN MARINE CARGO CLAUSES (ALL RISKS) AND OCEAN MARINE CARGO WAR RISK CLAUSES OF THE PEOPLE'S INSURANCE CO. OF CHINA OF 1981. CLAIMS PAYABLE IN JAPAN IN CURRENCY OF DRAFT(S).
4) PACKING LIST IN 2 COPIES.
5) G. S. P. CERTIFICATE OF ORIGIN FORM A IN 2 COPIES.

COVERING SHIPMENT:
"RABBIT" BRAND SHOVEL WITH METAL HANDLE
S501MH 210 DOZ @ USD38.00/DOZ
S503MH 200 DOZ @ USD39.50/DOZ
AS PER S/C NO. A97JP19900247　　CIF YOKOHAMA

OTHER MATERIALS:
INV. NO.: 97GD003511　　INV. DATE: NOV. 2, 1997
B/L DATE: NOV. 25, 1997　　POLICY NO.: AA3546897
NAME OF STEAMER: NEDLLOYD HONSHU V. 3165　　PACKING: 1DOZ/CTN
SHIPPING MARK: SK/YOKOHAMA/NOS. 1 - 410

中保财产保险有限公司
The People's Insurance (Property) Company of China, Ltd.

PICC PROPERTY

发票号码
Invoice No. 97GD003511

保险单号次
Policy No.

海 洋 货 物 运 输 保 险 单
MARINE CARGO TRANSPORTATION INSURANCE POLICY

被保险人：
Insured: GUANGDONG MACHINERY IMP. & EXP. CORP. (GPOUP)

中保财产保险有限公司（以下简称本公司）根据被保险人的要求，及其所缴付约定的保险费，按照本保险单承担险别和背面所载条款与下列特别条款承保下列货物运输保险，特签发本保险单。

This policy of Insurance witnesses that the People's Insurance (Property) Company of China, Ltd. (hereinafter called "the Company"), at the request of the Insured and in consideration of the agreed premium paid by the Insured, undertakes to insure the undermentioned goods in transportation subject to the conditions of this Policy as per the Clauses printed overleaf and other special clauses attached hereon.

保险货物项目 Descriptions of Goods	包装　单位　数量 Packing　Unit　Quantity	保险金额 Amount Insured
"RABBIT" BRAND SHOVEL WITH METAL HANDLE TOTAL: 410CTNS	410CTNS	USD17,468.00

承保险别
Conditions

COVERING OCEAN MARINE CARGO CLAUSES (ALL RISKS) AND OCEAN MARINE CARGO WAR RISK CLAUSES OF THE PEOPLE'S INSURANCE CO. OF CHINA OF 1981

货物标记
Marks of Goods

SK
TOKYO
NOS. 1 - 410

总保险金额：
Total Amount Insured: US DOLLARS SEVENTEEN THOUSAND FOUR HUNDRED AND SIXTY EIGHT ONLY.

保费
Premium as arranged

载运输工具
Per conveyance S. S. HEDLLOYD HONSHU V. 3165

开航日期
Slg. on or abt NOV. 25, 1997

起运港
From GUANGZHOU

目的港
to YOKOHAMA

所保货物，如发生本保险单项下可能引起索赔的损失或损坏，应立即通知本公司下述代理人查勘。如有索赔，应向本公司提交保险单正本（本保险单共有　　份正本）及有关文件。如一份正本已用于索赔，其余正本则自动失效。

In the event of loss or damage which may result in a claim under this Policy, immediate notice must be given to the Company's Agent as mentioned hereunder. Claims, if any, one of the Original Policy which has been issued in ONE Original(s) together with the relevant documents shall be surrendered to the Company. If one of the Original Policy has been accomplished, the others to be void.

中保财产保险有限公司
THE PEOPLE'S INSURANCE (PROPERTY) COMPANY OF CHINA, LTD.

赔款偿付地点
Claim payable at TOKYO

日期
Date NOV. 24, 1997

在
at GUANGZHOU

地址：
Address:

2. 单据改错二

请根据以下材料修改一份保险单。

A. 信用证条款。

APPLICANT	: HALSSEN & LYON GMBH PICKHUBEN 9, 20457 HAMBURG
BENEFICIARY	: CHINA TUHSU GUANGDONG TEA IMP. & EXP. CORP. 26-30 FLOOR, GUANGDONG FOREIGN ECONOMICS & TRADE BUILDING 351 TIANHE ROAD, GUANGZHOU, CHINA
AMOUNT	: DEM31,428. OO (DEUTSCHE MARK THIRTY ONE THOUSAND FOUR HUNDRED AND TWENTY EIGHT ONLY.)
PARTIAL SHIPMENTS	: NOT PERMITTED
TRANSSHIPMENT	: PERMITTED
LOADING IN CHARGE	: GUANGZHOU/HUANGPU, CHINA
FOR TRANSPORT TO	: HAMBURG
DESCRIPT. OF GOODS	: 4439 CHINA BLACK TEA ABT. 8,000 KGS @ DEM4. 05/KG CIFC3% HAMBURG (1 ×20' FCL/200 PAPERSACKS) PACKED IN PAPERSACKS, PALLETIZED AND CONTAINERIZED AS PER THE SALES CONFIRMATION NO. BT7095 THE PRICE IS TO BE UNDERSTOOD PER KILO NET SHIPPED WEIGHT CIF HAMBURG LESS 3 PERCENT COMMISSION, INCLUDING PACKING
DOCUMENTS REQUIRED	: MARINE INSURANCE POLICY/CERTIFICATE, COVERING ALL RISKS AND WAR RISKS, ISSUED FOR 110 PERCENT OF THE CIF INVOICE VALUE

B. 其他资料。

INVOICE NO. : TA7149　　INV. DATE: AUGUST 11, 1997

B/L NO. : GSG97 - 723　　B/L DATE: AUGUST 23, 1997

PACKING: 200 PAPERSACKS

SHIPPING MARKS: H&L/HAMBURG/6580

POLICY NO. : 1997A512

NAME OF STEAMER: PUDONG SENATOR WN743

PICC PROPERTY

中保财产保险有限公司

The People's Insurance (Property) Company of China, Ltd.

发票号码
Invoice No.

保险单号次
Policy No. 1997A512

海 洋 货 物 运 输 保 险 单
MARINE CARGO TRANSPORTATION INSURANCE POLICY

被保险人:
Insured: CHINA TUSHU GUANGDONG TEA IMPORT & EXPORT CORP.(被保险人背书转让)

中保财产保险有限公司(以下简称本公司)根据被保险人的要求,及其所缴付约定的保险费,按照本保险单承担险别和背面所载条款与下列特别条款承保下列货物运输保险,特签发本保险单。

This policy of Insurance witnesses that the People's Insurance(Property)Company of China, Ltd.(hereinafter called "the Company"), at the request of the Insured and in consideration of the agreed premium paid by the Insured, undertakes to insure the undermentioned goods in transportation subject to the conditions of this Policy as per the Clauses printed overleaf and other special clauses attached hereon.

保险货物项目 Descriptions of Goods	包装 单位 数量 Packing Unit Quantity	保险金额 Amount Insured
4439 CHINA BLACK TEA TOTAL:200 PAPERSACKS	200 PAPERSACKS	DEM34,571.00

承保险别
Conditions

COVERING ALL RISKS AND WAR RISKS AS PER OCEAN MARINE CARGO CLAUSES(1/1/1981)(WAREHOUSE TO WAREHOUSE CLAUSE IS INCLUDED)

货物标记
Marks of Goods

H&L
HAMBURG
65805

总保险金额:
Total Amount Insured: DEUTSCHE MARK THIRTY ONE THOUSAND FOUR HUNDRED AND TWENTY EIGHT ONLY.

保费
Premium as arranged

载运输工具
Per conveyance S. S. PUDONG SENATOR WN743

开航日期
Slg. on or abt. SEPT. 23,1997

起运港
From GUANGZHOU

目的港
to HAMBURG

所保货物,如发生本保险单项下可能引起索赔的损失或损坏,应立即通知本公司下述代理人查勘。如有索赔,应向本公司提交保险单正本(本保险单共有　份正本)及有关文件。如一份正本已用于索赔,其余正本则自动失效。

In the event of loss or damage which may result in a claim under this Policy, immediate notice must be given to the Company's Agent as mentioned hereunder. Claims, if any, one of the Original Policy which has been issued in ONE Original(s) together with the relevant documents shall be surrendered to the Company. If one of the Original Policy has been accomplished, the others to be void.

中保财产保险有限公司
THE PEOPLE'S INSURANCE(PROPERTY) COMPANY OF CHINA,LTD.

赔款偿付地点
Claim payable at HAMBURG

日期
Date SEPT. 22,1997

在
at GUANGZHOU

地址:
Address:

（八）单据填制

1. 单据填制一

请根据以下材料填制一份保险单。

A. 信用证条款。

Applicant	*50	: ZELLERS INC., ATTN. IMPORT DEPT. 401 BAY STREET, 10/FL. TORONTO ON MJH. 2Y4, CANADA
Beneficiary	*59	: G. M. G. HARDWEAR & TOOLS IMP. & EXP. COMPANY LTD. 726 DONGFENG ROAD EAST, GUANGZHOU, CHINA
Loading in Charge	44 A	: GUANG ZHOU, CHINA
For Transport to...	44 B	: VANCOUVER, CANADA
Descript. of Goods	45 A	: HANDLE TOOLS

ITEM NO.	QUANTITY	UNTI PRICE
A 0214	2,000 DOZ	USD 10.50
A 0012	1,000 DOZ	USD 11.50
M 0102	500 DOZ	USD 28.00

AS PER SALES CONFIRMATION NO. 02GP520471
DD 03 JAN. 02
CIF VANCOUVER CANADA

Documents required 46 A :

+MARINE INSURANCE POLICY OR CERTIFICATE IN DUPLICATE, ENDORSED IN BLANK, FOR FULL INVOICE VALUE PLUS 10 PERCENT, STATING CLAIM PAYABLE IN CANADA COVERING INSTITUTE CARGO CLAUSES(A) AND WAR RISKS.

B. 其他资料。

发票号码：KW-030419　　发票日期：2002年4月10日

发票金额：USD46500.00　　提单日期：2002年4月19日

船名：CHAOHE /ZIM CANADA V. 44E（在香港转运）

唛头：ZELLERS CANADA/VANCOUVER　　保险单号码：KC03-85362

货物装箱情况：10DOZ/PACKAGE　350 PACKAGES

中保财产保险有限公司

The People's Insurance (Property) Company of China, Ltd.

PICC PROPERTY

发票号码　　　　　　　　　　　　保险单号次

Invoice No.　　　　　　　　　　　　Policy No.

海　洋　货　物　运　输　保　险　单

MARINE CARGO TRANSPORTATION INSURANCE POLICY

被保险人：

Insured: ____________________

中保财产保险有限公司（以下简称本公司）根据被保险人的要求，及其所缴付约定的保险费，按照本保险单承担险别和背面所载条款与下列特别条款承保下列货物运输保险，特签发本保险单。

This policy of Insurance witnesses that the People's Insurance (Property) Company of China, Ltd. (hereinafter called "the Company"), at the request of the Insured and in consideration of the agreed premium paid by the Insured, undertakes to insure the undermentioned goods in transportation subject to the conditions of this Policy as per the Clauses printed overleaf and other special clauses attached hereon.

保险货物项目 Descriptions of Goods	包装　单位　数量 Packing　Unit　Quantity	保险金额 Amount Insured

承保险别　　　　　　　　　　　　货物标记

Conditions　　　　　　　　　　　　Marks of Goods

总保险金额：

Total Amount Insured: ____________________

保费　　　　　　　　载运输工具　　　　　　　　开航日期

Premium ___as arranged___　Per conveyance S. S. __________　Slg. on or abt __________

起运港　　　　　　　　　　　　目的港

From ____________________　to ____________________

所保货物，如发生本保险单项下可能引起索赔的损失或损坏，应立即通知本公司下述代理人查勘。如有索赔，应向本公司提交保险单正本（本保险单共有　　份正本）及有关文件。如一份正本已用于索赔，其余正本则自动失效。

In the event of loss or damage which may result in a claim under this Policy, immediate notice must be given to the Company's Agent as mentioned hereunder. Claims, if any, one of the Original Policy which has been issued in 　　　Original(s) together with the relevant documents shall be surrendered to the Company. If one of the Original Policy has been accomplished, the others to be void.

中保财产保险有限公司

THE PEOPLE'S INSURANCE (PROPERTY) COMPANY OF CHINA, LTD.

赔款偿付地点

Claim payable at ____________________

日期　　　　　　　　在

Date __________　at __________

地址：

Address:

2. 单据填制二

请根据以下材料填制一份保险单。

A. 信用证条款。

Applicant　＊50　: INTERCONTOR, ZENTRALEINKAUF UND HANDELS
SIGMUND STR. 220
90431 NUERNBERG

Beneficiary　＊59　: GUANGDONG TEXTILES IMP. & EXP.
COTTON MANUFACTURED GOODS COMPANY LTD.
14/F., GUANGDONG TEXTILES MANSION
NO. 168 XIAOBEI ROAD, GUANGZHOU

Loading in Charge　44 A : GUANGZHOU

For Transport to...　44 B : HAMBURG

Descript. of Goods　45 A : GUITAR

ITEM NO.	QUANTITY	UNTI PRICE
948	1,700 PCS	USD 7.42

AS PER SALES CONFIRMATION NO. 2002MCGS02007
DD 8.3.2002
TOTAL AMOUNT USD12,614.00
CIF HAMBURG

Documents Required　46 A :

MARINE INSURANCE POLICY OR CERTIFICATE IN DUPLICATE, ENDORSED IN BLANK, FOR FULL INVOICE VALUE PLUS 10 PERCENT, STATING CLAIM PAYABLE IN HAMBURG COVERING INSTITUTE CARGO CLAUSES (A) AND WAR RISKS, MARKED PREMIUM PAID.

B. 其他资料。

发票号码：020603GTB　　发票日期：2002 年 6 月 20 日
发票金额：USD12,614.00　　提单日期：2002 年 6 月 25 日
保险单号码：KC53696265　　唛头：KCHCSB /HAMBURG
船名：NANTU V. 832　　货物装箱情况：10PCS/CTN

中保财产保险有限公司
The People's Insurance (Property) Company of China, Ltd.
PICC PROPERTY

发票号码 保险单号次
Invoice No. Policy No.

海 洋 货 物 运 输 保 险 单
MARINE CARGO TRANSPORTATION INSURANCE POLICY

被保险人:
Insured: ______________________________

中保财产保险有限公司（以下简称本公司）根据被保险人的要求，及其所缴付约定的保险费，按照本保险单承担险别和背面所载条款与下列特别条款承保下列货物运输保险，特签发本保险单。

This policy of Insurance witnesses that the People's Insurance (Property) Company of China, Ltd. (hereinafter called "the Company"), at the request of the Insured and in consideration of the agreed premium paid by the Insured, undertakes to insure the undermentioned goods in transportation subject to the conditions of this Policy as per the Clauses printed overleaf and other special clauses attached hereon.

保险货物项目 Descriptions of Goods	包装 单位 数量 Packing Unit Quantity	保险金额 Amount Insured

承保险别 货物标记
Conditions Marks of Goods

总保险金额:
Total Amount Insured: ______________________________

保费 载运输工具 开航日期
Premium as arranged Per conveyance S. S. ______ Slg. on or abt ______

起运港 目的港
From ______________ to ______________

所保货物，如发生本保险单项下可能引起索赔的损失或损坏，应立即通知本公司下述代理人查勘。如有索赔，应向本公司提交保险单正本（本保险单共有 份正本）及有关文件。如一份正本已用于索赔，其余正本则自动失效。

In the event of loss or damage which may result in a claim under this Policy, immediate notice must be given to the Company's Agent as mentioned hereunder. Claims, if any, one of the Original Policy which has been issued in Original(s) together with the relevant documents shall be surrendered to the Company. If one of the Original Policy has been accomplished, the others to be void.

中保财产保险有限公司
THE PEOPLE'S INSURANCE (PROPERTY) COMPANY OF CHINA, LTD.

赔款偿付地点
Claim payable at ______________________________

日期 在
Date ______________ at ______________

地址:
Address:

二、练习题参考答案

（一）中英文术语、短语互译

1. 中译英

（1）Insurance Policy

（2）Open Policy

（3）Air Transportation Risk

（4）Warehouse to Warehouse Clause

（5）F. P. A.（Free From Particular Average）

（6）Strike Risks

（7）Particular Average

（8）Fresh and/or Water Damage

（9）Ocean Marine Cargo Clauses of the People's Insurance Company of China

（10）Premium

2. 英译中

（1）保险凭证　　（2）联合保险凭证

（3）投保一切险和战争险　　（4）保险金额

（5）协会货物条款　　（6）制成“凭指示”

（7）偷窃提货不着险　　（8）不计免赔率

（9）共同海损　　（10）被保险人

（二）单项选择题

1. B。理由：以 CIF 术语成交，装船前由出口方向保险公司投保，保险单的被保险人一栏一般填写出口方的名称，只有这样，保险公司的承保范围才是“仓至仓”。

2. A。理由：所加一成作为进口方的经营管理费用和预期利润。

3. D。理由：由于信用证条款只规定按 CIC 条款投保海洋运输险，所以出口公司投保平安险、水渍险及一切险中的任一种都符合信用证条款的规定。

4. D。理由：根据中国人民保险公司《海洋货物运输保险条款》的规定，其保险起讫采用“仓至仓”条款。

5. A。理由：信用证条款规定“所有单据都应该显示唛头”，所以只能填写实际唛头。

6. C。理由：保单的开航日期可填写提单签发日，或填写“AS PER B/L”，也可填写提单签发日前后各五天之内的任一天，答案 C 超出了这一范围。

7. B。理由：一般赔付地点在目的港（地），以利进口方向保险公司办理索赔手续。

8. D。理由：由于进口时通常采取的是“预约保险”的做法，进口方与保险公司签订有预约保险合同，合同中规定以国外寄来的装运通知替代投保单，保险公司在收到进口方交来的装运通知后，即负自动承保的责任。

9. C。理由：由于信用证中没有规定具体的投保险别，按惯例，我方只需投保最低险别——平安险，又由于出口商品是陶瓷制品，所以附加投保碰损破碎险。

10. C。理由：由于运输由两程运输完成，所以该栏应同时填写第一程船和第二程船的船名。

（三）多项选择题

1. ABC。理由：根据伦敦保险协会制定的《协会货物条款》，只有恶意损害险属于附加险别，不能单独投保。

2. BD。理由：按照我国《海洋货物运输保险条款》的规定，偷窃提货不着险及甲板险都属于一般附加险别。

3. ABCD。理由：T. P. N. D. LOSS 是指偷窃提货不着险，DAMAGE CAUSED BY HEAT，SHIP'S SWEAT 是指受潮受热险，DAMAGE CAUSED BY ODOUR 是指串味险，DAMAGE CAUSED BY BREAKAGE OF PACKING 是指破碎险。

4. AC。理由：按照我国《海洋货物运输保险条款》的规定，属于我国海洋运输货物保险中的基本险有 FPA、WPA 和 ALL RISKS。

5. ABD。理由：共同海损分摊时，涉及的受益方有船方、货方、运费方。

（四）判断题

1. 错误。理由：保险单和保险凭证具有相同的法律效力。

2. 正确。理由：保险单的签发日期应该早于海运提单的签发日期，否则，银行有权拒付。

3. 错误。理由：按照我国《海洋货物运输保险条款》的规定，一切险的承保范围不包括由于特殊外来原因造成的损失。

4. 错误。理由：以 CFR 术语进口钢材，我方公司承担货物在装运港越过船舷之后的风险，所以保险公司的承保责任范围为“船至仓”。

5. 错误。理由：如信用证规定按 ICC 条款投保，根据中国人民保险公司的现行做法是可以接受的。

6. 错误。理由：根据《UCP600》的规定，应提交一正一副或两份正本保单。

7. 正确。理由：按照我国现行的《海洋货物运输保险条款》的规定，保险公司对于海运战争险的保险责任起讫是仅负责水上风险。

8. 错误。理由：按照我国现行的《海洋货物运输保险条款》的规定，投保水渍险时，保险公司仅负责由于海水造成的损失。

9. 错误。理由：按照我国《海洋货物运输保险条款》的规定，战争险与罢工险作为特殊附加险，均不能单独投保。

10. 正确。理由：保险公司按伦敦保险协会制定的《协会货物条款》中的 ICCA、IC-CB 和 ICCC 三种险别承保的责任范围与按我国《海洋货物运输保险条款》中 ALL RISKS、WPA 和 FPA 承保的责任范围大致相同。

（五）案例分析题

1. 分析：保险公司对于该损失不应该赔偿。因为保单的被保险人为买方，而以 CFR

条件成交，根据《2010 通则》的规定，买方承担货物自装运港装上船之后的风险，所以保险公司的保险责任范围不再是“仓至仓”，其仅对货物自装运港装上船之后由于承保范围内的风险造成的损失进行赔偿。货物是用驳船从广州乌冲码头运往盐田港装船时，由于触礁而全部灭失，不在保险公司的保险责任范围内，所以保险公司不负责赔偿。

2. 分析：保险公司对于该损失不予赔偿。因为投保罢工险，保险公司只对因罢工造成的直接损失进行赔偿，而对于间接损失不予赔偿。本案例中，羊肉变质是由于码头工人罢工而致无人卸货，一个星期后由于无法补充燃料，货轮上的冷冻设备停止运转而造成的，属于间接损失，所以保险公司不予赔偿。

（六）阅读理解

1. 阅读理解一

（1）该笔交易是出口贸易。理由：根据保单记载，装运港是我国的广州港，目的港是希腊的派瑞斯港。

（2）受益人到银行办理议付前需要对该保单进行背书转让。理由：G M G HARDWARE & TOOLS IMP. &EXP. COMPANY LTD. 是出口公司，该交易以 CIF 条件达成，根据《2010 通则》的规定，该公司只承担货物在广州港越过船舷前的风险，广州港越过船舷后的风险由进口方承担。由于保单的被保险人一栏填写的是出口方的名称，所以受益人到银行办理议付前需要对该保单进行背书转让，否则银行不予议付。

（3）该金额不是发票金额。因为该交易以 CIF 条件达成，根据《2010 通则》的有关 CIF 章节 A3 款的规定，卖方有义务按合同规定的价款加 10% 投保。

2. 阅读理解二

（1）保险货物的名称是“MEN”/WOMEN'S SWEATERS”。

（2）该保单投保“一切险”，采取的是“中国人民保险公司的《海洋货物运输保险条款》”。

（3）保险货物在运输过程中没有发生转运。理由：保单记载的装运港是广东盐田港，目的港是加拿大的多伦多港，没有转运港口名称。

（七）单据改错

1. 单据改错一

保险单存在如下问题：

（1）Policy No.：AA3546897；

（2）被保险人在保险单背面进行背书转让；

（3）Marks of Goods：SK/YOKOHAMA /NOS. 1 –410；

（4）Per conveyance S. S.：NEDLLOYD HONSHU V. 3165；

（5）Claim Payable at：YOKOHAMA。

2. 单据改错二

保险单存在如下问题：

（1）Invoice No.：TA7149；

（2）Marks of Goods：H&L/HAMBURGA/6580；

（3）Total Amount Insured：DEUTSCHE MARK THIRTY FOUR THOUSAND FIVE HUNDRED AND SEVENTY-ONE ONLY.；

（4）Slg. on or abt.：AUG. 23，1997；

（5）Date：AUG. 22，1997。

（八）单据填制

1. 单据填制一

PICC PROPERTY

中保财产保险有限公司

The People's Insurance (Property) Company of China, Ltd.

发票号码
Invoice No. KW－030419

保险单号次
Policy No. KC 03－85362

海 洋 货 物 运 输 保 险 单
MARINE CARGO TRANSPORTATION INSURANCE POLICY

被保险人：
Insured: G. M. G. HARDWEAR & TOOLS IMP. & EXP. COMPANY LTD.（被保险人背面进行空白背书）

中保财产保险有限公司（以下简称本公司）根据被保险人的要求，及其所缴付约定的保险费，按照本保险单承担险别和背面所载条款与下列特别条款承保下列货物运输保险，特签发本保险单。

This policy of Insurance witnesses that the People's Insurance (Property) Company of China, Ltd. (hereinafter called "the Company"), at the request of the Insured and in consideration of the agreed premium paid by the Insured, undertakes to insure the undermentioned goods in transportation subject to the conditions of this Policy as per the Clauses printed overleaf and other special clauses attached hereon.

保险货物项目 Descriptions of Goods	包装 单位 数量 Packing Unit Quantity	保险金额 Amount Insured
HANDLE TOOLS TOTAL: 350 PACKAGES	350 PACKAGES	USD51,150.00

承保险别
Conditions

COVERING INSTITUTE CARGO CLAUSES(A)
AND WAR RISKS

货物标记
Marks of Goods

ZELLERS CANADA
VANCOUVER

总保险金额：
Total Amount Insured: US DOLLARS FIFTY-ONE THOUSAND ONE HUNDRED AND FIFTY ONLY.

保费 载运输工具 开航日期
Premium as arranged Per conveyance S. S. CHAO HE/ZIM CANADA V. 44E Slg. on or abt APR. 19, 2002

起运港 目的港
From GUANGZHOU to VANCOUVER W/T HONG KONG

所保货物，如发生本保险单项下可能引起索赔的损失或损坏，应立即通知本公司下述代理人查勘。如有索赔，应向本公司提交保险单正本（本保险单共有 份正本）及有关文件。如一份正本已用于索赔，其余正本则自动失效。

In the event of loss or damage which may result in a claim under this Policy, immediate notice must be given to the Company's Agent as mentioned hereunder. Claims, if any, one of the Original Policy which has been issued in ONE Original(s) together with the relevant documents shall be surrendered to the Company. If one of the Original Policy has been accomplished, the others to be void.

中保财产保险有限公司
THE PEOPLE'S INSURANCE (PROPERTY) COMPANY OF CHINA, LTD.

赔款偿付地点
Claim payable at CANADA

日期 在
Date APR. 19, 2002 at GUANGZHOU

地址：
Address:

2. 单据填制二

PICC PROPERTY

中保财产保险有限公司

The People's Insurance (Property) Company of China, Ltd.

发票号码 保险单号次

Invoice No. 020603GTB Policy No. KC53696265

海 洋 货 物 运 输 保 险 单

MARINE CARGO TRANSPORTATION INSURANCE POLICY

被保险人:

Insured: GUANGDONG TEXTILES IMP. & EXP. COTTON MANUFACTURED GOODS COMPANY LTD.

中保财产保险有限公司(以下简称本公司)根据被保险人的要求,及其所缴付约定的保险费,按照本保险单承担险别和背面所载条款与下列特别条款承保下列货物运输保险,特签发本保险单。

This policy of Insurance witnesses that the People's Insurance (Property) Company of China, Ltd. (hereinafter called "the Company"), at the request of the Insured and in consideration of the agreed premium paid by the Insured, undertakes to insure the undermentioned goods in transportation subject to the conditions of this Policy as per the Clauses printed overleaf and other special clauses attached hereon.

保险货物项目 Descriptions of Goods	包装 单位 数量 Packing Unit Quantity	保险金额 Amount Insured
GUITAR ITEM NO. 948	170CTNS	USD13,875.00

承保险别 货物标记

Conditions Marks of Goods

COVERING INSTITUTE CARGO CLAUSES (A) KCHCSB

AND WAR RISKS HAMBURG

总保险金额:

Total Amount Insured: US DOLLARS THIRTEEN THOUSAND EIGHT HUNDRED AND SEVENTY-FIVE ONLY.

保费 载运输工具 开航日期

Premium PAID Per conveyance S. S. NANTU V. 832 Slg. on or abt JUNE 25, 2002

起运港 目的港

From GUANGZHOU to HAMBURG

所保货物,如发生本保险单项下可能引起索赔的损失或损坏,应立即通知本公司下述代理人查勘。如有索赔,应向本公司提交保险单正本(本保险单共有 份正本)及有关文件。如一份正本已用于索赔,其余正本则自动失效。

In the event of loss or damage which may result in a claim under this Policy, immediate notice must be given to the Company's Agent as mentioned hereunder. Claims, if any, one of the Original Policy which has been issued in ONE Original (s) together with the relevant documents shall be surrendered to the Company. If one of the Original Policy has been accomplished, the others to be void.

中保财产保险有限公司

THE PEOPLE'S INSURANCE (PROPERTY) COMPANY OF CHINA, LTD.

赔款偿付地点

Claim payable at HAMBURG

日期 在

Date JUNE25, 2002 at GUANGZHOU

地址:

Address:

注:被保险人空白背书。

第五节　原产地证明书

一、练习题

（一）中英文术语、短语互译

1. 中译英

（1）目的地国家（地区）
（2）发票号码和日期
（3）签证机构
（4）工业联合会
（5）货物的原产地在中国
（6）回签
（7）成分
（8）代表处
（9）影印本
（10）与以色列没有任何直接或间接关系

2. 英译中

（1）Certificate of Origin
（2）GSP
（3）Origin Criterion
（4）Chamber of Commerce
（5）Competent Authorities
（6）For Official Use
（7）Means of Transport and Route
（8）H. S. Code
（9）Number and Kind of Packages
（10）Declaration by the Exporter

（二）单项选择题

1. 根据我国的规定，企业最迟于货物报关出运前（　　）向签证机构申请办理原产地证。

A. 7 天　　B. 3 天
C. 10 天　　D. 5 天

2. 在我国，签发普惠制原产地证 FORM A 的机构是（　　）。

A. 海关总署及各省市海关
B. 中国质检总局及各省市出入境检验检疫局
C. 商务部及各省市经贸厅
D. 各省市对外贸易促进委员会

3. 普惠制原产地证明书 FORM A 原产地标准栏目，如果出口商品完全是出口国自产的，不含有进口成分的商品，出口到所有给惠国，填写（　　）。

A. “P”　　B. “W”
C. “Y”　　D. “F”

4. 信用证条款：GSP Certificate of Origin, Form A, certifying goods of origin in China, issued by competent authorities，根据该条款，FORM A 的签发机构为（　　）。

A. 对外贸易促进委员会　　B. 出入境检验检疫局
C. 公证处　　D. 海关

5. 信用证条款：Certificate of Origin in two fold indicating that goods are of Chinese origin

issued by Chamber of Commerce，根据该条款，原产地证的签发机构为（　　）。

A. 商会　　B. 出入境检验检疫局

C. 公证处　　D. 海关

6. 普惠制是（　　）对发展中国家出口产品给予的一种关税优惠制度。

A. 发达国家　　B. 发展中国家

C. 美国　　D. 欧盟

7. 下列不属于普惠制原则的是（　　）。

A. 普遍原则　　B. 非互惠原则

C. 严格符合原则　　D. 非歧视原则

8. 下列不属于普惠制原产地规则的是（　　）。

A. 原产地标准　　B. 直接运输规则

C. 书面证明　　D. 单边优惠规则

（三）多项选择题

1. 出口企业在办理原产地证时，必须提交的单证有（　　）。

A.《中华人民共和国出口货物原产地证书/加工装配证明申请书》

B.《中华人民共和国出口货物原产地证书》一式四份

C. 出口货物商业发票

D. 签证机构认为必要的其他证明文件

2. 在我国，签发原产地证的机构包括（　　）。

A. 海关总署及各省市海关　　B. 各省市出入境检验检疫局

C. 商务部及各省市经贸厅　　D. 各省市对外贸易促进委员会

3. 下列国家中，给予我国普惠制待遇的是（　　）。

A. 保加利亚　　B. 美国

C. 新西兰　　D. 加拿大

4. 普惠制原产地证明书 FORM A 原产地标准栏目，如果出口商品完全是出口国自产的，不含有进口成分的商品，出口到澳大利亚、新西兰，该栏目可填写（　　）。

A. “P”　　B. “W”

C. “Y”　　D. 留空

5. 普惠制原产地证明书 FORM A 的申报日期，可以（　　）。

A. 早于发票日期　　B. 不得早于发票日期

C. 与发票日期同日　　D. 与提单日期同日

（四）判断题

1. 普惠制原产地证明书 FORM A 一般使用英文填制，应进口商的要求，也可使用法文，除此之外，证书不得使用其他文种。（　　）

2. 普惠制原产地证明书 FORM A 的收货人应填写最终收货人的名称。如果信用证未明确最终收货人，可以填写商业发票的抬头人，也可填写中间商的名称。（　　）

3. 含有进口成分的产品，出口到加拿大，普惠制原产地证明书 FORM A 的原产地标

准栏目填“W”。(　　)

4. 根据日本政府的规定，普惠制原产地证明书 FORM A 的有效期为自进口之日起 4 个月内。(　　)

5. 普惠制的原则有非普遍原则、非互惠原则和非歧视原则。(　　)

6. 非互惠原则是指非对等的，发达国家应单方面给予发展中国家优惠关税待遇，而不要求发展中国家给予同等待遇。(　　)

7. 非歧视原则是指应对所有的发展中国家都给予优惠待遇，不应区别对待，不应有例外。(　　)

（五）阅读理解

1. 阅读理解一

ORIGINAL

1. Exporter GUANGDONG TEXTILES IMPORT AND EXPORT KNITWEARS COMPANY LTD.15/F GUANGDONG TEXTILES MANSION 168 XIAOBEI ROAD, GUANGZHOU 510045, CHINA TEL 83856391 FAX NO.83866713	Certificate No. 971697422 CERTIFICATE OF ORIGIN OF THE PEOPLE' S REPUBLIC OF CHINA
2. Consignee H/S ALAMOUDI SPORT CENTER P.O.BOX 40616 JEDDAH 21511 K.S.A. TEL 6447453 FAX NO.6447433	
3. Means of transport and route FROM GUANGZHOU CHINA TO JEDDAH BY VESSEL	5. For certifying authority use only
4. Country / region of destination JEDDAH	

6. Marks and numbers	7. Number and kind of packages;description of goods	8. H.S.Code	9. Quantity	10. Number and date of invoices
ALAMOUDI SPORT CENTER JEDDAH	ONE HUNDRED AND FIFTY (150) CARTONS OF BOY'S SPORT SUIT THE NAME OF THE MANUFACTURERS:SAME AS EXPORTER GOODS EXPORTED ARE WHOLLY OF DOMESTIC ORIGIN. **	6112	600 DOZ	97229KES OCT. 28, 1997

11. Declaration by the exporter	12. Certification
The undersigned hereby declares that the above details and statements are correct, that all the goods were produced in China and that they comply with the Rules of Origin of the People's Republic of China. 广东省纺织品进出口针织品有限公司 GUANGDONG TEXTILES IMPORT & EXPORT KNITWEARS COMPANY LIMITED 林树宗 GUANGZHOU NOV. 01,1997	It is hereby certified that the declaration by the exporter is correct. 中国国际贸易促进委员会 CHINA COUNCIL FOR THE PROMOTION OF INTERNATIONAL TRADE (GUANGZHOU) GUANGZHOU NOV. 01,1997
Place and date. signature and stamp of authorized signatory	Place and date, signature and stamp of certifying authority

请根据上面的原产地证回答问题：
（1）出口商：
（2）收货人：
（3）运输方式和路线：
（4）目的地国家（地区）：
（5）运输标志：
（6）商品名称：
（7）包装数量：
（8）商品编码：
（9）发票号码：
（10）发票日期：
（11）申请日期：
（12）签发日期：
（13）签证机构：

2. 阅读理解二

请根据下面的 FORM A 回答问题：
（1）出口商：
（2）收货人：
（3）运输方式和路线：
（4）FORM A 号码：
（5）运输标志：
（6）商品名称：
（7）包装数量：
（8）原产地标准：
（9）发票号码：
（10）发票日期：
（11）申请日期：
（12）签发日期：
（13）签证机构：

ORIGINAL

1. Goods consigned from (Exporter's business name, address, country)
GUANGDONG TEXTILES IMP. AND EXP. COTTON
MANUFACTURED GOODS COMPANY LTD.
14/F,GUANGDONG TEXTILES MANSION NO.168
XIAOBEI ROAD, GUANGZHOU CHINA

2. Goods consigned to (Consignee's name, address, country)
BRUSSELS LACES AND GIFTS SERV.SA
RUE DE LUSAMBO,21/23
1190 BRUXELLES,BELGIUM

Reference No. GZ8/80293/0120

GENERALIZED SYSTEM OF PREFERENCES
CERTIFICATE OF ORIGIN
(Combined declaration and certificate)
FORM A
Issued in THE PEOPLE'S REPUBLIC OF CHINA
(country)
See Notes overleaf

3. Means of transport and route (as far as known)
ON/AFTER APR.24 1998 FROM GUANGZHOU
GUANGDONG CHINA TO ANTWERP BELGIUM VIA
HONGKONG BY SEA

4. For official use
THIS IS TO CERTIFY THAT THE GOODS STATED IN THIS CERTIFICATE HAD NOT BEEN SUBJECTED TO ANY PROCESSING DURING THEIR STAY/TRANSHIPMENT IN HONG KONG.
SIGNATURE
DATE: 14 MAY 1998

5. Item number	6. Marks and numbers of packages	7. Number and kind of packages; description of goods	8. Origin criterion (see Notes overleaf)	9. Gross weight or other quantity	10. Number and date of invoices
1.	BLGS VIA ANTWERP P.O.NO.970366 ART.NR... BEACH TOWELS C.C. SIZE:75X150 CM QTY.:24 PCS	ONE HUNDRED AND SIXTY-FOUR (164) CARTONS OF COTTON PRINTED VELVET TOWELS(WOVEN) *******************************	"P"	3 936 PCS	98422CBS APR.21, 1998

11. Certification
It is hereby certified, on the basis of control carried out, that the declaration by the exporter is correct.

GZ APR.23,1998

Place and date, signature and stamp of certifying authority

12. Declaration by the exporter
The undersigned hereby declares that the above details and statements are correct; that all the goods were produced in
CHINA
(country)
and that they comply with the origin requirements specified for those goods in the Generalized System of Preferences for goods exported to
BELGIUM
(importing country)
GUANGZHOU APR.22,1998

Place and date, signature of authorized signatory

（六）单据改错

广东省东风进出口公司（GUANGDONG DONGFENG IMPORT AND EXPORT CORP. 122 DONGFENG ROAD EAST，GUANGZHOU）与 SANYEI HONG KONG 14/F.，KAISER ESTATE 1，MANYUE STREET，HUNG HOM，SYDNEY，AUSTRALIA 达成一笔交易，内容主要有：2 400 件不锈钢铲头（STAINLESS STEEL SPADE HEAD），每 12 件扎成 1 捆，2002 年 12 月 1 日出运，该公司填制好如下“FORM A”，请审核并修改。

ORIGINAL

1. Goods consigned from (Exporter's business name, address, country) GUANGDONG DONGFENG IMPORT AND EXPORT CORP. 122 DONGFENG ROAD EAST, GUANGZHOU	Reference No. GZ9/12078/6311 GENERALIZED SYSTEM OF PREFERENCES CERTIFICATE OF ORIGIN (Combined declaration and certificate) FORM A issued in THE PEOPLE'S REPUBLIC OF CHINA (COUNTRY) See Notes overleaf
2. Goods consigned to (Consignee's name, address, country) SANYEI HONG KONG 14/F., KAISER ESTATE 1, MANYUE STREET, HUNG HOM, SYDNEY	
3. Means of transport and route (as far as known) ON/AFTER NOV. 11, 2002 FROM GUANGZHOU TO SYDNEY BY VESSEL	4. For official use

5. Item number	6. Marks and numbers of packages	7. Number and kind of packages; description of goods	8. Origin criterion (see Notes overleaf)	9. Gross weight or other quantity	10. Number and date of invoices
1	KMART SYDNEY NO. 1 - 200	TWO THOUDAND FOUR HUNDRED (2,400) PCS OF STAINLESS STEEL SPADE HEAD * * * * * * * * * * * * * * * * * * *	"P"	2,400PCS	YSM199901 NOV. 11, 2002

11. Certification It is hereby certified, on the basis of control carried out, that the declaration by the exporter is correct. GUANGZHOU NOV. 20, 2002 Place and date, signature and stamp of certifying authority	12. Declaration by the exporter The undersigned hereby declares that the above details and statements are correct; that all the goods were produced in GUANGZHOU (country) and that they comply with the origin requirements specified for those goods in the Generalized System of Preferences for goods exported to SYDNEY (importing country) GUANGZHOU NOV. 21, 2002 Place and date, signature of authorized signatory

（七）单据填制

1．单据填制一

广东省纺织品进出口针织品有限公司向希腊某商出口一批塑胶玩具，该出口公司产地证申报员张强拟于2003年10月7日向广州检验检疫局申报，公司电话：78787878。请你根据下面的商业发票帮张强填制“一般原产地证明书”。

广东省纺织品进出口针织品有限公司

GUANGDONG TEXTILES IMP. & EXP. KNITWEARS COMPANY LIMITED 15/F.,
GUANGDONG TEXTILES MANSION 168 XIAOBEI ROAD, GUANGZHOU, CHINA

商业发票
COMMERCIAL INVOICE

Messrs:
JOHNSON
KREONTOS 30 STR.
GREECE

INVOICE NO. : YSM1999B
INVOICE DATE : OCT. 05, 2003
L/C NO. : KDTT524250
L/C DATE : AUG. 20, 2003
S/C NO. : GD－98TX2509

Exporter:
GUANGDONG TEXTILES IMP. & EXP.
KNITWEARS COMPANY LIMTIED
15/F., GUANGDONG TEXTILES MANSION
168 XIAOBEI ROAD, GUANGZHOU, CHINA

Transport details:
FROM GUANGZHOU TO PIRAEUS GREECE
BY VESSEL SAILING DATE: OCT. 15, 2003

Terms of Payment:
BY L/C

MARKS AND NUMBERS	DESCRIP. OF GOODS	QUANTITY	UNIT PRICE	AMOUNT
JOHNSON 97KCS05111 NO. 1－500 MADE IN CHINA	H. S. NO.: 9503. 90 PLASTIC TOYS	10,000PCS	USD0. 60/PC	USD6,000. 00

FOB GUANGZHOU USD6,000. 00

TOTAL QUANTITY: 10,000PCS PACKING: 500CARTONS

TOTAL: US DOLLARS SIX THOUSAND ONLY.

广东省纺织品进出口针织品有限公司
GUANGDONG TEXTILES IMP. & EXP.
KNITWEARS COMPANY LIMITED
（签章）

ORIGINAL

1. Exporter	Certificate No. CERTIFICATE OF ORIGIN OF THE PEOPLE'S REPUBLIC OF CHINA
2. Consignee	
3. Means of transport and route	5. For Certifying authority use only
4. Country/region of destination	

6. Marks and numbers of packages	7. Number and kind of packages; Description of goods	8. H. S. Code	9. Quantity	10. Number and date of invoices

11. Declaration by the exporter The undersigned hereby declares that the above details and statements are correct, that all the goods were produced in China and that they comply with the Rules of Origin of the People's Republic of China. -- Place and date, signature and stamp of certifying authority	12. Certification It is hereby certified that the declaration by the export is correct. -- Place and date, signature of authorized signatory

2. 单据填制二

广东省轻工家电有限公司出口一批产品到比利时，该产品完全为我国江西浪花毛织厂自产，不含任何进口成分，请你根据下面的商业发票帮该公司产地证申报员张强（2005年3月18日申报，预定出口装运日期为3月22日）填制"普惠制产地证明书 FORM A"。

广东省轻工家电有限公司

GUANGDONG LIGHT ELECTRICAL APPLIANCES COMPANY LIMITED

52 DEZHENG ROAD SOUTH, GUANGZHOU, CHINA

商业发票

COMMERCIAL INVOICE

MESSRS.:	INVOICE NO. : GD05753
BRUSSELSLACES AND GIFTS SERV. SA	INVOICE DATE : FEB. 28, 2005
RUE DE LUSAMBO. 21/23	L/C NO. : 21036414276424
1190 BRUXELLES, BE	S/C NO. : D/269/97

EXPORTER:

GUANGDONG LIGHT ELECTRICAL

APPLIANCES COMPANY LIMITED

TRANSPORT DETAILS:	TERMS OF PAYMENT:
FROM GUANGZHOU TO ANTWERP BELGIUM	BY L/C
W/T HONG KONG BY VESSEL	

MARKS & NUMBERS	DESCRIP. OF GOODS	QUANTITY	UNIT PRICE	AMOUNT
AL SHAMALI ANTWERP	COTTON PRINTED VELVET TOWELS H. S. CODE: 6302. 5900	3,936PCS	@USD3. 64/PC	USD14,327. 04
			CIF ANTWERP	USD14,327. 04

TOTAL QUANTITY: 3,936PCS　PACKING: 160CTNS

TOTAL: US DOLLARS FOURTEEN THOUSAND AND THREE HUNDRED TWENTY-SEVEN POINT FOUR ONLY.

GUANGDONG LIGHT ELECTRICAL

APPLIANCES COMPANY LIMITED

（签章）

ORIGINAL

1. Goods consigned from (Exporter's business name, address, country)	Reference No. GENERALIZED SYSTEM OF PREFERENCES CERTIFICATE OF ORIGIN (Combined declaration and certificate) FORM A issued in THE PEOPLE'S REPUBLIC OF CHINA (COUNTRY) See Notes overleaf
2. Goods consigned to (Consignee's name, address, country)	
3. Means of transport and route (as far as known)	4. For official use

5. Item number	6. Marks and numbers of packages	7. Number and kind of packages; description of goods	8. Origin criterion (see Notes overleaf)	9. Gross weight or other quantity	10. Number and date of invoices

11. Certification It is hereby certified, on the basis of control carried out, that the declaration by the exporter is correct. -- Place and date, signature and stamp of certifying authority	12. Declaration by the exporter The undersigned hereby declares that the above details and statements are correct; that all the goods were produced in -- (country) and that they comply with the origin requirements specified for those goods in the Generalized System of Preferences for goods exported to -- (importing country) -- Place and date, signature of authorized signatory

二、练习题参考答案

（一）中英文术语、短语互译

1. 中译英

（1）Country/Region of Destination
（2）Number and Date of Invoice
（3）Certificate Authority
（4）Union of Industry
（5）Goods of Origin in China
（6）Issued Retrospectively
（7）Component
（8）The Representative Office
（9）Photocopy
（10）Has No Direct or Indirect Connection Whatsoever with Israel

2. 英译中

（1）原产地证
（2）普惠制（Generalized System of Preference）
（3）原产地标准
（4）商会
（5）授权当局
（6）供官方使用
（7）运输方式和航行
（8）商品编码
（9）包装种类和数量
（10）出口方声明

（二）单项选择题

1. B。理由：根据我国的规定，企业最迟于货物报关出运前3天向签证机构申请办理原产地证。

2. B。理由：根据我国的规定，签发普惠制原产地证 FORM A 的机构是中国质量监督检验检疫局及各省市出入境检验检疫局。

3. A。理由：按联合国贸发会议优惠问题特别委员会的规定，应填写“P”。

4. B。理由：我国授权签发 FORM A 的机构为出入境检验检疫局。

5. A。理由：“Chamber of Commerce”指中国商会。

6. A。理由：普惠制是发达国家对发展中国家出口产品给予的一种关税优惠制度。

7. C。理由：普惠制原则包括普遍原则、非互惠原则和非歧视原则。

8. D。理由：普惠制原产地规则包括原产地标准、直接运输规则和书面证明。

（三）多项选择题

1. ABCD。理由：根据我国的规定，出口企业在办理原产地证时，必须真实、完整、正确地提交《中华人民共和国出口货物原产地证书/加工装配证明申请书》、《中华人民共和国出口货物原产地证书》（一式四份）以及出口货物商业发票和签证机构认为必要的其他证明文件。

2. BD。理由：根据我国的规定，签发原产地证的机构包括中国质量监督检验检疫总局及各省市出入境检验检疫局和各省市贸易促进委员会。

3. CD。理由：世界上有29个发达国家是我国的给惠国，其中包括新西兰和加拿大。

4. AD。理由：按联合国贸发会议优惠问题特别委员会的规定，输往澳大利亚、新西兰的商品，如果出口商品完全是出口国自产的，不含有进口成分，则普惠制原产地证明书 FORM A 中的原产地标准栏目可填写“P”，也可以留空不填。

5. BCD。理由：按联合国贸发会议优惠问题特别委员会的规定，普惠制原产地证明书 FORM A 的申报日期不得早于发票日期。

（四）判断题

1. 错误。理由：普惠制原产地证明书 FORM A 在特殊情况下，第二栏可以使用给惠国的文种。

2. 错误。理由：普惠制原产地证明书 FORM A 的收货人不可填写中间商的名称。

3. 错误。理由：按联合国贸发会议优惠问题特别委员会的规定，含有进口成分的产品，出口到加拿大，普惠制原产地证明书 FORM A 的原产地标准栏目填“F”。

4. 错误。理由：根据日本政府的规定，普惠制原产地证明书 FORM A 的有效期为自签发机关签发之日起 4 个月内。

5. 错误。理由：普惠制的原则有普遍原则、非互惠原则和非歧视原则。

6. 正确。

7. 正确。

（五）阅读理解

1. 阅读理解一

（1）出口商：GUANGDONG TEXTILES IMPORT AND EXPORT KNITWEARS
COMPANY LTD. 15/F., GUANGDONG TEXTILES MANSION
168 XIAOBEI ROAD, GUANGZHOU 510045, CHINA
TEL 83856391 FAX NO. 83866713

（2）收货人：H/S ALAMOUDI SPORT CENTER P. O. BOX
40616 JEDDAH 21511 K. S. A.
TEL 6447453 FAX NO. 6447433

（3）运输方式和路线：FROM GUANGZHOU CHINA TO JEDDAH
BY VESSEL

（4）目的地国家（地区）：JEDDAH

（5）运输标志：ALAMOUDI SPORT CENTER
JEDDAH

（6）商品名称：BOY'S SPORT SUIT

（7）包装数量：ONE HUNDRED AND FIFTY（150）CARTONS

（8）商品编码：6112

（9）发票号码：97229KES

（10）发票日期：OCT. 28, 1997

（11）申请日期：NOV. 01, 1997

（12）签发日期：NOV. 01, 1997

（13）签证机构：中国国际贸易促进委员会

2. 阅读理解二

(1) 出口商: GUANGDONG TEXTILES IMP. AND EXP. COTTON
MANUFACTURED GOODS COMPANY LTD.
14/F., CUANGDONG TEXTILES MANSION NO. 168
XIAOBEI ROAD, GUANGZHOU, CHINA

(2) 收货人: BRUSSELS LACES AND GIFTS SERV. SA
RUE DE LUSAMBO, 21/23
1190 BRUXELLES, BELGIUM

(3) 运输方式和路线: ON/AFTER APR. 24, 1998
FROM GUANGHOU GUANGDONG CHINA TO ANTWERP
BELGIUM VIA HONGKONG BY SEA

(4) FORM A 号码: GZ8/80293/0120

(5) 运输标志: BLGS VIA ANTWERP
P. O. NO. 970366
ART. NR...
BEACH TOWELS C. C.
SIZE: 75×150 CM
QTY.: 24PCS

(6) 商品名称: COTTON PRINTED VELVET TOWELS (WOVEN)

(7) 包装数量: ONE HUNDRED AND SIXTY-FOUR (164) CARTONS

(8) 原产地标准: "P"

(9) 发票号码: 98422CBS

(10) 发票日期: APR. 21, 1998

(11) 申请日期: APR. 22, 1998

(12) 签发日期: APR. 23, 1998

(13) 签证机构: 中华人民共和国进出口商品检验局

(六) 单据改错

FORM A 存在如下主要问题:

(1) 第一项出口公司缺填写出口国家名,应增加"CHINA";

(2) 第二项进口公司缺填写进口国家名,应增加"AUSTRALIA";

(3) 第三项应将发票日期改为出运日期,同时,增加运输方式的内容,加填"BY VESSEL";

(4) 第七项包装数量及货物描述有错,应将计价数量改为运输包装数量;

(5) 第十二项应改填为出口国家和进口国家的名称,而不是装运港和目的港名称。

(6) 第十一、十二项的日期有错,一般情况下,申请日期应早于签发日期。两日期对调位置即可。

单据改正如下:

ORIGINAL

1. Goods consigned from (Exporter's business name, address, country) GUANGDONG DONGFENG IMPORT AND EXPORT CORP. 122 DONGFENG ROAD EAST, GUANGZHOU, CHINA	Reference No. GZ9/12078/6311 GENERALIZED SYSTEM OF PREFERENCES CERTIFICATE OF ORIGIN (Combined declaration and certificate) FORM A issued in THE PEOPLE'S REPUBLIC OF CHINA (COUNTRY) See Notes overleaf
2. Goods consigned to (Consignee's name, address, country) SANYEI HONG KONG 14/F., KAISER ESTATE 1, MANYUE STREET, HUNG HOM, SYDNEY, AUSTRALIA	
3. Means of transport and route (as far as known) ON/AFTER DEC. 01, 2002 FROM GUANGZHOU TO SYDNEY BY VESSEL	4. For official use

5. Item number	6. Marks and numbers of packages	7. Number and kind of packages; description of goods	8. Origin criterion (see Notes overleaf)	9. Gross weight or other quantity	10. Number and date of invoices
1	KMART SYDNEY NO. 1 - 200	TWO HUNDRED (200) BUNDLES OF STAINLESS STEEL SPADE HEAD *	"P"	2,400PCS	YSM199901 NOV. 11, 2002

11. Certification It is hereby certified, on the basis of control carried out, that the declaration by the exporter is correct. GUANGZHOU NOV. 21, 2002 Place and date, signature and stamp of certifying authority	12. Declaration by the exporter The undersigned hereby declares that the above details and statements are correct; that all the goods were produced in CHINA (country) and that they comply with the origin requirements specified for those goods in the Generalized System of Preferences for goods exported to AUSTRALIA (importing country) GUANGZHOU NOV. 20, 2002 Place and date, signature of authorized signatory

（七）单据填制

1．单据填制一

ORIGINAL

1. Exporter GUANGDONG TEXTILES IMP. & EXP. KNITWEARS COMPANY LIMTIED 15/F., GUANGDONG TEXTILES MANSION 168 XIAOBEI ROAD, GUANGZHOU, CHINA	Certificate No. CERTIFICATE OF ORIGIN OF THE PEOPLE'S REPUBLIC OF CHINA
2. Consignee JOHNSON KREONTOS 30 STR. GREECE	
3. Means of transport and route FROM GUANGZHOU TO PIRAEUS GREECE BY VESSEL	5. For Certifying authority use only
4. Country/region of destination GREECE	

6. Marks and numbers of packages	7. Number and kind of packages; description of goods	8. H. S. Code	9. Quantity	10. Number and date of invoices
JOHNSON 97KCS05111 NO. 1－500 MADE IN CHINA	FIVE HUNDRED (500) CARTONS OF PLASTIC TOYS * * * * * * * * * * * * * * * *	9503	10,000PCS	YSM1999B OCT. 05, 2003

11. Declaration by the exporter	12. Certification
The undersigned hereby declares that the above details and statements are correct, that all the goods were produced in China and that they comply with the Rules of Origin of the People's Republic of China. GUANGZHOU OCT. 07, 2003　张强 Place and date, signature and stamp of certifying authority	It is hereby certified that the declaration by the export is correct. GUANGZHOU OCT. 08, 2003 Place and date, signature of authorized signatory

2. 单据填制二

ORIGINAL

1. Goods consigned from (Exporter's business name, address, country) GUANGDONG LIGHT ELECTRICAL APPLIANCES COMPANY LIMITED 52, DEZHENG ROAD SOUTH, GUANGZHOU, CHINA	Reference No. GENERALIZED SYSTEM OF PREFERENCES CERTIFICATE OF ORIGIN (Combined declaration and certificate) FORM A issued in THE PEOPLE'S REPUBLIC OF CHINA (COUNTRY) See Notes overleaf
2. Goods consigned to (Consignee's name, address, country) BRUSSELS LACES AND GIFTS SERV. SA RUE DE LUSAMBO. 21/23 1190 BRUXELLES, BE	
3. Means of transport and route (as far as known) ON/AFTER MAR. 22, 2005 FROM GUANGZHOU TO ANTWERP BELGIUM W/T HONGKONG BY VESSEL	4. For official use

5. Item number	6. Marks and numbers of packages	7. Number and kind of packages; description of goods	8. Origin criterion (see Notes overleaf)	9. Gross weight or other quantity	10. Number and date of invoices
1	AL SHAMALI ANTWERP	ONE HUNDRED AND SIXTY (160) CARTONS OF COTTON PRINTED VELVET TOWELS * * * * * * * * * * * * * * * * * * *	"P"	3,936PCS	GD05753 FEB. 28, 2005

11. Certification	12. Declaration by the exporter
It is hereby certified, on the basis of control carried out, that the declaration by the exporter is correct GUANGZHOU MAR. 20, 2005 Place and date, signature and stamp of certifying authority	The undersigned hereby declares that the above details and statements are correct; that all the goods were produced in CHINA (country) and that they comply with the origin requirements specified for those goods in the Generalized System of Preferences for goods exported to BELGIUN (importing country) GUANGZHOU MAR. 18, 2005 Place and date, signature of authorized signatory

第六节　装箱单

一、练习题

（一）中英文术语、短语互译

1. 中译英

（1）装箱单/重量单/尺码单　（2）集装包和集装袋

（3）托盘　（4）散装

（5）习惯包装　（6）麻袋装

（7）每袋一打

2. 英译中

（1）Bundle　（2）Roll

（3）Drum　（4）Teu

（5）Sea-Worthy Packing　（6）Packed in Wooden Case

（7）Each Carton Cotains 2 Sets

（二）单项选择题

1. 对于价值较低的农产品，买卖双方往往采用（　　）计算其重量。

A. 法定重量　B. 理论重量

C. 净重　D. 以毛作净

2. 买卖双方以 CIF 条件达成 10 万吨散装小麦的交易合同，卖方如不希望在交货时因数量产生纠纷，最好在合同中订立（　　）。

A. 品质机动幅度　B. 仓至仓条款

C. 溢短装条款　D. 禁止转运条款

3. 某贸易公司向英国客商出口平纹印花纯棉坯布，信用证中规定"数量约为 100 000 码"，根据《UCP600》的规定，卖方可以理解为交货数量有不超过（　　）的增减幅度。

A. 3%　B. 5%　C. 10%　D. 15%

4. 信用证中规定"PACKING LIST IN FIVE COPIES"，则受益人提交的装箱单的份数为（　　）。

A. 5 份副本　B. 1 份正本 4 份副本

C. 不需提交正本　D. 5 份正本及 5 份副本

5. 某公司出口货物，从黄埔港发运，运往汉堡，在香港转船，在装箱单"TRANSPORT DETAILS"一栏填写错误的是（　　）。

A. FROM HUANGPU TO HAMBURG W/T HONGKONG

B. FROM HUANGPU TO HAMBURG VIA HONGKONG

C. FROM HUANGPU TO HONGKONG AND THENCE TO HAMBURG

D. FROM HUANGPU TO HAMBURG WITH TRANSSHIPMENT AT HONGKONG

(三) 多项选择题

1. 印刷在运输包装上的唛头，其作用是在运输过程中使有关人员易于辨认货物，便于核对单证，按习惯做法，唛头由（　　）提供。

A. 卖方　　B. 买方
C. 船方　　D. 货代公司

2. 根据在流通过程中所起作用不同，商品包装可分为（　　）。

A. 运输包装　　B. 装卸包装
C. 储存包装　　D. 销售包装

3. 买卖双方在合同中对交货数量规定了溢短装条款，溢短装的选择权可以在合同中规定由（　　）行使。

A. 买方　　B. 卖方
C. 拖车公司　　D. 船公司

4. 当合同中规定采用净重计算商品重量时，对于如何计算包装的重量，国际上通常采用以下几种做法（　　）。

A. 按实际皮重计算　　B. 按约定皮重计算
C. 按平均皮重计算　　D. 按习惯皮重计算

5. 运输包装分为单件运输包装和集合运输包装，以下哪些包装属于集合运输包装(　　)。

A. 托盘　　B. 箱
C. 集装箱　　D. 包

(四) 判断题

1. 装箱单的主要作用是补充商业发票内容的不足，便于买方掌握商品的包装、数量及供进口国海关检查和核对货物。(　　)

2. 某工厂出口货物一批，合同中规定使用纸箱包装，为了更好地保护商品，卖方在交货时没有经过买方的同意就采用了木箱包装，这种替客户着想的做法是对的。(　　)

3. 信用证中规定包装采用“SEAWORTHY PACKING”，受益人在出口时根据货物情况采用了纸箱作为运输包装，在制作装箱单时，包装材料一栏应填制为“SEAWORTHY PACKING”。(　　)

4. 国际贸易中的习惯做法是将包装包括在货价以内，不另计收。(　　)

5. 受益人在制作相关单据时，必须将运输包装上的标志都注明在单据上。(　　)

(五) 案例分析

1. 某公司出口羊肉罐头到科威特，合同规定使用木箱装，每箱 24 听。卖方按合同规定的数量交付了货物，但其中部分包装使用的是 12 听的小箱。货到目的港后，买方以包装与合同不符为由拒绝收取货物，卖方却坚持要买方收取全部货物，其称：根据我方在科威特市场的销售人员及客户的反映，不论是使用每箱 24 听的包装还是使用每箱 12 听的包装，并不影响羊肉罐头的市场销售价格。请问买方有无权利拒收货物？为什么？

2. 我某外贸公司从日本进口鱼粉 5 000 公吨，合同条款如下：价格为 CIF 广州每公吨 100 美元，单层新麻袋包装，每袋 50 千克，以即期信用证方式付款。货到广州港后，我方发现货物扣除麻袋重量后不足 5 000 公吨，于是要求卖方将短量部分的货款退还。问我方要求是否合理？为什么？

（六）单据改错

1. 单据改错一

请根据以下材料修改装箱单。

A. 信用证条款。

Date of Issue	: 971020
Form of Doc. Credit	: IRREVOCABLE
Doc. Credit Number	: M20K2710NS00032
Expiry	: Date 971115 Place IN BENEFICIARY'S COUNTRY
Applicant	: SE BANG TRADING CO., LTD. 148 NAMCHEON - 2 DONG, SUYOUNG - KU PUSAN, KOREA
Beneficiary	: GUANGZHOU ARTS & CRAFTS IMP. & EXP. CORP. 628 GUAGNZHOU DADAO ZHONG ROAD, GUANGZHOU, CHINA
Partial Shipments	: ALLOWED
Transshipment	: ALLOWED
Loading in Charge	: GUANGZHOU, CHINA
For Transport to...	: PUSAN, KOREA
Latest Date of Ship.	: 971105
Descript. of Goods	: CHINA ORIGIN CIF PUSAN ARTIFICIAL FLOWERS AB - 06001　　5,184DOZ @ USD2.50/DOZ AB - 07049　　2,880DOZ @ USD2.50/DOZ AS PER S/C NO. 97A/KF002A DATE OCT. 15, 1997, ISSUED BY GUANGZHOU ARTS & CRAFTS IMP. & EXP. CORP.
Documents Required	: PACKING LIST IN TRIPLICATE
Additional Cond.	: ALL DOCUMENTS MUST INDICATE THIS CREDIT NUMBER THE DETAILS SUCH AS ART NO. COLOR, Q'TY SHOULD BE MARKED ON THE EACH INNER BOX AND CARTON EXACTLY

B. 其他资料。

INV. NO.: 97KF335　　INV. DATE: OCT. 28, 1997

B/L NO.: DSA97 - 1102　　SHIPPING MARKS: SE BANG/PUSAN

PACKING: AB - 06001 36DOZ/CTN　G. W.: 23KGS/CTN　N. W.: 18KGS/CTN

AB - 07049 36DOZ/CTN　G. W.: 19KGS/CTN　N. W.: 13KGS/CTN

NAME OF STEAMER: SUI 301/NORASIA V.49 - 3　W/T HONGKONG

CONTAINER NO. MSCU 4097560（20'）　MSCU 4097615（40'）

MEASUREMENT:（40 × 50 × 80）CM/CTN

广州工艺品进出口公司

GUANGZHOU ARTS & CRAFTS IMP. & EXP. CORP.

628 GUANGZHOU DADAO ZHONG ROAD, GUANGZHOU, CHINA

装 箱 单

PACKING LIST

ORIGINAL

Exporter:
GUANGZHOU ARTS & CRAFTS IMP. & EXP. CORP.
628 GUANGZHOU DADAO ZHONG ROAD,
GUANGZHOU, CHINA

DATE: OCT. 28, 1997
INVOICE NO.: 97KF335
B/L NO.: OCT. 31, 1997
S/C NO.: 97A/KF002A
L/C NO.: M20K2710NS00032

TRANSPORT DETAILS:
FROM GUANGZHOU TO PUSAN
BY VESSEL

标记 Marks & numbers	货名 description of goods	件数 Quantity	净重 N. W.	毛重 G. W.	尺码 Measurement
SE BANG	ARTIFICIAL FLOWERS				
PUSAN	ART NO.: AB－06	36DOZ/CTN	@18.00KGS	@23.00KGS	@(40×50×80)CM
	5,184DOZ	144CTNS	2,592.00KGS	3,312.00KGS	23.04CBMS
	ART NO.: AB－07049	36DOZ/CTN	@13.00KGS	@19.00KGS	@(40×50×80)CM
	2,880DOZ	80 CTNS	1,040.00KGS	1,520.00KGS	12.80CBMS
		224CTNS	3,632.00KGS	4,832.00KGS	35.84CBMS

TOTAL QUANTITY: 224CTNS
TOTAL: TWO HUNDRED AND TWENTY-FOUR CARTONS ONLY.

GUANGZHOU ARTS & CRAFTS IMP. & EXP. CORP.
628 GUANGZHOU DADAO ZHONG ROAD, GUANGZHOU, CHINA

2. 单据改错二

请根据以下材料修改装箱单。

A. 信用证条款。

NANYANG COMMERCIAL BANK LTD. , HONGKONG

HONGKONG 1ST MARCH, 1997

TO: BANK OF CHINA, GUANGZHOU, CHINA

DOCUMENTARY CREDIT NO. 97 - 34985

FOR THE ACCOUNT OF ABC TRADING CO. , LTD. , 312 SOUTHBRIDGE STREET, HONGKONG

DEAR SIRS,

WE OPEN AN IRREVOCABLE DOCUMENTARY CREDIT IN FAVOUR OF GUANGDONG FOREIGN TRADE IMP. AND EXP. CORP. , 267 TIANHE ROAD, GUANGZHOU, CHINA. FOR A SUM NOT EXCEEDING HKD980, 000. 00 (SAY HONGKONG DOLLARS NINE HUNDRED AND EIGHTY THOUSAND ONLY.) AVAILABLE BY THE BENEFICIARY'S DRAFT (S) AT SIGHT DRAWN ON US, BEARING THE CLAUSE: "DRAWN UNDER NANYANG CMMERCIAL BANK LTD. , HONGKONG IRREVOCABLE DOCUMENTARY CREDIT NO. 97 - 34985 DATED 1ST MARCH, 1997." ACCOMPANIED BY THE FOLLOWING DOCUMENTS:

...

(4) PACKING LIST IN TRIPLICATE.

(5) CERTIFICATE OF ORIGIN ISSUED BY GUANGZHOU IMPORT AND EXPORT COMMODITY INSPECTION BUREAU OF THE PEOPLE'S REPUBLIC OF CHINA IN TRIPLICATE. EVIDENCING SHIPMENT OF THE FOLLOWING MERCHANDISE:

AIR CONDITIONER (HUALING BRAND), 500 SETS KF - 23GW AND 500 SETS KF - 25GW, PACKING: IN CARTON BOX, 50 KILOS NET EACH CARTON, 1SET/CTN, @ HKD1, 000/SET, CIFC2% DUBAI, OTHER TERMS AND CONDITIONS AS PER S/C NO. AB44001, FROM GUANGZHOU TO DUBAI VIA HONGKONG. PARTIAL SHIPMENT PERMITIED. TRANSSHIPMENT PROHIBITED. LATEST DATE FOR SHIPMENT: 30TH APPIL, 1997. EXPIRY DATE: 15TH MAY, 1997. IN PLACE OF BENEFICIARY FOR NEGOTIATION.

WE HEREBY ENGAGE WITH THE DRAWERS, ENDORSERS AND BONAFIDE HOLDERS OF DRAFT(S) DRAWN UNDER AND COMPLIANCE WITH THE TERMS OF THIS CREDIT THAT SUCH DRAFT(S) SHALL BE DULLY HONOURED ON DUE PRESENTATION.

BENEFICIARY'S DECLARATION ON THE INVOICE THAT THE PRODUCTION COMPANY IS A STATE-OWNED ENTERPRISE AND IS NO RELATION WITH ISRAEL WHATSOEVER.

SHIPPING MARKS: ABC/DUBAI/NOS1 - 1000

THIS CREDIT IS SUBJECT TO "UNIFORM CUSTOMS AND PRACTICE FOR DOCUMENTARY CREDITS" (1993 REVISION) INTERNATIONAL CHAMBER OF COMMERCE PUBLICATION NO. 500.

YOURS FAITHFULLY,

NANYANG COMMERCIAL BANK LTD. , HONGKONG

B. 其他资料。

发票号码	GDF - 97 - 22341	发票日期	APR. 15, 1997	船　名	MECUE/DONGFENG M0123
毛　重	55 KGS/CTN	提单号码	SWHK - 970156	尺　码	(50 × 80 × 100) CM/CTN

广东对外贸易进出口公司

GUANGDONG FOREIGN TRADE IMP. AND EXP. CORP.
267 TIANHE ROAD, GUANGZHOU, CHINA

装 箱 单
PACKING LIST

ORIGINAL

Exporter:
GUANGDONG FOREIGN TRADE IMP. AND EXP. CORP.
267 TIANHE ROAD,
GUANGZHOU, CHINA

DATE: APR. 15, 1997
INVOICE NO.: GDF-97-2234
B/L NO.: SWHK-970156
S/C NO.: AB44001
L/C NO.: 97-34985

TRANSPORT DETAILS:
FROM GUANGZHOU TO DUBAI VIA
HONGKONG BY VESSEL

标记 Marks & numbers	货名 description of goods	件数 Quantity	净重 N. W.	毛重 G. W.	尺码 Measurement
ABC	AIR CONDITIONER (HUALING BRAND)				
DUBAI	ART NO.: KF-23GW	1SET/CTN	@50.00KGS	@55.00KGS	@ (50×80×100) CM
NOS1-100	500SETS	500CTNS	2,500.00KGS	2,750.00KGS	200CBMS
	ART NO.: KF-25GW	1SET/CTN	@50.00KG	@55.00KGS	@(50×80×100)CM
	500SETS	500CTNS	2,500.00KGS	2,750.00KGS	200CBMS
		1,000CTNS	5,000.00KGS	5,500.00KGS	400CBMS

TOTAL QUANTITY: 1,000SETS
TOTAL: ONE THOUSAND PIECES ONLY.

GUANGDONG FOREIGN TRADE IMP. AND EXP. CORP.
267 TIANHE ROAD, GUANGZHOU, CHINA

（七）单据填制

1. 单据填制一

请根据以下材料填制一份装箱单。

A. 信用证条款。

WE HEREBY ESTABLISH OUR IRREVOCABLE DOCUMENTARY CREDIT（DC NO.：FK28093）FOR AMOUNT OF USD8,335.00 US DOLLARS EIGHT THOUSAND THREE HUNDRED THIRTY FIVE ONLY.
CFR KARACHI

AVAILABLE BY BENEFICIARY'S MANUALLY SIGNED DRAFTS DRAWN ON US IN DUPLICATE ACCOUNT OPENERS AT SIGHT FOR FULL INVOICE VALUE OF SHIPMENT PURPORTING TO BE：
（H. S. CODE NO. 8539.2900）FILAMENT LAMPS
TW－3050（1.5M） 3,000 PCS AT USD0.65 PER PC
TW－3018（3YD） 3,800 PCS AT USD0.65 PER PC
TW－8031（2YD） 3,000 PCS AT USD0.98 PER PC
TW－6013（2YD） 500 PCS AT USD0.65 PER PC

AS PER BENEFICIARIES FAX PROFORMA INVOICE NO. 97SGQ469011 DTD 26/4/97

ACCOMPANIED BY THE FOLLOWING DOCUMENTS：
+PACKING LIST IN DUPLICATE
...
PARTIAL SHIPMENT PROHIBITED
TRANSSHIPMENT ALLOWED
SHIPMENT FROM P. R. OF CHINA TO KARACHI BY VESSEL

ALL DOCUMENTS TO EVIDENCE SHIPMENT AS INDICATED ABOVE
B/L MUST BE DATED NOT BEFORE THE DATE OF THIS CREDIT
AND NOT LATER THAN 30/30/97.

B. 其他资料。

发票号码：97SGP7528	发票日期：1997年6月20日
提单号码：CANE124004	装运港：黄埔港
船名：HANJIN V. 008W	尺码：（40×40×50）CM/CTN
净重：10.00KGS/CTN	毛重：12.00KGS/CTN
货物装箱情况：100PCS/CTN	

广东轻工家电有限公司

GUANGDONG LIGHT ELECTRICAL APPLIANCES CO., LTD.

52 DEZHENG ROAD SOUTH, GUANGZHOU, CHINA

装 箱 单
PACKING LIST

ORIGINAL

Exporter:

DATE :

INVOICE NO. :

B/L NO. :

S/C NO. :

L/C NO. :

TRANSPORT DETAILS:

标记 Marks & numbers	货名 description of goods	件数 Quantity	净重 N. W.	毛重 G. W.	尺码 Measurement

2. 单据填制二

请根据以下材料填制一份装箱单。

A. 信用证条款。

DOC. Credit Number	*20		: KRT2899302
Date of Issue	31	C	: 970912
Expiry	*31	D	: Date 971205 place CHINA
Applicant	*50		: CURRENT FUNDS LIMITED ROOM 1110 CHINACHEM GOLDEN PLAZA NO. 77 MODY ROAD, TSIM SHA TSUI EAST, KOWLOON, HONG KONG
Beneficiary	*59		: GUANGDONG TEXTILES IMPORT AND EXPORT KNITWEARS COMPANY LIMITED 15/F., GUANGDONG TEXTILES MANSION, 168 XIAOBEI ROAD, GUANGZHOU, CHINA
Amount	*32	B	: CURRENCY USD AMOUNT 30, 384. 00
Available with / by	*41	D	: CREDIT ISSUING OFFICE BY PAYMENT
Partial Shipments	43	P	: FORBIDDEN
Transshipment	43	T	: PROHIBITED
Loading in Charge	44	A	: GUANGDONG, CHINA
For Transport to...	44	B	: SANTOS, BRAZIL
Latest Date of ship.	44	C	: 971115
Descript. of Goods	45	A	:

DESCRIPTION: CHILDREN'S 65 PERCENT COTTON 35 PERCENT POLYESTER KNITTED JOGGING SUIT

QUANTITY: 720 DOZEN SETS

UNIT PRICE: USD42. 2 PER DOZEN SET

FOB GUANGDONG, CHINA

ALL OTHER DETAILS AS PER CONFIRMATION NO. DY - 039

SHIPMENT TO BE EFFECTED BY 1 × 20 CONTAINER (FCL)

Documents Required 45 A :

PACKING LIST IN TRIPLICATE SHOWING DETAILS OF PACKING.

BREAKDOWN OF QUANTITY, GROSS WEIGHT, NET WEIGHT AND MEASUREMENT OF EACH CARTON.

B. 其他资料。

发票号码: 9703SP023　　发票日期: 1997 年 11 月 2 日

提单号码: SA75214　　货物装箱情况: 30DOZ/BALE

船名: FANDU V. 336　　装运港: 广州港

净重: 180. 00KGS/BALE　　毛重: 195. 00KGS/BALE

尺码: (100 × 100 × 120) CM/BALE

广东纺织品进出口针织品有限公司

GUANGDONG TEXTILES IMPORT & EXPORT KNITWEARS COMPANY LIMITED

15/F., GUANGDONG TEXTILES MANSION, 168 XIAOBEI ROAD, GUANGZHOU, CHINA

装 箱 单

PACKING LIST

ORIGINAL

Exporter:

DATE:

INVOICE NO.:

B/L NO.:

S/C NO.:

L/C NO.:

TRANSPORT DETAILS:

标记 Marks & numbers	件数 Quantity	货名 Description of goods	净重 Net weight	毛重 Gross weight	尺码 Measurement

二、练习题参考答案

（一）中英文术语、短语互译

1. 中译英

（1）Packing List /Weight List/Measurement List
（2）Flexible Container
（3）Pallet
（4）In Bulk
（5）Customary Packing
（6）Packed In Gunny Bag
（7）One Dozen Per Bag

2. 英译中

（1）捆
（2）卷
（3）桶
（4）20 英尺等量单位
（5）适于海运的包装
（6）木箱装
（7）每箱装 2 套

（二）单项选择题

1. D。理由：由于农产品价值较低，所以买卖双方通常把产品的毛重当成净重以计算其重量。

2. C。理由：由于该交易属于大批量的散装货，交货数量易因运输、装卸等发生溢短装的情况，卖方通常要求在合同中订立“溢短装条款”，以使自己的交货数量具有一定的机动幅度。

3. C。理由：根据《UCP600》第 30 条 A 款的规定，凡“约”或类似意义的词语用于涉及信用证规定的数量时，应解释为允许有关数量有 10% 的增减。

4. B。理由：根据《UCP600》第 17 条 E 款的规定，如信用证要求一式多份单据，除非单据本身另有表明，只需提交一份正本，其余份数为副本。

5. C。理由：在香港转船的正确表述是“W/T OR VIA HONGKONG”，而“W/T”是“WITH TRANSSHIPMENT AT”的缩略形式。

（三）多项选择题

1. AB。理由：按国际贸易习惯，唛头一般由卖方决定，如买方要求，也可在合同中作出具体规定。

2. AD。理由：根据商品包装在流通过程中所起作用不同，可分为运输包装和销售包装。

3. ABD。理由：合同中对交货数量规定了溢短装条款，大多数由买方决定伸缩量，特别是在买方派船装运时，可由买方决定。而在采用程租船时，可授权船方根据轮船的实际运载能力决定伸缩幅度。

4. ABCD。理由：这四种均是国际贸易中常用的去除皮重的方法。

5. AC。理由：箱和包都属于单件运输包装。

（四）判断题

1. 正确。理由：装箱单就是通过表内的包装件数、净重、毛重等项目的描写，补充商业发票内容的不足，便于买方掌握商品的包装、数量及供进口国海关检查和核对货物。

2. 错误。理由：根据《联合国国际货物销售合同公约》第35条的规定，卖方必须按照合同规定的方式装箱或包装。

3. 正确。理由：由于信用证中规定包装采用“SEAWORTHY PACKING”，所以在制作装箱单时应照抄信用证的规定。

4. 正确。理由：商品的包装是商品的重要组成部分，在作价时一般都包括了水平包装的费用。

5. 错误。理由：运输包装上的标志有运输标志、指示性标志、警告性标志，受益人在制作相关单据时，只需将运输标志（即唛头）填制在单据上。

（五）案例分析

1. 答：买方没有权利拒收货物，但可以要求减低价格。虽然卖方所交货物有部分包装与合同不符，但根据《联合国国际货物销售合同公约》第51条的规定，买方只有在卖方完全不交付货物或不按照合同规定交付货物等于根本违反合同时，才可以宣布整个合同无效。而根据第50条的规定，如果货物不符合同，不论价款是否已付，买方都可以减低价格，减价按实际交付的货物在交货时的价值与符合合同的货物在当时的价值两者之间的比例计算。

2. 答：我方的要求是合理的。因为根据《联合国国际货物销售合同公约》第51条的规定，如果价格是按货物的重量规定的，如有疑问，应按净重确定。所以我方发现扣除麻袋重量后不足5 000公吨，可以要求对方将短量部分的货款退还。

（六）单据改错

1. 单据改错一

单据主要存在如下错误：

（1）B/L NO.：DSA97－1102；

（2）TRANSPORT DETAILS：FROM GUANGZHOU TO PUSAN W/T HONGKONG；

（3）TOTAL QUANTITY：8,064DOZ；

（4）ART NO.：AB－06001。

2. 单据改错二

单据主要存在如下错误：

（1）INVOICE NO.：GDF－97－22341；

（2）Marks & numbers：ABC/ DUBAI/NOS1－1000；

（3）TOTAL：ONE THOUSAND CTNS ONLY.；

（4）N. W.：25,000.00KGS.　　G. W.：27,500.00KGS
50,000.00KGS　　55,000.00KGS。

（七）单据填制

1. 单据填制一

广 东 轻 工 家 电 有 限 公 司

GUANGDONG LIGHT ELECTRICAL APPLIANCES CO. , LTD.

52DEZHENG ROAD SOUTH, GUANGZHOU, CHINA

装 箱 单

PACKING LIST

ORIGINAL

Exporter:

GUANGDONG LIGHT ELECTRICAL APPLIANC-
ESCO. , LTD.
52 DEZHENG ROAD SOUTH, GUANGZHOU,
CHINA

DATE : JUNE 20, 1997
INVOICE NO. : 97SGP7528
B/L. NO. : CANE124004
S/C NO. : 97SGQ469011
L/C NO. : FK28093

TRANSPORT DETAILS:

FROM HUANGPU TO KARACHI
BY VESSEL

标记 Marks & numbers	件数 Quantity	货名 Description of goods	净重 Net wieght	毛重 Gross weight	尺码 Measurement
	100PCS/CTN	FILAMENT LAMPS	@10KGS	@12KGS	@ (40×40×50) CM
N/M	30CTNS	TW-3050 (1.5M)	300KGS	360KGS	2.4M^3
	38CTNS	TW-3018 (3 YD)	380KGS	456KGS	3.04M^3
	30CNTS	TW-8013 (2 YD)	300KGS	360KGS	2.4M^3
	5CTNS	TW-6013 (2 YD)	50KGS	60KGS	0.40M^3
	103CTNS		1,030KGS	1,236KGS	8.24M^3

TOTAL QUANTITY: 10,300PCS

TOTAL: ONE HUNDRED AND THREE CTNS ONLY.

GUANGDONG LIGHT ELECTRICAL APPLIANCES
CO. , LTD.

2. 单据填制二

广东纺织品进出口针织品有限公司

GUANGDONG TEXTILES IMPORT & EXPORT KNITWEARS COMPANY LIMITED

15/F., GUANGDONG TEXTILES MANSION, 168 XIAOBEI ROAD, GUANGZHOU, CHINA

装箱单

PACKING LIST

ORIGINAL

Exporter:

GUANGDONG TEXTILES IMPORT & EXPORT
KNITWEARS COMPANY LIMITED

DATE : NOV. 2, 1997
INVOICE NO.: 9703SP023
B/L. NO. : SA75214
S/C NO. : DY-039
L/C NO. : KRT2899302

TRANSPORT DETAILS:

FROM GUANGZHOU, CHINA TO SANTOS, BRAZIL
BY VESSEL

标记 Marks & numbers	件数 Quantity	货名 Description of goods	净重 Net wieght	毛重 Gross weight	尺码 Measurement
		CHILDREN'S 65 PERCENT COTTON			
N/M	30DOZ/BALE	35 PERCENT POLYESTER KNITTED	@180.00KGS	@195.00KGS	@ (100×100×120)
	24BALES	JOGGING SUIT	4,320.00KGS	4,680.00KGS	28.8M^3
	24BALES		4,320.00KGS	4,680.00KGS	28.8M^3

TOTAL QUANTITY: 720 DOZ SETS
TOTAL: TWENTY-FOUR BALES ONLY.

GUANGDONG TEXTILES IMPORT & EXPORT
KNITWEARS COMPANY LIMITED

第三章
其他结汇单据

第一节　商检证书

一、练习题

（一）中英文术语、短语互译

1. 中译英

（1）商品检验　　（2）品质检验证书

（3）重量/体积检验证书　　（4）数量检验证书

（5）开证人的代表

2. 英译中

（1）Inspection Certificate of Sanitary or Health

（2）Inspection Certificate of Disinfection

（3）Inspection Certificate of fumigation

（4）Inspection Certificate of Hold

（5）China Commodity Inspection Bureau

（二）单项选择题

1. 根据《联合国国际货物销售合同公约》的规定，买方向卖方提出索赔的最后期限是(　　)。

A. 货物在装运港经检验机构检验并签发检验证书之日起两年内

B. 货物到达目的港经检验机构检验并签发检验证书之日起两年内

C. 买方在实际收到货物之日起两年内

D. 货物到达目的港（地）进入买方仓库之日起两年内

2. 根据出入境检验检疫局的规定，出境货物最迟应于报关或装运前(　　)天报验。

A. 3 天　　B. 7 天

C. 10 天　　D. 15 天

3. 以下哪一项不是国家质量监督检验检疫总局的主要职责(　　)。

A. 主管全国质量、计量　　B. 出入境商品检疫
C. 出入境卫生检疫　　D. 流通领域商品质量监督管理

4. 有关商品检验的时间和地点比较公平合理，能够兼顾买卖双方的利益的规定是(　　)。
A. 离岸质量、重量（或数量）为准　　B. 到岸质量、重量（或数量）为准
C. 出口国检验、目的国复验　　D. 提交第三国检验机构进行检验

5. 对于规格复杂、精密程度高，需要在一定操作条件下用精密仪器或设备检验的货物一般在(　　)进行检验。
A. 生产设备的工厂　　B. 设备在装运港装船前
C. 进口国卸货地　　D. 最终用户所在地

（三）多项选择题

1. 根据我国《商检法》，地方检验检疫机构在进出口商品检验方面的基本任务是(　　)。
A. 实施法定检验　　B. 办理鉴定业务
C. 实施监督管理　　D. 发放检验证书

2. 在合同中规定买方有检验权的情况下，商检条款中应进一步明确以下问题(　　)。
A. 复验地点　　B. 复验时间
C. 复验机构　　D. 复验方法

3. 在合同中商品检验时间和地点的规定的基本做法有(　　)。
A. 在出口国检验　　B. 将货物运到双方同意的第三国检验
C. 在进口国检验　　D. 出口国检验，进口国复验

4. 在国际贸易中，检验证书所起的作用有(　　)。
A. 公证证明的作用
B. 买卖双方交接货物、结算货款和进行索赔和理赔的依据
C. 通关的有效凭证
D. 以信用证支付时，通常是银行议付货款的依据

5. 根据国家质量监督检验检疫总局的规定，出境货物报验时须提交的有关单据是(　　)。
A. 外贸合同（确认书）　　B. 信用证
C. 提单　　D. 发票

（四）判断题

1. 根据《进出口商品检验法》的规定，列入《种类表》的进出口商品，必须经过商检机构的检验。(　　)

2. 根据《联合国国际货物销售合同公约》的规定，若买方没有利用合理的机会检验货物，就是放弃了选择权，从而丧失了声称货物不符合同的权利。(　　)

3. 在合同中规定为“离岸品质，离岸重量”时，买方在货物到达目的港或目的地

后，可自行委托检验机构对货物进行复验，并有权在规定的时间内凭复验证书向卖方提出异议和索赔。(　　)

4.“出口国检验，进口国复验”是国际货物买卖中最常见的一种规定检验时间和地点的方法。(　　)

5. 根据《中华人民共和国进出口商品检验法》的规定，对出口食品的卫生检验不属于我国法定检验的范围。

6. 凡属法定检验范围的商品，在办理进出口清关手续时，必须向海关提供检验检疫机构签发的检验证书，海关方予以验放。(　　)

7. 已在所在地检验检疫机构办理报验登记备案的单位，可以自行办理报验或代理他人报验。(　　)

8. 经商检机构检验合格发给检验证单的出口商品，应当在商检机构规定的期限内报关出口；超过期限的，可向商检机构申请延长检验证单的期限。(　　)

9.《中华人民共和国进出口商品检验法》规定，必须经商检机构检验的进出口商品以外的进出口商品，根据国家规定全部免予检验。(　　)

10. 实行“到岸品质、重量”检验条件时，买方无须分清卖方、船公司或保险公司的责任，而有权根据货物到达目的港时的检验结果，直接向卖方提出索赔。(　　)

（五）案例分析

1. 我某出口企业以 CIF 旧金山向美国 A 公司出口了 400 套家具，该公司又将货物转手出售给了加拿大 B 公司。货物抵达旧金山后，A 公司发现家具质量存在问题，但仍将货物转运至加拿大。B 公司收到家具后，在合同规定的索赔期限内凭加拿大商检机构签发的检验证书，向我出口企业提出索赔。问我方企业是否需要进行赔偿？为什么？

2. 我方公司以 FOB 条件向法国某经销商出口 5 000 打男式衬衣，合同规定：“货物在黄埔港装运前由中国出入境检验检疫局进行检验，交货品质以该机构出具的检验证书为准。”我方在货物装运后制作了整套结汇单据，其中的品质检验证书声明我方所交货物符合合同规定。我方在办理完结汇手续后，收到了法国经销商的传真，声称我方所交衬衣的质量与和合同严重不符，要求我方赔偿，法方还提交了该国检验机构出具的检验证明。问我方公司是否要进行赔偿？为什么？

（六）阅读理解

根据下面的单据，找出下列内容：

（1）货物名称及 H. S. 编码：
（2）货物总值：
（3）包装种类及数量：
（4）运输工具名称号码：
（5）贸易方式：
（6）货物存放地点：
（7）合同号：
（8）用途：
（9）发货日期：
（10）输往国家（地区）：
（11）起运地：
（12）到达口岸：
（13）标记及号码：
（14）领取单证日期：
（15）需要证单名称：
（16）检验检疫费：

中华人民共和国出入境检验检疫
出境货物报检单

2-6035

报检单位(加盖公章)：广东育华实业发展有限公司　　　　*编　　号 442200205000589E

报检单位登记号：4401004824　联系人：吴会芳　电话：82170725　报检日期：2005 年 05 月 20 日

发货人	(中文)	广东育华实业发展有限公司
	(外文)	***
收货人	(中文)	***
	(外文)	***

货物名称(中/外文)	H.S. 编码	产地	数/重量	货物总值	包装种类及数量
木雕	44201090.90 P/Q	广东省	4,000件 4,000千克	20,000 港币	200纸箱
木家具	94036099.00 P/Q	广东省	60件 2,500千克	12,000 港币	60捆装
木家具	94016900.00 P/Q	广东省	80件 2,000千克	12,000 港币	80纸箱
竹雕	44201010.90 P/Q	广东省	100件 500千克	4,000 港币	50纸箱
				USD 60,000.-	

运输工具名称号码	船舶	贸易方式	一般贸易	货物存放地点	永业码头
合同号	DH050322	信用证号	***	用途	其他
发货日期	2005-06-20	输往国家(地区)	中国台湾	许可证/审批号	***
启运地	天河永业码头口岸	到达口岸	中国台湾省	生产单位注册号	***
集装箱规格、数量及号码	***				

合同、信用证订立的检验检疫条款或特殊要求	标 记 及 号 码	随附单据(划"✓"或补填)	
***	N/M	□合同 □信用证 □发票 □换证凭单 □装箱单 □	□包装性能结果单 □许可/审批文件 □ □ □ □

需要证单名称(划"✓"或补填)			*检验检疫费	
□品质证书 ＿正＿副	□植物检疫证书 ＿正＿副		总金额(人民币元)	66.-
□重量证书 ＿正＿副	□熏蒸/消毒证书 ＿正＿副			
□数量证书 ＿正＿副	□出境货物换证凭单 1 2		计费人	李平
□兽医卫生证书 ＿正＿副	□出境货物通关单			
□健康证书 ＿正＿副	□		收费人	欧阳文
□卫生证书 ＿正＿副	□			
□动物卫生证书 ＿正＿副	□			

报检人郑重声明：	领 取 证 单	
1. 本人被授权报检。 2. 上列填写内容正确属实，货物无伪造或冒用他人的厂名、标志、认证标志，并承担货物质量责任。 签名：吴会芳	日期	05.6.20
	签名	[illegible]

注：有"*"号栏由出入境检验检疫机关填写　　　　◆国家出入境检验检疫局制
[1-2(2004)-1]

（七）单据改错

请根据以下资料修改一份出境货物报检单。

广东纺织品进出口针织品有限公司

GUANGDONG TEXTILES IMPORT & EXPORT KNIT WEARS COMPANY LIMITED

15/F., GUANGDONG TEXTILES MANSION, 168 XIAO BEI ROAD, GUANGZHOU CHINA

COMMERCIAL INVOICE

ORIGINAL

Messrs.:	INVOICE NO.: 9703S9023
CURRENT FUNDS LIMITED	INVOICE DATE: NOV. 2, 1997
ROOM 1110 CHINACHEM GOLDEN PLAZA	L/C NO.: WFH515950F
NO. 77 MODY ROAD, TSIM SHA TSUI EAST	L/C DATE: AUG. 26, 1997
KOWLOON, HONGKONG	S/C NO.: DY-039
Transport details:	Terms of payment:
FROM GUANGZHOU TO SANTOS W/T HONGKONG	BY L/C
BY VESSEL	

Marks & numbers	Description of goods	Quantity	Unit price	Amount
N/M	MEN'S 100 PCT COTTON WOVEN UNDER PANTS	7,200 DOZ	USD 4.2/DOZ	USD 30,240.00
			CIF SANTOS	USD 30,240.00

TOTAL QUANTITY: 7,200 DOZ　　PACKING: 240CTNS

TOTAL WEIGHT: N. W.: 720 KGS　　G. W.: 800 KGS

TOTAL: US DOLLARS THIRTY THOUSAND TWO HUNDRED AND FORTY ONLY.

SHIPPED PER: XINDA/FANDU V. 336

SHIPPED ON BOARD: NOV. 10, 1997

GUANGDONG TEXTILES IMPORT & EXPORT
KNITWEARS COMPANYLIMITED

Remarks:

商品编码：6207.1100　　用途：其他

货物存放地点：大朗仓库　　产地：广州

报检人：何涛　　报检日期：1997 年 11 月 3 日

报验时提交的随附单据：合同、信用证、发票、装箱单

需要的证单：品质证书 1 正 1 副

中华人民共和国出入境检验检疫
出境货物报检单

报检单位（加盖公章）：　　　　　　　　　　　　＊编　号________

报检单位登记号：　　　联系人：何涛　　　电话：　　　报检日期：1997 年 11 月 3 日

发货人	（中文）	广东纺织品进出口针织品有限公司
	（外文）	GUANGDONG TEXTILES IMPORT & EXPORT KNITWEARS COMPANY LIMITED
收货人	（中文）	
	（外文）	CURRENT FUNDS LTMTTED

货物名称（中外文）	H. S. 编码	产地	数/重量	货物总值	包装种类及数量
男式内裤 MEN'S 100 PCT COTTON WOVEN UNDER PANTS		广东省广州市	7 ,200 件	30, 240 美元	240 纸箱

运输工具名称号码	XINDA/FANDU V. 336	贸易方式	来料加工	货物存放地点	大朗仓库
合同号	DY －093	信用证号	WFH5159590F	用途	其他
发货日期	1997 年 11 月 10 日	输往国家(地区)	巴西	许可证/审批号	/
启运地	广州	到达口岸	圣保罗	生产单位注册号	/
集装箱规格、数量及号码	/				

合同、信用证订立的检验检疫条款或特殊要求	标 记 及 号 码	随附单据（划“√”或补填）	
/	N/M	√合同 √信用证 √发票 □换证凭单 √装箱单 □厂检单	□包装性能结果单 □许可/审批文件 □ □ □ □

需要证单名称（划“√”或补填）				＊检验检疫费	
☑品质证书	1 正 1 副	□植物检疫证书	__正__副	总金额（人民币元）	
□重量证书	__正__副	□熏蒸/消毒证书	__正__副		
□数量证书	__正__副	□出境货物换证凭单	__正__副		
□兽医卫生证书	__正__副	□		计费人	
□健康证书	__正__副	□			
□卫生证书	__正__副	□		收费人	
□动物卫生证书	__正__副	□			

报检人郑重声明：	领 取 证 单	
1. 本人被授权报检。 2. 上列填写内容正确属实，货物无伪造或冒用他人的厂名、标志、认证标志，并承担货物质量责任。	日期	
签名：何涛	签名	

注：有“＊”号栏由出入境检验检疫机关填写

(八) 单据填制

1. 单据填制一

请根据以下材料填制一份出境货物报检单。

四川长虹电器股份有限公司

SICHUAN CHANGHONG ELECTRIC CO., LTD.

35, EAST MIANXING ROAD, HIGH-TECH PARK, MIANYANG, CHINA

COMMERCIAL INVOICE

Messrs:
YOUTA TRADING COMPANY LTD.
52 JULAN SULTAN
ROOM 1510 KOONA PLAZA
SINGAPORE

INVOICE NO : TB－M85062
INVOICE DATE : JULY 25, 2003
S/C NO. : SM9806263
L/C NO. : HU65926

Transport details:
FROM SHENZHEN TO SINGAPORE BY VESSEL
PER S. S.: TAO LA V. 441

Terms of payment:
BY L/C

Marks & numbers	Description of goods	Quantity	Unit price	Amount
			CIF SINGAPORE	
YOUTA SINGAPORE NOS. 1－500	"CHANGHONG" BRAND COLOUR TELEVISION SET MODEL RT560 WITH REMOTE CONTROL, PACKED IN EXPORT CARTONS OF ONE SET EACH	500SETS	USD160.00 PER SET	USD 80,000.00

四川长虹电器股份有限公司
SICHUAN CHANGHONG ELECTRIC CO., LTD.

Remarks:

商品编码：8528.1291　　CONTAINER NO.：1＊40'COSU829234－2

发货日期：AUG. 10, 2003　　货物存放地点：中山南头

用途：其他　　产地：四川省绵阳市

报检人：李明　　报检日期：2003 年 7 月 27 日

报验时提交的随附单据：合同、信用证、发票、装箱单

需要的证单：品质证书（1 正 2 副）日出境货物换证凭单（1 正 1 副）

中华人民共和国出入境检验检疫
出境货物报检单

报检单位（加盖公章）：　　　　　　　　　　　　　＊编　号________________

报检单位登记号：　　　联系人：　　　电话：　　　报检日期：　　年　　月　　日

发货人	（中文）						
	（外文）						
收货人	（中文）						
	（外文）						

货物名称（中外文）	H. S. 编码	产地	数/重量	货物总值	包装种类及数量

运输工具名称号码		贸易方式		货物存放地点	
合同号		信用证号		用途	
发货日期		输往国家(地区)		许可证/审批号	
启运地		到达口岸		生产单位注册号	
集装箱规格、数量及号码					

合同、信用证订立的检验检疫条款或特殊要求	标 记 及 号 码	随附单据（划“√”或补填）	
		□合同	□包装性能结果单
		□信用证	□许可/审批文件
		□发票	□
		□换证凭单	□
		□装箱单	□
		□厂检单	□

需要证单名称（划“√”或补填）				＊检验检疫费	
□品质证书	__正__副	□植物检疫证书	__正__副	总金额（人民币元）	
□重量证书	__正__副	□熏蒸/消毒证书	__正__副		
□数量证书	__正__副	□出境货物换证凭单	__正__副		
□兽医卫生证书	__正__副	□		计费人	
□健康证书	__正__副	□			
□卫生证书	__正__副	□		收费人	
□动物卫生证书	__正__副	□			

报检人郑重声明：	领 取 证 单	
1. 本人被授权报检。 2. 上列填写内容正确属实，货物无伪造或冒用他人的厂名、标志、认证标志，并承担货物质量责任。	日期	
签名：______________	签名	

注：有“＊”号栏由出入境检验检疫机关填写

2. 单据填制二

请根据以下材料填制一份出境货物报检单。

厦门富乐贸易发展公司

FULE TRADE DEVELOPMENT CO. LTD.

INVOICE

L/C NO.: KC－65284　　　INVOICE NO.: FL69536874

S/C NO.: TL652C063　　　DATE: MARCH 15, 2002

MESSRS.: L. Y. CONSULTANT CO., LTD.

ADDRESS: 21 OTEMON CHUO—KU FUKUODA, JAPAN

PER S. S.: HONG YAN V. 5021　DATE OF DEPARTURE: APR. 25, 2002

FROM XIAMEN　TO MOJI

MARK	PACKAGE	DESCRIPTION	QUANTITY	UNIT PRICE	AMOUNT
N/M	15,000CTNS	FRESH WINTER BAMBOO SHOOTS	15,000KGS	USD1.60/KG	USD24,000.00
				CFR MOJI	

Remarks:

集装箱号码：CCLU 850114－5（20’）　CCLU850500－6（20’）

商品编码：0709.9010

货物存放地点：石狮　　用途：食用

报验人：王雅丽　　报检日期：2002 年 4 月 15 日

产地：福建省厦门特区

报验时提交的随附单据：信用证、合同、发票、装箱单

需要的证单：品质证书 1 正 1 副、卫生检验证书 1 正 1 副、出境货物换证凭单 1 正 2 副

中华人民共和国出入境检验检疫
出境货物报检单

报检单位（加盖公章）：　　　　　　　　　　　　＊编　号________________

报检单位登记号：　　　联系人：　　　电话：　　　报检日期：　年　月　日

发货人	（中文）	
	（外文）	
收货人	（中文）	
	（外文）	

货物名称（中外文）	H. S. 编码	产地	数/重量	货物总值	包装种类及数量

运输工具名称号码		贸易方式		货物存放地点	
合同号		信用证号		用途	
发货日期		输往国家（地区）		许可证/审批号	
启运地		到达口岸		生产单位注册号	
集装箱规格、数量及号码					

合同、信用证订立的检验检疫条款或特殊要求	标 记 及 号 码	随附单据（划“√”或补填）	
		□合同 □信用证 □发票 □换证凭单 □装箱单 □厂检单	□包装性能结果单 □许可/审批文件 □ □ □ □

需要证单名称（划“√”或补填）				＊检验检疫费	
□品质证书	__正__副	□植物检疫证书	__正__副	总金额（人民币元）	
□重量证书	__正__副	□熏蒸/消毒证书	__正__副		
□数量证书	__正__副	□出境货物换证凭单	__正__副		
□兽医卫生证书	__正__副	□		计费人	
□健康证书	__正__副	□			
□卫生证书	__正__副	□		收费人	
□动物卫生证书	__正__副	□			

报检人郑重声明：	领 取 证 单	
1．本人被授权报检。 2．上列填写内容正确属实，货物无伪造或冒用他人的厂名、标志、认证标志，并承担货物质量责任。	日期	
签名：____________	签名	

注：有“＊”号栏由出入境检验检疫机关填写

二、练习题参考答案

（一）中英文术语、短语互译

1. 中译英

（1）Commodity Inspection

（2）Inspection Certificate of Quality

（3）Inspection Certificate of Weight/Measurement

（4）Inspection Certificate of Quantity

（5）Applicant's Representive

2. 英译中

（1）卫生（健康）检验证书　（2）消毒检验证书　（3）熏蒸证书

（4）验舱证书　（5）中国商品检验局

（二）单项选择题

1. C。理由：《联合国国际货物销售合同公约》第39条（2）款规定："无论如何，如果买方不在实际收到货物之日起两年内将货物不符合同情形通知卖方，他就丧失声称货物不符合同的权利，除非这一时限与合同规定的保证期限不符。"

2. B。理由：国家质量监督检验检疫总局规定，出境货物最迟应于报关或装运前7天报验。

3. D。理由：流通领域商品质量监督管理工作由国家工商总局负责。

4. C。理由：因为这种检验办法既承认卖方提供的检验证书是有效的文件，作为交接货物和结算货款的依据之一，又让买方有复验权。

5. D。理由：精密仪器或设备不能在使用前开拆包装检验，或需要具备一定的检验条件和检验设备才能检验，在最终用户所在地进行检验有利于保障买方利益。

（三）多项选择题

1. ABC。理由：根据我国《商检法》，地方检验检疫机构在进出口商品检验方面的基本任务有三项，发放检验证书不是基本任务之一。

2. ABCD。理由：有利于避免日后发生争议。

3. ACD。理由：合同中商品检验时间和地点的规定方法主要有三种：在出口国检验、在进口国检验和出口国检验、进口国复验。

4. ABCD。理由：国际贸易中，检验证书起着公证的作用，作为买卖双方交接货物、结算货款和进行索赔和理赔的依据之一，也是通关、征收关税和优惠减免关税、结算运费等的有效凭证，以信用证支付时，通常是银行议付货款和出口收汇的依据。

5. AB。理由：根据国家质量监督检验检疫总局的规定，出境货物报验时须提交的单据有外贸合同（确认书）、信用证、许可证、厂检单等。

（四）判断题

1. 正确。理由：根据我国《进出口商品检验法》的规定，列入《种类表》的进出口商品，属于法定检验的范畴。

2. 正确。理由：买方对货物的检验权并不是表示对货物接受的前提条件，买方对收到的货物可以进行检验，也可以不进行检验，若买方没有利用合理的机会检验货物，就是放弃了选择权，从而丧失了声称货物不符合同的权利。

3. 错误。理由：当合同中规定商品检验的时间和地点的方法为“离岸品质，离岸重量”时，货物是在装运港装运前经由双方所约定的检验机构对货物的质量和重量或数量进行检验，并由其出具的检验证书作为决定交货质量和重量或数量的最后依据。

4. 正确。理由：因为这种方法对买卖双方较公平合理。

5. 错误。理由：根据《中华人民共和国进出口商品检验法》的规定，对出口食品的卫生检验属于我国法定检验的范围。

6. 正确。理由：根据《中华人民共和国进出口商品检验法》第 15 条的规定，对本法规定必须实施检验的出口商品，海关凭商检机构签发的货物通关证明验放。

7. 错误。理由：代理报验单位必须向所在地检验检疫结构申请办理代理报验单位注册登记手续，取得代理报验注册登记证明书的单位方可代理他人报验。

8. 错误。理由：根据《中华人民共和国进出口商品检验法》第 16 条的规定，超过期限的，应当重新报验。

9. 错误。理由：根据《中华人民共和国进出口商品检验法》第 19 条的规定，本法规定必须经商检机构检验的进出口商品以外的进出口商品，根据国家规定实施抽查检验。

10. 错误。理由：即使实行“到岸品质、重量”检验条件，只有货物品质与合同不符是由于卖方的责任时，买方才能向卖方提出索赔。

（五）案例分析

1. 分析：我方企业不需要进行赔偿。理由：①由于货物抵达旧金山后，A 公司已经发现家具质量存在问题，但仍将货物转运至加拿大交给 B 公司，并未向我方提出异议，也没有要求当地的检验机构进行复验，根据《联合国国际货物销售合同公约》的规定，由于买方没有在发现货物不符合同后一段合理时间内通知卖方，说明不符合同情形的性质，所以 A 公司就丧失了声称货物不符合同的权利。②至于 B 公司由于不是与我方签订合同的买方，其只能凭加拿大商检机构签发的检验证书向卖方 A 公司提出异议与索赔的要求。

2. 分析：我方公司不需要进行赔偿。理由：我方与法国经销商所签订的合同中规定：“货物在黄埔港装运前由中国出入境检验检疫局进行检验，交货品质以该机构出具的检验证书为准。”而我方提交的品质检验证书声明我方所交货物符合合同规定，所以法方无权对货物品质进行复验，也无权根据该国检验机构出具的检验证明要求我方进行赔偿。

（六）阅读理解

1. 货物名称及 H. S. 编码：木雕（44201090. 90）、木家具（94036099. 00）、骨雕

（44201010.90）

2. 货物总值：HKD48,000.00
3. 包装种类及数量：390 纸箱
4. 运输工具名称号码：船舶
5. 贸易方式：一般贸易
6. 货物存放地点：永业码头
7. 合同号：DH050322
8. 用途：其他
9. 发货日期：2005－06－20
10. 输往国家（地区）：中国台湾
11. 启运地：天河永业码头口岸
12. 到达口岸：中国台湾省
13. 标记及号码：N/M
14. 领取单证日期：05．06．20
15. 需要证单名称：出境货物通关单
16. 检验检疫费：66 人民币元

（七）单据改错

（1）货物名称不够具体，应为：全棉男式内裤；
（2）数量单位为打，应改为：7,200 打；
（3）贸易方式错，应改为：一般贸易；
（4）合同号错，应改为：DY－039；
（5）到达口岸错，应改为：桑托斯；
（6）缺商品编码，应在 H．S． 编码栏目中填写 6207.1100。

（八）单据填制

1. 单据填制一

中华人民共和国出入境检验检疫
出境货物报检单

报检单位（加盖公章）：　　　　　　　　　　　　　　　　　＊编　号________

报检单位登记号：　　　联系人：李明　　　电话：　　　　报检日期：2003 年 7 月 27 日

发货人	（中文）	四川长虹电器股份有限公司
	（外文）	SICHUAN CHANGHONG ELECTRIC CO. , LTD.
收货人	（中文）	/
	（外文）	YOUTA TRADING COMPANY LTD.

货物名称（中外文）	H. S. 编码	产地	数/重量	货物总值	包装种类及数量
“长虹”牌遥控彩色电视机 型号：RT560 “CHANGHONG” BRAND COLOUR TELEVISION SET MODEL RT560 WITH REMOTE CONTROL	8528. 1291	四川省绵阳市	500 台	80, 000 美元	500 纸箱

运输工具名称号码	TAO LAV. 441	贸易方式	一般贸易	货物存放地点	中山南头
合同号	SM9806263	信用证号	HU65926	用途	其他
发货日期	2003. 08. 10	输往国家(地区)	新加坡	许可证/审批号	/
启运地	深圳	到达口岸	新加坡	生产单位注册号	/
集装箱规格、数量及号码	1＊40'COSU829234－2				

合同、信用证订立的检验检疫条款或特殊要求	标记及号码	随附单据（划“√”或补填）	
/	YOUTA SINGAPORE NOS. 1－500	☑合同 ☑信用证 ☑发票 □换证凭单 ☑装箱单 □厂检单	□包装性能结果单 □许可/审批文件 □ □ □ □

需要证单名称（划“√”或补填）				＊检验检疫费	
☑品质证书	1 正 2 副	□植物检疫证书	__正__副	总金额（人民币元）	
□重量证书	__正__副	□熏蒸/消毒证书	__正__副		
□数量证书	__正__副	☑出境货物换证凭单	1 正 1 副		
□兽医卫生证书	__正__副	□		计费人	
□健康证书	__正__副	□			
□卫生证书	__正__副	□		收费人	
□动物卫生证书	__正__副	□			

报检人郑重声明：	领取证单	
1. 本人被授权报检。 2. 上列填写内容正确属实，货物无伪造或冒用他人的厂名、标志、认证标志，并承担货物质量责任。 签名：李明	日期	
	签名	

注：有“＊”号栏由出入境检验检疫机关填写

2. 单据填制二

中华人民共和国出入境检验检疫
出境货物报检单

报检单位（加盖公章）：　　　　　　　　　　　　　　＊编　号＿＿＿＿＿＿

报检单位登记号：　　　联系人：王雅丽　　电话：　　　　报检日期：2002 年 4 月 15 日

发货人	（中文）厦门富乐贸易发展公司				
	（外文）FULE TRADE DEVELOPMENT CO., LTD.				
收货人	（中文）/				
	（外文）L. Y. CONSULTANT CO. LTD				
货物名称（中外文）	H. S. 编码	产地	数/重量	货物总值	包装种类及数量
鲜冬笋 FRESH WINTER BAMBOO SHOOTS	0709. 9010	福建省 厦门特区	15, 000KGS	24, 000. 00 美元	15, 000 纸箱

运输工具名称号码	HONG YAN V. 5021	贸易方式	一般贸易	货物存放地点	石狮
合同号	TL652C063	信用证号	KC－65284	用途	食用
发货日期	2003 年 4 月 25 日	输往国家（地区）	日本	许可证/审批号	/
启运地	厦门	到达口岸	门司	生产单位注册号	/
集装箱规格、数量及号码	2×20’CCLU 850114－5，CCLU850500－6				

合同、信用证订立的检验检疫条款或特殊要求	标 记 及 号 码	随附单据（划“√”或补填）	
/	N/M	☑合同 ☑信用证 ☑发票 ☐换证凭单 ☑装箱单 ☐厂检单	☐包装性能结果单 ☐许可/审批文件 ☐ ☐ ☐ ☐

需要证单名称（划“√”或补填）				＊检验检疫费	
☑品质证书	1 正 1 副	☐植物检疫证书	＿正＿副	总金额（人民币元）	
☐重量证书	＿正＿副	☐熏蒸/消毒证书	＿正＿副		
☐数量证书	＿正＿副	☑出境货物换证凭单	1 正 2 副		
☐兽医卫生证书	＿正＿副	☐		计费人	
☐健康证书	＿正＿副	☐			
☑卫生检验证书	1 正 1 副	☐		收费人	
☐动物卫生证书	＿正＿副	☐			

报检人郑重声明：	领 取 证 单	
1. 本人被授权报检。	日期	
2. 上列填写内容正确属实，货物无伪造或冒用他人的厂名、标志、认证标志，并承担货物质量责任。		
签名：王雅丽	签名	

注：有“＊”号栏由出入境检验检疫机关填写

第二节　受益人证明书

一、练习题

（一）单据填制

1. 单据填制一

请根据以下材料制作一份受益人证明书。

A. 信用证条款。

BENEFICIARY: SHANGHAI MACHINERY IMP. & EXP. CORPORATION

L/C NO.: HU65926

DOCUMENTS REQUIRED:

* BENEFICIARY'S CERTIFICATE CERTIFYING THAT COMMERCIAL INVOICE, PACKING LIST AND ORIGINAL EXPORT LICENCE HAVE BEEN DESPATCHED BY COURIER DIRECTLY TO YOUTA TRADING COMPANY.

B. 其他资料。

INVOICE NO.: TB – M85062

DATE OF ISSUING THE BENEFICIARY'S CERTIFICATE: AUG. 3, 2003

2. 单据填制二

请根据以下材料制作一份受益人证明书。

A. 信用证条款。

BENEFICIARY: FULE TRADE DEVELOPMENT CO., LTD.

L/C NO.: KC – 65284

DOCUMENTS REQUIRED:

* BENEFICIARY'S CERTIFICATE CERTIFYING THAT FIVE COPIES OF YOUR SAMPLE BOOK HAVE BEEN SENT BY REGISTERED AIRMAIL TO L. Y. CONSULTANT CO., LTD., 21 OTEMON CHUO-KU FUKUODA, JAPAN.

B. 其他资料。

INVOICE NO.: FL69536874

DATE OF ISSUING THE BENEFICIARY'S CERTIFICATE: MARCH 30, 2002

3. 单据填制三

请根据以下材料制作一份受益人证明书。

A. 信用证条款。

BENEFICIARY: GUANGDONG TEXTILES I/E (GROUP) GARMENTS CO.

L/C NO.: P – 67971

DOCUMENTS REQUIRED:

* BENEFICIARY'S CERTEFICATE STATING THAT ALL THE SHIPPED GOODS ARE STRICTLY IN COMPLIANCE WITH THE TERMS OF THE RELATIVE SALES CONTRACT (NO. 98GTB0602).

B. 其他资料。

INVOICE NO.: 980602GTB

DATE OF ISSUING THE BENEFICIARY'S CERTIFICATE: SEP. 25, 1998

（二）单据改错

1. 单据改错一

请根据以下材料修改一份受益人证明书。

A. 信用证条款。

ISSUE OF A DOCUMENTARY CREDIT

APPLICANT: HALSSEN & LYON GMBH, GERMANY

BENEFICIARY: CHINA TUHSU GUANGDONG TEA IMP. & EXP. CORP.

L/C NO.: 6005729745H3

DOCUMENTS REQUIRED:

* BENEFICIARY'S CERTIFICATE CERTIFYING THAT ONE COPY OF COMMERCIAL INVOICE, N/N B/L HAVE BEEN FAXED TO APPLICANT TO FAX NO. 78 - 025 - 605 WHITHIN 3 DAYS AFTER SHIPMENT.

B. 其他资料。

INVOICE NO.: TA7149

DATE OF ISSUING THE BENEFICIARY' S CERTIFICATE: AUGUST 28, 1997

BENEFICIARY'S CERTIFICATE

DATE: AUG. 28, 1997

INVOICE NO.: TAT149　　L/C NO.: 6005729745H3

WE HEREBY CERTIFY THAT ONE COPY OF COMMERCIAL INVOICE NO. B/L HAVE BEEN FAXED TO APPLICANT TO FAX NO. 78 - 025 - 605 WHITHIN 3 DAYS AFTER SHIPMENT.

中国土畜产广东茶叶进出口公司
CHINA TUHSU GUANGDONG TEA IMP. & EXP. CORP.
(SIGNATURE)

2. 单据改错二

请根据以下材料修改一份受益人证明书。

A. 信用证条款。

ISSUE OF A DOCUMENTARY CREDIT

APPLICANT: DU PONT SINGAPORE FIBRES PTE LTD.

BENEFICIARY: SHANGHAI HUAYUAN TRADE ENTERPRISE LTD.

L/C NO.: XCBS07258

DOCUMENTS REQUIRED:

* BENEFICIARY'S CERTIFICATE CERTIFYING THAT ALL THE GOODS ARE PACKED IN STRONG SEAWORTHY CARTONS AND EACH CASE CLEARLY INDICATES THE SHIPPING MARKS AND NOS.: DU PONT/NO. 1-420/SINGAPORE.

B. 其他资料。

INVOICE NO.: IG20303465

DATE OF ISSUING THE BENEFICIARY'S CERTIFICATE: JULY 18, 2001

BENEFICIARY'S CERTIFICATE

JULY 8, 2001

INVOICE NO.: IG20303465　　L/C NO.: XCBS07258

TO WHOM IF MAY CONCERN:

WE HEREBY CERTIFY THAT ALL THE GOODS ARE PACKED IN CARTONS AND EACH CASE CLEARLY INDICATES THE SHIPPING MARKS AND NOS.: DU PONT/NO. 1-420/SINGAPORE.

上海华源贸易有限公司

SHANGHAI HUAYUAN TRADE ENTERPRISE LTD.

(SIGNATURE)

二、练习题参考答案

（一）单据填制

1. 单据填制一

BENEFICIARY'S CERTIFICATE

AUG. 3, 2003

INVOICE NO.: TB－M85062　　L/C NO.: HU65926

WE HEREBY CERTIFY THAT COMMERCIAL INVOICE, PACKING LIST AND ORIGINAL EXPORT LICENCE HAVE BEEN DESPATCHED BY COURIER DIRECTLY TO YOUTA TRADING COMPANY.

上海机械进出口公司
SHANGHAI MACHINERY IMP. & EXP. CORPORATION
(SIGNATURE)

2. 单据填制二

BENEFICIARY'S CERTIFICATE

MARCH 30, 2002

INVOICE NO.: FL69536874　　L/C NO.: KC－65284

TO WHOM IT MAY CONCERN:

WE HEREBY CERTIFY THAT WE HAVE SENT OUR FIVE COPIES OF OUR SAMPLE BOOK BY REGISTERED AIRMAIL TO L. Y. CONSULTANT CO., LTD., 21 OTEMON CHUO－KU FUKUODA, JAPAN.

富乐贸易发展有限公司
FULE TRADE DEVELOPMENT CO., LTD.
(SIGNATURE)

3. 单据填制三

BENEFICIARY'S CERTIFICATE

SEP. 25, 1998

INVOICE NO.: 980602GTB L/C NO.: P-67971

TO WHOM IT MAY CONCERN:

WE HEREBY STATE THAT ALL THE SHIPPED GOODS ARE STRICTLY IN COMPLIANCE WITH THE TERMS OF THE RELATIVE SALES CONTRACT (NO. 98GTB0602).

广东纺织品进出口(集团)服装公司
GUANGDONG TEXTILES I/E (GROUP) GARMENTS CO.
(SIGNATURE)

(二)单据改错

1. 单据改错一

(1) INVOICE NO.: TA7149;

(2) NO. B/L 应改为N/N B/L;

(3) APPLICANT 应改为 HALSSEN & LYON GMBH, GERMANY。

2. 单据改错二

(1) 出证日期应改为 JULY 18, 2001;

(2) ARE PACKED IN CARTONS 应改为 ARE PACKED IN STRONG SEAWORTHY CARTONS。

第三节　航空运单

一、练习题

（一）中英文术语、短语互译

1. Airway Bill
2. Airline Code Number
3. Declared Value for Customs
4. Airport of Destination
5. Chargeable Weight
6. Accounting Information
7. IATA
8. NCV
9. NVD
10. CHGS Code
11. AS
12. PPD
13. FC
14. COLL
15. IN
16. GT
17. RCP
18. NIL

（二）单项选择题

1. 航空运单正本按国际惯例为(　　)。
   A. 一式两份　　B. 一式三份
   C. 一份　　D. 一式六份
2. 中国民航的代号为(　　)。
   A. 999　　B. 131
   C. 160　　D. 988
3. 香港机场代号为(　　)。
   A. HGH　　B. HRB
   C. HKG　　D. HAK
4. 广州机场的代号为(　　)。
   A. SHA　　B. PEK
   C. SZX　　D. CAN
5. 大阪机场的代号为(　　)。
   A. TYO　　B. OSA
   C. OKA　　D. NGO
6. 曼谷机场的代号为(　　)。
   A. SIN　　B. PEN
   C. MNL　　D. BKK
7. 巴黎机场的代号为(　　)。
   A. LON　　B. PAR
   C. HAM　　D. FRA
8. 旧金山的机场代号为(　　)。
   A. SFO　　B. NYK
   C. WAS　　D. LAX

9. 在航空运输中，当托运的货物中含有危险货物时，应分别填写，并把危险货物填列在(　　)。

A. 第一项　B. 第二项

C. 任意项　D. 最后一项

10. 在航空运单中的“Executed on date”栏目表示的日期，一般应是(　　)。

A. 航空公司接受托运货物的日期　B. 签发航空运单的日期

C. 信用证规定的最后装运日期　D. 实际起飞的日期

(三) 多项选择题

1. 航空运单可分为(　　)。

A. 出票航空公司标志的航空货运单　B. 指示航空运单

C. 无承运人任何标志的中性货运单　D. 记名航空运单

2. 航空运单的作用包括(　　)。

A. 航空运单是航空运输承运人与托运人之间的运输合同

B. 航空运单是航空公司或其代理人收运货物的证明文件

C. 航空运单是承运人核收运费的依据

D. 航空运单是承运人处理货物运输过程情况的依据

3. 下列机场代号中，属于我国机场的是(　　)。

A. LAS　B. TSN

C. SEL　D. XMN

4. 下列表述正确的是(　　)。

A. 航空运单不是物权凭证　B. 航空运单是物权凭证

C. 航空运单不可转让　D. 航空运单经背书后可以转让

5. 航空运单的托运人名称和地址栏目，一般填写(　　)。

A. 托运人的名称和地址　B. 托运人的国家（或国家两字代号）

C. 托运人的传真、电传号码　D. 托运人的电话号码

(四) 判断题

1. 航空运单不是物权凭证，不能通过背书转移货物的所有权，但只有航空运单的持有人才能对货物要求所有权。(　　)

2. 航空运单正本按国际惯例为一式三份，每份都印有背面条款。交单议付时必须提交全部三份正本航空运单。(　　)

3. 与海运提单相同，航空运单只是运输契约的证明，它本身不是运输契约。(　　)

4. 一张航空运单可用于一个托运人在同一时间、同一地点托运货物，运往不同目的站的不同收货人。(　　)

5. 航空运单的货物运价细目，当一票货物中如含有两种或两种以上不同运价类别计费的货物应分别填写，每填写一项另起一行，如果含有危险品，则该危险货物应列在第一项。(　　)

（五）阅读理解

988-2191 7184　　　　DYN-8800845

Shipper's Name and Address　　Shipper's Account Number

GUANGDONG TEXTILES I/E WOOLEN KNITWEARS
CO.,LTD.13/F GUANGDONG TEXTILES MANSION
168,XIAOBEI ROAD,GUANGZHOU CHINA

Not negotiable
Air Waybill*
issued by
DYNASTY INTERNATIONAL, INC.

Copies 1, 2 and 3 of this Air Waybill are originals and have the same validity.

Consignee's Name and Address　　Consignee's Account Number

TO Q.T.SERVICES GROUP,INC.

It is agreed that the goods described herein are accepted in apparent good order and condition (except as noted) for carriage SUBJECT TO THE CONDITIONS OF CONTRACT ON THE REVERSE HEREOF. ALL GOODS MAY BE CARRIED BY ANY OTHER MEANS INCLUDING ROAD OR ANY OTHER CARRIER UNLESS SPECIFIC CONTRARY INSTRUCTIONS ARE GIVEN HEREON BY THE SHIPPER, AND SHIPPER AGREES THAT THE SHIPMENT MAY BE CARRIED VIAINTERMEDIATE STOPPING PLACES WHICH THE CARRIER DEEMS APPROPRIATE. THE SHIPPER'S ATTENTION IS DRAWN TO THE NOTICE CONCERNING CARRIER'S LIMITATION OF LIABILITY. Shipper may increase such limitation of liability by declaring a higher value for carriage and paying a supplemental charge if required.

Issuing Carrier's Agent Name and City

DYNASTY INTERNATIONAL, INC.

Accounting Information
ALSO NOTIFY:
DYNASTY CHB,INC.
365 CHELSEA ST., EAST BOSTON, MA
02128,PHONE 617.569.5969

Agent's IATA Code　　Account No.

Airport of Departure (Addr. of first Carrier) and requested Routing
SHANGHAI,CHINA

to	By first Carrier / Routing and Destination	to	by	to	by	Currency	Chgs. Code	WT/VAL PPD	WT/VAL COLL	OTHER PPD	OTHER COLL	Declared Value for Carriage	Declared Value for Customs
						USD		PP		PP		N.V.D	AS PER INV

Airport of Destination	Flight/Date (For Carrier Use Only) Flight/Date	Amount of Insurance	INSURANCE – If carrier offers insurance and such insurance is requested in accordance with conditions on reverse hereof indicate amount to be insured in figures in box marked Amount of Insurance.
BOSTON,MA	OZ364/2OCT		

Handling Information including marks, numbers and mehtods of packaging.
THIS SHPT CONTAINS NO SOLID WOOD PACKING MATERIALS.
A/S/D

SCI

No. of Pieces RCP	Gross Weight	kg lb	Rate Class / Commodity Item No.	Chargeable Weight	Rate / Charge	Total	Nature and Quantity of Goods (Incl. Dimensions or Volume)
103 CTNS	691.00	K	FREIGHT	1,371.00 PREPAID			WOMEN'S APPAREL (WOMEN'S 100% CASHMERE KNITTED SWEATERS) PO#703307,703308,703309 STYLE#44-3375M,44-3375P,44-3375W VOL:8.226CBM (60.5×40×33)CM×103

SHIPPING MARKS:
TO:QT SERVICES GROUP,INC
A J.JILL COMPANY
ATTN: RECEIVING DEPT
100 BIRCH POND DRIVE
TILTON, NH03276
TEL: 603-279-7051
FROM: DZ TRADING LTD
110 EAST 9TH STREET, SUITE A1103
LOS ANGELES, CA90079
TEL: 213-532-8000
MADE IN P.R.CHINA

Prepaid	Weight Charge	Collect	Other Charges
AS ARRANGED			
	Valuation Charge		
	Tax		
	Total other CHarges Due Agent		
AS ARRANGED			
	Total other CHarges Due Carrier		
Total prepaid		Total collect	
AS ARRANGED			
Currency Conversion Rates		cc Charges in Dest. Currency	
For Carriers Use only at Destination		Charges at Destination	Total Collect Charges

Shipper certifies that the particulars on the face hereof are correct and that insofar as any part of the consignment contains dangerous goods such part is properly described by name and is in proper condition for carriage by air according to the applicable Dangerous Goods Regulations.

Signature of Shipper or His Agent

Executed on 2,OCT 2004 (date) at SHANGHAI (place)　Signature of Issuing Carrier or its Agent

DYN-8800845

3.ORIGINAL (FOR SHIPPER)

1. 阅读理解一

根据以上的单据找出有关内容：

（1）收货人：

（2）代理人的名称和地址：

（3）财务说明：

（4）始发站：

（5）到达站：

（6）航班：

（7）货币：

（8）供运输用声明价值：

（9）供海关用声明价值：

（10）处理情况：

（11）货物件数：

（12）计费重量：

（13）运费缴付方式：

（14）货物品名和数量：

（15）货物体积：

（16）航空运单填开日期：

（17）航空运单填开地点：

2. 阅读理解二

根据以下的单据找出有关内容：

（1）托运人的名称及地址：

（2）收货人：

（3）航班日期：

（4）财务说明：

（5）始发站：

（6）到达站：

（7）航班：

（8）货币：

（9）供运输用声明价值：

（10）供海关用声明价值：

（11）货物件数：

（12）计费重量：

（13）运费缴付方式：

（14）货物品名和数量：

（15）货物体积：

（16）航空运单填开日期：

（17）航空运单填开地点：

（18）所附文件：

160 HKG 36877175 FILE NO : AE05-02-0016

House Air Waybill Number: IFS-31661

Shipper's Name and Address:
STEP ELEGANT LTD.
RM201,2/F,WAI CHING COMM BLDG,
77 WAI CHING ST,KLN,HONG KONG
27812910 DEREK CHENG

Shipper's Account Number:

Not negotiable
Air Waybill
(Air Consignment note)
issued by
IFS 運航國際空運有限公司 IFS INTERNATIONAL AIR CARGO LIMITED

Copies 1, 2 and 3 of this Air Waybill are originals and have the same validity.

Consignee's Name and Address: TO ORDER OF BNP PARIBAS (CANADA)

Consignee's Account Number:

It is agreed that the goods described herein are accepted in apparent good order and condition (except as noted) for carriage SUBJECT TO THE CONDITIONS OF CONTRACT ON THE REVERSE HEREOF. THE SHIPPER'S ATTENTION IS DRAWN TO THE NOTICE CONCERNING CARRIERS' LIMITATION OF LIABILITY. Shipper may increase such limitation of liability by declaring a higher value for carriage and paying a supplemental charge if required.

FREIGHT PREPAID
NOTIFY COSACO INC
9600 RUE MEILLEUR,MONTREAL,
QC H2N 2E3
CONTACT PERSON:KAREN CRAWLEY
TEL:(514)3824860 FAX:(514)3878086

Airport of Departure (Addr. of First Carrier) and Requested Routing: HONG KONG

to	By First Carrier	Routing and Destination	Air Waybill Number	Currency	CHGS Code	WT/VAL PPD	WT/VAL COLL	Other PPD	Other COLL	Declared Value for Carriage	Declared Value for Customs
YUL	CX			HKD		P		P		N.V.D.	AS PER INV

Airport of Destination	Flight/Date	For Carrier Use only	Flight/Date	Amount of Insurance
MONTREAL	CX828	05 FEB.2005		NIL

INSURANCE - If Carrier offers insurance and such insurance is requested in accordance with conditions on reverse hereof, indicate amount to be insured in figures in box marked amount of insurance.

Handling information:
THIS SHIPMENT,INCLUDING ITS CONTAINERS,DOES NOT CONTAIN ANY NON-MANUFACTURED WOODEN PACKING MATERIAL,DUNNAGE,BRACING MATERIAL,PALLETS, CRATING OR OTHER NON-MANUFACTURED WOODEN PACKING MATERIAL.

No. of Pieces RCP	Gross Weight	kg/lb	Rate Class / Commodity Item No.	Chargeable Weight	Rate / Charge	Total	Nature and Quantity of Goods (incl. Dimensions or Volume)
22	189.0	K		189.0	PREPAID AS ARRANGED		LADIES' 95% COTTON 5% SPANDEX KNITTED SWEATER PO. C9588 STYLE NO.52309D5S/LD QTY:800PCS [D34×60×31CM×14] [D54×31×31CM×8] VOL. = 1300512.0CM BY VOL. 186.0K

MARKS:
OUR MARK
OUR P/O NO.
CONCECUTIVE
PACKAGE NUMBER
STYLE NO.
COLOR
SIZE
QTY
MADE IN CHINA
WEIGHT
MEASURMENT

INVOICE,PACKING LIST,ORIGINAL CHINA
C/O#040551659 ATT'D
E/L : E501221500005

Prepaid	Weight Charge	Collect
AS ARRANGED		PREPAID

Valuation Charge

Tax

Total other Charges Due Agent

Total other Charges Due Carrier

Other Charges

Shipper certifies that the particulars on the face hereof are correct and that insofar as any part of the consignment contains restricted articles, such part is properly described by name and is in proper condition for carriage by air according to the applicable Dangerous Goods Regulations.

IFS INTERNATIONAL AIR CARGO LIMITED
Signature of Shipper or his Agent

IFS INTERNATIONAL AIR CARGO LIMITED 運航國際空運有限公司

Total Prepaid	Total Collect
Currency Conversion Rates	CC Charges in Dest. Currency

03 FEB.2005 HONG.KONG LE06
Executed on (Date) at (Place) Signature of Issuing Carrier or its Agent

ORIGINAL 1 (FOR SHIPPER)

House Air Waybill Number: IFS-31661

（七）单据填制

1. 单据填制一

根据给出的资料填制单据。

A. 信用证条款。

Applicant　*50　: YYY TRADING CO., LTD.
220 SIGMUND STR.
80035 NOLA (ITALY)

Beneficiary　*59　: GUANGDONG ABC IMPORT & EXPORT COMPANY LTD.
NO. 188 XIAOGANG ROAD, GUANGZHOU

Loading in Charge　44 A : FROM ANY CHINESE AIRPORT

For Transport to ...　44 B : MILAN, ITALY

Descript. of Goods　45 A :

1,700 PCS OF LADIES' 55% RAMIE 36% WOOL 9% NYLON KNITTED SWEATER
CFR MILAN AIRPORT
AS PER SALES CONFIRMATION NO. 2002MCGS02007 DD 8.3.2002
TOTAL AMOUNT USD12,614.00

Documents Required　46 A :

CLEAN AIRWAYBILL FOR GOODS AIRFREIGHTED TO YYY TRADING CO., LTD. 220 SIGMUND STR. 80035 NOLA (ITALY) MARKED FREIGHT PREPAID AND EVIDENCING THAT ORIGINAL INVOICE AND PACKING LIST ACCOMPANY THE GOODS, NOTIFY APPLICANT

B. 其他资料。

航空运单填开日期：2005 年 5 月 25 日　　航空运单填开地点：广州
始发站：广州　　货物装箱情况：1,700PCS/40CTNS
航班号及日期：CA1234/26, MAY. 2005　　总毛重：400KGS
唛头：YYY/MILAN/NOS1 - 40　　计费重量：420KGS
计费货币：美元　　航空运单号码：03030030509
空运单注明没有声明价值和没有商业价值　　尺码：(30 × 40 × 20) CM

999 | | 999—

Shipper's Name and Address	Shipper's Account Number	NOT NEGOTIABLE 中国民航 CAAC AIR WAYBILL AIR CONSIGNMENT NOTE ISSUED BY:THE CIVIL AVIATION ADMINIASTRATION OF CHINA BEIJING CHINA Copies 1, 2 and 3 of this Air Waybill are originals and have the same validity.
Consignee's Name and Address	Consignee's Account Number	It is agreed that the goods described herein are accepted in apparent good order and condition (except as noted) for carriage SUBJECT TO THE CONDITIONS OF CONTRACT ON THE REVERSE HEREOF.THE SHIPPER' S ATTENTION IS DRAWN TO THE NOTICE CONCERNINC CARRIER'S LIMITATION OF LIABILITY. Shipper may increase such limitation of liability by declaring a higher value for carriage and paying a supplemental charge if required. ISSUING CARRIER MAINTAINS CARGO ACCIDENT LIABILITY INSURANCE
Issuing Carrier's Agent Name and City Agent's IATA Code	Account No.	Accounting Information
Airport of Departure(Addr. of First Carrier)and Requested Routing		

to	By First Carrier / Routing and Destination	to	by	to	by	Currency	CHGS Code	WT/NAL PPD	WT/NAL COLL	Other PPD	Other COLL	Declared Value for Carriage	Declared Value for Customs

Airport Destination	Flight/Date	For Carrier Use only	Flight/Date	Amount of Insurance	INSURANCE if carrier offers insurance, and such insurance is requested in accordance with conditions on reverse here of, indicate amount to be insured in figure in box marked amount of insurance.

Handling Information

(for USA only)Those commodities licensed by US for ultimate destination...Diversion contray to US law is prohibited.

No.of Pieces RCP	Gross Weight	Kg Lb	Rate Class / Commodity Item No.	Chargeable Weight	Rate / Charge	Total	Nature and Quantity of Goods (incl.Dimensions or Volume)

Prepaid / Weight Charge / Collect	Other Charges
Valuation Charge	
Tax	
Total Other Charges Due Agent	Shipper certifies that the particulars on the face hereof are correct and that insofar as any part of the consignment contains dangerous goods, such part is properly described by name and is in proper condition for carriage by air according to the applicable Dangerous Goods Regulations.
Total Other Charges Due Carrier	.... Signature of Shipper or his Agent
Total Prepaid / Total Collect	
Currency Conversion Rates / CC Charges in Dest.Currency	.... Executed on (date) at (place) Signature of Issuing carrier or its Agent

For Carrier's use only at Destination	Charges at Destination	Total Collect Charges	999—

2. 单据填制二

根据给出的国际货物托运书填制单据。

国际货物托运书（SHIPPERS LETTER OF INSTRUCTION）

<table>
<tr><td colspan="2">托运人姓名及地址
SHIPPER'S NAME AND ADDRESS</td><td colspan="2">托运人账号
SHIPPER'S ACCOUNT NUMBER</td><td colspan="2">供承运人用
FOR CARRIAGE USE ONLY</td></tr>
<tr><td colspan="4" rowspan="3">GUANGDONG FOREIGN TRADE IMP. & EXP. CORP. 15 - 18/F. ,
GUANGDONG FOREIGN ECONOMIC AND TRADE BUILDING 351
TIANHE ROAD, GUANGZHOU, CHINA</td><td>班期/日期
FLIGHT/DAY</td><td>航班/日期
FLIGHT/DAY</td></tr>
<tr><td colspan="2">CA253/MAY 28,2004</td></tr>
<tr><td colspan="2"></td></tr>
<tr><td colspan="2">收货人姓名及地址
CONSIGNEE'S NAME AND ADDRESS</td><td colspan="2">收货人账号
CONSIGNEE'S ACCOUNT NUMBER</td><td colspan="2">已预留吨位
BOOKED</td></tr>
<tr><td colspan="4">ABC COMPANY LIMITED
BLUE BIRD STREET, NEW YORK, USA</td><td colspan="2">运费 CHARGES
FREIGHT PREPAID</td></tr>
<tr><td colspan="4">代理人的名称和城市
ISSUING CARRIER'S AGENT NAME AND CITY

XYZ SHIPPING CO. ,LTD.</td><td colspan="2" rowspan="3">ALSO NOTIFY</td></tr>
<tr><td colspan="4">始发站 AIRPORT OF DEPARTURE
GUANGZHOU AIRPORT</td></tr>
<tr><td colspan="4">到达站 AIRPORT OF DESTINATION
JOHN KENNEDY AIRPORT(JEK)</td></tr>
<tr><td colspan="2">托运人声明价值
SHIPPER'S DECLARED VALUE</td><td colspan="2" rowspan="2">保险金额
AMOUNT OF INSURANCE

NIL</td><td colspan="2" rowspan="2">所附文件
DOCUMENT TO ACCOMPANY AIR WAYBILL

1 COMMERCIAL INVOICE AND 1PACKING LIST</td></tr>
<tr><td>供运输用
FOR CARRIAGE
NVD</td><td>供海关用
FOR CUSTOMS
NCV</td></tr>
<tr><td colspan="6">处理情况（包括包装方式、货物标志及号码）
HANDLING INFORMATION（INGL METHOD OF PACKING IDENTIFYING AND NUMBERS）

KEEP UPSIDE</td></tr>
<tr><td>件数
NO. OF PACKAGES</td><td>实际毛重
ACTUAL GROSS WEIGHT(KG.)</td><td>运价种类
RATE CLASS</td><td>收费重量
CHARGEABLE WEIGHT</td><td>费率
RATE/ CHARGE</td><td>货物品名及数量（包括体积或尺寸）
NATUER AND QUANTITY OF GOODS（INCL. DIMENSION OF VOLUME）
480PCS OF MEN'S SWEATERS</td></tr>
<tr><td>10</td><td>100</td><td></td><td>100</td><td>18.00</td><td>DIMS：
(40 × 30 × 25) CM × 10</td></tr>
</table>

999　　　　　　　　　　　　　　　　　　　　　　　　999—

Shipper's Name and Address	Shipper's Account Number	NOT NEGOTIABLE 中国民航 CAAC AIR WAYBILL AIR CONSIGNMENT NOTE ISSUED BY: THE CIVIL AVIATION ADMINIASTRATION OF CHINA BEIJING CHINA
		Copies 1, 2 and 3 of this Air Waybill are originals and have the same validity.
Consignee's Name and Address	Consignee's Account Number	It is agreed that the goods described herein are accepted in apparent good order and condition (except as noted) for carriage SUBJECT TO THE CONDITIONS OF CONTRACT ON THE REVERSE HEREOF. THE SHIPPER' S ATTENTION IS DRAWN TO THE NOTICE CONCERNINC CARRIER'S LIMITATION OF LIABILITY. Shipper may increase such limitation of liability by declaring a higher value for carriage and paying a supplemental charge if required. ISSUING CARRIER MAINTAINS CARGO ACCIDENT LIABILITY INSURANCE
Issuing Carrier's Agent Name and City		Accounting Information
Agent's IATA Code	Account No.	
Airport of Departure (Addr. of First Carrier) and Requested Routing		

to	By First Carrier / Routing and Destination	to	by	to	by	Currency	CHGS Code	WT/NAL PPD	WT/NAL COLL	Other PPD	Other COLL	Declared Value for Carriage	Declared Value for Customs

Airport Destination	Flight/Date	For Carrier Use only	Flight/Date	Amount of Insurance	INSURANCE if carrier offers insurance, and such insurance is requested in accordance with conditions on reverse here of, indicate amount to be insured in figure in box marked amount of insurance.

Handling Information

(for USA only) Those commodities licensed by US for ultimate destination... Diversion contray to US law is prohibited.

No. of Pieces RCP	Gross Weight	Kg Lb	Rate Class / Commodity Item No.	Chargeable Weight	Rate / Charge	Total	Nature and Quantity of Goods (incl. Dimensions or Volume)

Prepaid / Weight Charge / Collect		Other Charges
Valuation Charge		
Tax		
Total Other Charges Due Agent		Shipper certifies that the particulars on the face hereof are correct and that insofar as any part of the consignment contains dangerous goods, such part is properly described by name and is in proper condition for carriage by air according to the applicable Dangerous Goods Regulations.
Total Other Charges Due Carrier		.... Signature of Shipper or his Agent
Total Prepaid	Total Collect	
Currency Conversion Rates	CC Charges in Dest. Currency	.... Executed on (date)　at (place)　Signature of Issuing carrier or its Agent
For Carrier's use only at Destination	Charges at Destination	Total Collect Charges

999—

二、练习题参考答案

（一）中英文术语、短语互译

1. 航空运单
2. 航空公司数字代号
3. 海关申报价值
4. 目的地机场
5. 计费重量
6. 财务说明
7. （International Air Transport Association）国际航协
8. （No Commercial Value）没有商业价值
9. （No Value Declared）没有声明价值
10. 费用代码（Charges Code）
11. （Assembly Service Fee）集中货物服务费
12. （Prepaid ）预付
13. （Charges Collect Fee）运费到付手续费
14. （Collect）待付
15. （Insurance Premium）代办保险服务费
16. （Government Tax）政府捐税
17. （Rate Combination Point）运价组合点
18. （Nothing）零

（二）单项选择题

1. B。理由：航空运单正本按国际惯例为一式三份，每份都印有背面条款。

2. A。理由：中国民航的代号为999，131是日本航空公司代号。

3. C。理由：香港机场代号为HKG。HGH是杭州机场代号，HRB是哈尔滨机场代号，HAK是海口机场代号。

4. D。理由：广州机场的代号为CAN，SHA是上海机场的代号，PEK是北京机场的代号，SZX是深圳机场的代号。

5. B。理由：大阪机场的代号为OSA，TYO是东京机场的代号，OKA是冲绳机场的代号，NGO是名古屋机场的代号。

6. D。理由：曼谷机场的代号为BKK，SIN是新加坡机场的代号，PEN是槟城机场的代号，MNL是马尼拉机场的代号。

7. B。理由：巴黎机场的代号为PAR，LON是伦敦机场的代号，HAM是汉堡机场的代号，FRA是法兰克福机场的代号。

8. A。理由：旧金山的机场代号为SFO，NYK是纽约机场的代号，WAS是华盛顿机场的代号，LAX是洛杉矶机场的代号。

9. A。理由：按规定，在航空运输中，当托运的货物中含有危险货物时，应分别填写，并把危险货物填列在第一项。

10. B。理由："Executed on date"意指运单日期，该日期为签发航空运单的日期。如果信用证规定运单必须注明实际起飞日期，才以实际起飞日期作为装运日期填写。

（三）多项选择题

1. AC。理由：航空运单可分为出票航空公司标志的航空货运单和无承运人任何标志的中性货运单两种。

2. ABCD。理由：航空运单是航空运输承运人与托运人之间的运输合同；航空运单是航空公司或其代理人收运货物的证明文件；航空运单是承运人核收运费的依据；航空运单是承运人处理货物运输过程情况的依据。

3. BD。理由：TSN 表示天津机场，XMN 表示厦门机场，LAS 表示拉斯维加斯机场，SEL 表示首尔机场。

4. AC。理由：空运单不是物权凭证，不能通过背书进行转让。

5. ABCD。理由：航空运单的托运人名称和地址栏目，一般填写托运人的名称、地址、国家（或国家两字代号）、电话号码、传真、电传号码。

（四）判断题

1. 错误。理由：航空运单不是物权凭证，因此，持有航空运单并不能说明可以对货物要求所有权。

2. 错误。理由：航空运单正本一式三份，第一份由航空公司留存，第二份随货同行，第三份交托运人，因此，受益人到银行议付时只能提交一份正本航空运单。

3. 错误。理由：航空运单不仅是航空运输合同的证明，而且航空运单本身就是托运人与航空运输承运人之间签订的货物运输合同。

4. 错误。理由：一张航空运单只能用于一个托运人在同一时间、同一地点托运货物，运往同一目的站同一收货人。

5. 正确。

（五）阅读理解

1. 阅读理解一

（1）收货人：TO Q. T. SERVICES GROUP, INC.

（2）代理人的名称和地址：DYNASTY INTERNATIONAL, INC.

（3）财务说明：ALSO NOTIFY：
DYNASTY CHB, INC.,
365 CHEISEA ST., EAST BOSTON, MA
02128, PHONE 617.569.5969

（4）始发站：SHANGHAI, CHINA

（5）到达站：BOSTON, MA

（6）航班：OZ364/2OCT

（7）货币：USD

（8）供运输用声明价值：NVD（NO VALUE DECLARED）没有声明价值

（9）供海关用声明价值：AS PER INV（按照发票）

（10）处理情况：THIS SHPT CONTAINS NO SOLID WOOD PACKING MATERIALS.
A/S/D

（11）货物的件数：103CTNS

（12）计费重量：1,371.00KGS

（13）运费缴付方式：FREIGHT PREPAID

（14）货物品名和数量：WOMEN'S APPAREL（WOMEN'S 100% CASHMERE KNITTED

SWEATERS)
PO#703307, 703308, 703309
STYLE#44 -3375M, 44 -3375P, 44 -3375W

(15) 货物体积：VOL：8.226CBM
(60.5 ×40 ×33) CM ×103

(16) 航空运单填开日期：2, OCT. 2004

(17) 航空运单填开地点：SHANGHAI

2. 阅读理解二

(1) 托运人的名称及地址：STEP ELEGANT LTD.
RM201, 2/F, WAI CHING COMM BLDG,
77 WAI CHING ST, KLN, HONGKONG
27812910 DEREK CHENG

(2) 收货人：TO ORDER OF BNP PARIBAS (CANDA)

(3) 航班日期：05 FEB. 2005

(4) 财务说明：FREIGHT PREPAID
NOTIFY COSACO INC
9600 RUE MEILLEUR, MONTREAL,
QC H2N 2E3
CONTACT PERSON：KAREN CRAWLEY
TEL：(514) 3824860 FAX：(514) 3878086

(5) 始发站：HONGKONG

(6) 到达站：MONTREAL

(7) 航班：CX828

(8) 货币：HKD

(9) 供运输用声明价值：N. V. D.

(10) 供海关用声明价值：AS PER INV

(11) 货物的件数：22

(12) 计费重量：189.0

(13) 运费缴付方式：PREPAID AS ARRANGED

(14) 货物品名和数量：LADIES' 95% COTTON 5% SPANDEX KNITTED SWEATER
PO. C9588
STYLE NO. 52309D5S/LD
QTY：800PCS

(15) 货物体积：D34 ×60 ×31CM ×14
D54 ×31 ×31CM ×8
VOL. =1300512.0CM
BY VOL. 186.0K

(16) 航空运单填开日期：03 FEB. 2005

(17) 航空运单填开地点：HONGKONG

（18）所附文件：INVOICE，PACKING LIST，ORIGINAL CHINA
C/O#040551659 ATT' D
E/L：E501221500005

（七）单据填制

1. 单据填制一

999 | | 999—

Shipper's Name and Address | **Shipper's Account Number**

GUANGDONG ABC IMPORT & EXPORT
COMPANY LTD.
NO.188 XIAOGANG ROAD,GUANGZHOU

NOT NEGOTIABLE 中国民航 CAAC

AIR WAYBILL AIR CONSIGNMENT NOTE
ISSUED BY:THE CIVIL AVIATION ADMINIASTRATION OF CHINA
BEIJING CHINA

Copies 1, 2 and 3 of this Air Waybill are originals and have the same validity.

Consignee's Name and Address | **Consignee's Account Number**

YYY TRADING CO.,LTD.
220 SIGMUND STR.
80035 NOLA (ITALY)

It is agreed that the goods described herein are accepted in apparent good order and condition (except as noted) for carriage SUBJECT TO THE CONDITIONS OF CONTRACT ON THE REVERSE HEREOF.THE SHIPPER'S ATTENTION IS DRAWN TO THE NOTICE CONCERNINC CARRIER'S LIMITATION OF LIABILITY.Shipper may increase such limitation of liability by declaring a higher value for carriage and paying a supplemental charge if required.
ISSUING CARRIER MAINTAINS CARGO ACCIDENT LIABILITY INSURANCE

Issuing Carrier's Agent Name and City XYZ CARGO.

Agent's IATA Code | **Account No.**

Accounting Information

FRELGHT PREPALD
NOTIFY YYY TRADING CO.,LTD.
220 SIGMUND STR.80035 NOLA(ITALY)

Airport of Departure(Addr. of First Carrier)and Requested Routing

GUANGZHOU, CHINA

to	By First Carrier	Routing and Destination	to	by	to	by	Currency	CHGS Code	WT/NAL PPD	WT/NAL COLL	Other PPD	Other COLL	Declared Value for Carriage	Declared Value for Customs
							USD		P		P		N V D	N V C

Airport Destination	Flight/Date	For Carrier Use only / Flight/Date	Amount of Insurance	INSURANCE if carrier offers insurance, and such insurance is requested in accordance with conditions on reverse here of, indicate amount to be insured in figure in box marked amount of insurance.
MILAN	CA1234	MAY 26,2005	N I L	

Handling Information

MARKS:YYY/MILANO/NOS1- 40

(for USA only)Those commodities licensed by US for ultimate destination...Diversion contray to US law is prohibited.

No. of Pieces RCP	Gross Weight	Kg Lb	Rate Class / Commodity Item No.	Chargeable Weight	Rate / Charge	Total	Nature and Quantity of Goods (incl.Dimensions or Volume)
40CT N S	400	K		420			LADIES'55% RAMIE30% WOOL9% NYLON KNITTED SWEATER DIMS:(30×40×20)CM×40

Prepaid	Weight Charge	Collect
AS ARRANGED	Valuation Charge	PREPAID
	Tax	
	Total Other Charges Due Agent	
	Total Other Charges Due Carrier	

Other Charges

ORIGINAL INVOICE AND PACKING LIST, ACCOMPANY THE GOODS.

Shipper certifies that the particulars on the face hereof are correct and that insofar as any part of the consignment contains dangerous goods,such part is properly described by name and is in proper condition for carriage by air according to the applicable Dangerous Goods Regulations.

Signature of Shipper or his Agent

Total Prepaid	Total Collect
Currency Conversion Rates	CC Charges in Dest. Currency

MAY 25, 2005 GUANGZHOU

Executed on (date) at (place) Signature of Issuing carrier or its Agent

For Carrier's use only at Destination	Charges at Destination	Total Collect Charges

999—

2. 单据填制二

999 | |　　　　　　　　　　　　　　　　　　　　　　999—

Shipper's Name and Address / Shipper's Account Number	NOT NEGOTIABLE 中国民航 CAAC
GUANGDONG FOREIGN TRADE IMP. & EXP. CORP. 15 – 18/F., GUANGDONG FOREIGN ECONOMIC AND TRADE BUILDING 351 TIANHE ROAD, GUANGZHOU, CHINA	AIR WAYBILL AIR CONSIGNMENT NOTE ISSUED BY: THE CIVIL AVIATION ADMINIASTRATION OF CHINA BEIJING CHINA Copies 1, 2 and 3 of this Air Waybill are originals and have the same validity.
Consignee's Name and Address / Consignee's Account Number ABC COMPANY LIMITED BLUE BIRD STREET, NEW YORK, USA	It is agreed that the goods described herein are accepted in apparent good order and condition (except as noted) for carriage SUBJECT TO THE CONDITIONS OF CONTRACT ON THE REVERSE HEREOF. THE SHIPPER'S ATTENTION IS DRAWN TO THE NOTICE CONCERNINC CARRIER'S LIMITATION OF LIABILITY. Shipper may increase such limitation of liability by declaring a higher value for carriage and paying a supplemental charge if required. ISSUING CARRIER MAINTAINS CARGO ACCIDENT LIABILITY INSURANCE
Issuing Carrier's Agent Name and City XYZ SHIPPING CO., LTD. Agent's IATA Code / Account No.	Accounting Information FREIGHT PREPAID
Airport of Departure (Addr. of First Carrier) and Requested Routing GUANGZHOU AIRPORT	

to	By First Carrier \ Routing and Destination /	to	by	to	by	Currency	CHGS Code	WT/VAL PPD	WT/VAL COLL	Other PPD	Other COLL	Declared Value for Carriage	Declared Value for Customs
JEK	CAAC					USD		×		×		NVD	NCV

Airport Destination	Flight/Date \ For Carrier Use only / Flight/Date		Amount of Insurance	
JOHN KENNEDY AIRPORT (JEK)	CA253	MAY 28, 2004	×××	INSURANCE if carrier offers insurance, and such insurance is requested in accordance with conditions on reverse here of, indicate amount to be insured in figure in box marked amount of insurance.

Handling Information

KEEP UPSIDE

(for USA only) Those commodities licensed by US for ultimate destination...Diversion contray to US law is prohibited.

No. of Pieces RCP	Gross Weight	Kg Lb	Rate Class Commodity Item No.	Chargeable Weight	Rate / Charge	Total	Nature and Quantity of Goods (incl. Dimensions or Volume)
10	100	K		100	18.00		480 PCS OF MEN'S SWEATERS DIMS: (40×30×25)CM×10

Prepaid \ Weight Charge / Collect	Other Charges
AS ARRANGED \ Valuation Charge / PREPAID	1 COMMERCIAL INVOICE AND 1 PACKING LIST
Tax	
Total Other Charges Due Agent	Shipper certifies that the particulars on the face hereof are correct and that insofar as any part of the consignment contains dangerous goods, such part is properly described by name and is in proper condition for carriage by air according to the applicable Dangerous Goods Regulations.
Total Other Charges Due Carrier	.... Signature of Shipper or his Agent
Total Prepaid / Total Collect	MAY 27, 2004 GUANGZHOU
Currency Conversion Rates / CC Charges in Dest. Currency	.... Executed on (date)　at (place)　Signature of Issuing carrier or its Agent
For Carrier's use only at Destination / Charges at Destination	Total Collect Charges　　999—

第四节　装船通知

一、练习题

（一）单据填制一

根据有关资料填制装船通知。

A. 信用证资料。

Date of Issue	:	041020
Form of Doc. Credit	:	IRREVOCABLE
Doc. Credit Number	:	M20K2710NS00032
Expiry	:	Date 041115 Place IN BENEFICIARY'S COUNTRY
Applicant	:	SE BANG TRADING CO., LTD. 148 NAMCHEON - 2 DONG, SUYOUNG - KU PUSAN, KOREA
Beneficiary	:	GUANGZHOU ARTS & CRAFTS IMP. & EXP. CORP. 628 GUANGZHOU DADAO ZHONG ROAD, GUANGZHOU, CHINA
Partial Shipments	:	ALLOWED
Transshipment	:	ALLOWED
Loading in Charge	:	GUANGZHOU, CHINA
For Transport to...	:	PUSAN, KOREA
Latest Date of Ship.	:	041105
Descript. of Goods	:	CHINA ORIGIN ARTIFICIAL FLOWERS AB - 06001　　5,184DOZ @ USD2.50/DOZ AB - 07049　　2,880DOZ @ USD2.80/DOZ AS PER S/C NO. 97A/KF002A DATE OCT. 15, 2004 CIF PUSAN
Documents Required	:	SHIPMENT ADVICE IN FULL DETAILS INCLUDING SHIPPING MARKS, CONTAINER NUMBERS, VESSEL NAME, B/L NUMBER, VALUE AND QUANTITY OF GOODS MUST BE SENT ON THE DATE OF SHIPMENT TO APPLICANT.

B. 其他资料。

INV. NO.: 97KF335　　　　B/L DATE: OCT. 28, 2004

B/L NO.: DSA97 - 1102　　　　SHIPPING MARKS: SE BANG/PUSAN

PACKING: AB - 06001　36DOZ/CTN　G. W.: 23KGS/CTN　N. W.: 18KGS/CTN

　　　　AB - 07049　36DOZ/CTN　G. W.: 19KGS/CTN　N. W.: 13KGS/CTN

MEASUREMENT: (40×50×80) CM/CTN　DATE OF ADVICE: OCT. 29, 2004

CONTAINER NO. MSCU 4097561 (20') MSCU 4097615 (40')

NAME OF STEAMER: SUI 301/NORASIA V. 49 - 3 W/T HONGKONG

（二）单据填制二

根据有关资料填制装船通知。

A. 信用证资料。

Credit Number : LRT9802457
Date of Issue : 020505
Expiry : Date 020716 Place CHINA
Applicant : ABC CORP. AKEKSANTERINK AUTO
P. O. BOX 9, FINLAND
Beneficiary : GUANGDONG RONGHUA TRADE CO., LTD.
168, DEZHENG ROAD SOUTH, GUANGZHOU, CHINA
Amount : Currency USD Amount 36,480.00 (SAY US DOLLARS THIRTY SIX THOUSAND FOUR HUNDRED AND EIGHTY ONLY.)
Loading in Charge : GUANGZHOU
For Transport to : HELSINKI
Shipment Period : AT THE LATEST JULY 16, 2002
Descrip. of Goods : 9,600PCS OF WOMEN'S SWEATERS
UNIT PRICE: USD3.80/PC, PACKING: 12PCS/CTN
OTHER DETAILS AS PER S/C NO. 98SGQ468001
CFR HELSINKI
Documents Required:
ADVICE OF SHIPMENT MUST BE SENT BY FAX TO MARKE INSURANCE CO. HELSINKI, FINLAND (FAX NO. 33333) WITH DETAILS OF SHIPMENT INCLUDING VALUE, NAME OF VESSEL, DATE OF SHIPMENT, NAME OF COMMODITY, NUMBER OF PACKAGE; TOTAL NET AND GROSS WEIGHT QUOTING THEIR POLICY NO. 3RT20053. COPY OF THIS FAX TO BE PRESENTED WITH DOCUMENTS UPON NEGOTIATION.
Additional Cond. : 1. T. T. REIMBURSEMENT IS PROHIBITED.
2. ALL DOCUMENTS MUST BE MARKED THE S/C NO. AND THE L/C NO.
3. SHIPPING MARKS: ABC/HELSINKI/ NO. 1-UP

B. 其他资料。

INV. NO.: 2005PCI448　DATE OF SHIPMENT: MAY. 20, 2002
B/L NO.: FKK9078533　MEASUREMENT: (40×50×80) CM/CTN
G. W.: 23KGS/CTN　N. W.: 18KGS/CTN
NAME OF STEAMER: DONGFRNEG E003 DATE OF ADVICE: MAY 21, 2002

二、练习题参考答案

（一）单据填制一

广州工艺进出口公司

GUANGZHOU ARTS & CRAFTS IMP. & EXP. CORP.

628 GUANGZHOU DADAO ZHONG ROAD. GUANGZHOU, CHINA

INVOICE NO.: 97KF335

To Messrs.:

SE BANG TRADING CO., LTD.
148 NAMCHEON -2 DONG, SUYOUNG - KU
PUSAN, KOREA

SHIPPING ADVICE

Name of Commodity: CHINA ORIGIN
ARTIFICIAL FLOWERS
Quantity: 8,064DOZ, 224CTNS
Invoice Value: USD21,024.00
Name of Carrying Steamer: SUI 301/NORASIA V. 49 -3 W/T HONGKONG
Date of Shipment: OCT. 28, 2004
Shipping Marks: SE BANG/PUSAN
Credit No.: M20K2710NS00032
Port of Loading: GUANGZHOU, CHINA
Port of Discharge:: PUSAN, KOREA
B/L No.: DSA97 -1102
Container No.: MSCU 4097561 (20') MSCU 4097615 (40')

GUANGZHOU ARTS & CRAFTS IMP. & EXP. CORP.
628 GUAGNZHOU DADAO ZHONG ROAD,
GUANGHZOU, CHINA

（二）单据填制二

广东荣华贸易有限公司

GUANGDONG RONGHUA TRADE CO., LTD.

168 DEZHENG ROAD SOUTH, GUANGZHOU, CHINA

FAX NO.: 33333

INV. NO.: 2005PCI448

To Messrs.:

MARKE INSURANCE CO.

HELSINKI, FINLAND

ADVICE OF SHIPMENT

Name of Commodity: WOMEN'S SWEATERS
Quantity: 800CTNS
Invoice Value: USD36,480.00
Name of Carrying Steamer: DONGFRNEG E003
Date of Shipment: MAY 20, 2002
Shipping Marks: ABC/HELSINKI/ NO. 1 - UP
L/C No.: LRT9802457
Port of Loading: GUANGZHOU
Port of Discharge: HELSINKI
B/L No.: FKK9078533
S/C No.: 98SGQ468001
TOTAL NET WEIGHT: 14,400.00KGS
TOTAL GROSS WEIGHT: 18,400.00KGS
POLICY NO.: 3RT20053

GUANGDONG RONGHUA TRADE CO., LTD.
168 DEZHENG ROAD SOUTH, GUANGZHOU, CHINA

第四章
托　运　单

一、练习题

（一）中英文术语、短语互译

1. 中译英

(1) 托运人　　(2) 收货人
(3) 提货单　　(4) 分运
(5) 正本提单　　(6) 托运单
(7) 运费预付　　(8) 场站收据
(9) 运输标志　　(10) 运费待付

2. 英译中

(1) Place of Destination　　(2) Time of Shipment
(3) Booking Note　　(4) Transshipment
(5) Stowage Plan　　(6) Loading Port
(7) Description of Goods　　(8) Shipping Order
(9) Container Load Plan　　(10) Mate's Receipt

（二）单项选择题

1. 若货物从广州运往荷兰的鹿特丹港口后，再运至德国一内陆城市 SCHORNDORF，贸易术语为 CIF ROTTERDAM，则托运单的目的港应填(　　)

A. ROTTERDAM　　B. NETHERLAND
C. SCHORNDORF　　D. GERMANY

2. 开证行 HANGSENG BANK 开来的信用证中，要求 FULL SET OF B/L MADE OUT TO OUR ORDER，则填托运单时在 CONSIGNEE 一栏应填(　　)

A. TO ORDER
B. TO OUR ORDER
C. TO ORDER OF HANGSENG BANK
D. HANGSENG BANK

3. 下面集装箱交接方式中，(　　)是“整箱接，拆箱交”。

A. FCL/FCL　　B. FCL/LCL

C. LCL/FCL　　D. LCL/LCL

4. 托运单 CONSIGNEE 栏目中，若填写为(　　)，则提单必须由托运人背书方可转让。

A. TO ORDER　　B. TO ORDER OF ×××BANK

C. 开证人名称　　D. TO ORDER OF 开证人名称

5. 若信用证同时列明 3 个装运港 XINGANG/QINHUANGDAO/TANGSHANG，在填制托运单时应填(　　)

A. XINGANG/QINHUANGDAO/TANGSHANG

B. XINGANG

C. 根据 L/C 提供的港口，只填写实际装运港的名称

D. GUANGZHOU

（三）多项选择题

1. (　　)是结汇单据，如果缮制错漏、延误等，就会影响安全结汇。

A. 汇票　　B. 发票

C. 托运单　　D. 受益人证明书

2. 托运单收货人栏目填写为(　　)，则其对应的提单可通过背书转让。

A. ABC　CO.　　B. TO ORDER

C. TO ORDER OF SHIPPER　　D. TO ORDER OF×××BANK

3. 下面托运单栏目中，须由船公司填写的是(　　)。

A. 提单编号　　B. 船名

C. 船期　　D. 托运单编号

4. 托运单的运费缴付方式，根据实际情况可填写(　　)。

A. FREIGHT PREPAID　　B. FREIGHT PAID

C. FREIGHT COLLECT　　D. FREIGHT PAYABLE AT DESTINATION

5. 承运人从起运地到目的地都采用整箱交接货物方式的是(　　)。

A. CY TO CY　　B. CY TO CFS

C. DOOR TO CY　　D. CFS TO CY

（四）判断题

1. 如来证中要求两个或两个以上的公司为被通知人，若托运单栏内写不下，可只填写一个被通知人。(　　)

2. 货物装船后，大副在收货单上签收。托运人凭已签名的收货单向船公司或船代理换取全套正本提单。(　　)

3. 如在托运单收货人一栏留空，这种表示方法称为空白指示。(　　)

4. 被通知人的职责是及时接受船方发出的到货通知并及时提货。(　　)

5. 如出口 10 万码花布，分别用粗抷布捆成 100 捆，则填写数目这一栏时应填写 100 捆。(　　)

6. 如果买卖合同和信用证都没有规定唛头，则卖方不能自行选择一个合适的唛头。(　　)

7. 若一次装运货物中有几种不同的货物，那么在填写毛重这一栏目时，只需填写合计全部的毛重。(　　)

8. 若合同或信用证没有特别说明，通常情况下，托运单中的货物说明也必须详细列出货物的型号、规格，不能只写大类名称或统称。(　　)

9. 托运单号码一般就是提单号码。(　　)

10. 若信用证中规定装运港为 Chinese main port，则在托运单中的装运港应填 Chinese main port ，以保持单证一致。(　　)

（五）单据填制

1. 单据填制一

请根据以下材料填制一份托运单。

A. 信用证条款。

Credit Number	: SK/25067/2004
Date of Issue	: DEC. 27, 2004
Expiry	: Date 050327 Place CHINA
Applicant	: MAHARAJA DEIRA L. L. C, DUBAI (UAE) P. O. BOX No. 6093, DUBAI (UAE), FAX NO. 263745
Beneficiary	: GUANGDONG TEXTILES IMP. AND EXP. GRANDTON TRADING CO., LTD., 7/F., GUANGDONG TEXTILES MANSION, NO. 168 XIAOBEI ROAD, GUANGZHOU, CHINA
Amount	: USD 99,960.00
Patrial Shipments	: Allowed
Transshipment	: Allowed (AT HONGKONG PORT ONLY)
Shipment Period	: AT THE LATEST MARCH 27, 2005 (Shipment from CHINA Ports To DUBAI By Steamer)
Covering	: 4,000 DOZEN LADIES LYCRA LONG PANT CIFC2 DUBAI USD25.5 PER DOZEN ALL OTHER DETAILS ARE AS PER S/C No. 2004/2495 PACKING 10DOZ/CTN
Shipping Marks	: MAHARAJA / 264553/ DUBAI/NO. 1-400
Documents Required	: * Full set of clean "Shipped on board" ocean Bills of Lading made out to the order of Habib Bank AG Zurich DUBAI. U. A. E. and notify applicant, showing "freight Prepaid" mentioning L/C NO.
Additional Condition	: Shipment to be effected by 1×20' container (FCL).

B. 其他资料。

发票号码	GD-TX-9057	托运日期	JAN. 2, 2005
单位毛重	15KGS/CTN	单位净重	12KGS/CTN
单位尺码	(60×20×50) CM/CTN	货物堆存地点	大松岗

中　国　外　运　广　东　公　司
出口货物托运单

提单编号＿＿＿＿＿＿＿　托运日期＿＿＿＿＿＿＿　托运单位编号＿＿＿＿＿＿

合约编号＿＿＿＿＿＿

船　　名＿＿＿＿＿＿＿　船期＿＿＿＿＿＿＿　运往地点＿＿＿＿＿＿

托运人＿＿＿＿＿＿＿＿＿＿＿＿＿＿＿＿＿＿＿＿＿＿＿＿

受货人＿＿＿＿＿＿＿＿＿＿＿＿＿＿＿＿＿＿＿＿＿＿＿＿

通　知＿＿＿＿＿＿＿＿＿＿＿＿＿＿＿＿＿＿＿＿＿＿＿＿

标记及号码	件　　数	货　　名	重量（公斤）		容积吨
			净	毛	
合计			共重：		

特约事项					
可否转船			（托运人盖章）		
可否分批		需要提单正本　　份　副本　　份			
货物堆存地点		装船期限		结汇期限	
运费缴付方式			运费账单开送		
信用证号码		货　价	F. O. B.	C. I. F.	
运往香港船名		实际装船日期			
运费吨：		运费率：		运费金额：	

2. 单据填制二

请根据以下资料填制一份托运单。

A. 信用证条款。

DATE AND PLACE OF ISSUE: 97/09/28 IN JAPAN

DATE AND PLACE OF EXPIRY: 97/11/10 IN GUANGZHOU, CHINA

IRREVOCABLE DOCUMENTARY CREDIT NO.: D-22-P-31209

APPLICANT: SUNNY TRADE ENTERPRISE UNIT A 8/F., CHINA TRADE CTR 122 WAI YIP ST KWUN TONG KOWLOON, JAPAN	BINEFICIARY: GUANGDONG ARTS AND CRAFTS IMP. AND EXP. CORP. (GROUP) 318 DADE ROAD, GUANGZHOU, CHINA
AMOUNT: USD 30,000.00 (US DOLLARS THIRTY THOUSAND ONLY.)	
PARTIAL SHIPMENTS ARE ALLOWED TRANSSHIPMENT IS ALLOWED SHIPMENT FROM GUANGZHOU, CHINA TO TOKYO LATEST 97/10/25	CREDIT AVAILBLE WITH ANY BANK BY NEGOTIATION AGAINST PRESENTATION OF THE DOCS DETAILED HEREIN AND OF THE BENE'S DRAFT (S) AT SIGHT DRAWN ON US FOR FULL INVOICE VALUE

LIST OF DOCUMENTS TO BE PRESENTED:

FULL SET OF ORIGINAL CLEAN "SHIPPED ON BOARD" OCEAN BILLS OF LADING MADE OUT TO ORDER OF THE CHINA AND SOUTH SEA BANK LTD., MARKED "FREIGHT PREPAID", NOTIFYING APPLICANT

SHIPPING DOCUMENTS COVERING (AS PER S/C NO. GDF-97-44011128):

ENERGY SAVING LAMPS LES9W2U

QUANTITY: 20,000PCS

UNIT PRICE: @USD1.50/PC, CIF TOKYO, 100PCS/CTN

WEIGHT: N. W: 8.00KGS/CTN, G. W: 10.00KGS/CTN

MEASUREMENT (CTN): (46×24×38) CM

SPECIAL CONDITION:

THE NAME, ADDRESS, TELEPHONE NUMBER OF SHIPPING AGENT IN TOKYO MUST BE MENTIONED ON B/L.

ALL GOODS MUST BE SHIPPED IN 20' CONTIANER.

B. 其他资料。

发票号码	GDF-97-2503	托运日期	OCT. 20, 1997
唛头	SUNNY/TOKYO/NO. 1-200	集装箱号码	1*20' SOMU2234925
东京货代资料	NAME: ABC SHIPPING CO., LTD. ADDRESS: 222 ROSE STREET, TOKYO, JAPAN TEL: 222888		

中　国　外　运　广　东　公　司
出口货物托运单

提单编号__________　托运日期__________　托运单位编号__________

合约编号__________

船　　名__________　船期__________　运往地点__________

托 运 人____________________

受 货 人____________________

通　　知____________________

标记及号码	件　　数	货　　名	重量（公斤）		容积吨
			净	毛	

合计		共重：	

特约事项		

可 否 转 船				（托运人盖章）	
可 否 分 批		需要提单正本　　份　副本　　份			
货物堆存地点		装船期限		结汇期限	
运费缴付方式		运费账单开送			
信用证号码		货　价	F. O. B.	C. I. F.	
运往香港船名		实际装船日期			

运费吨：　　运费率：　　运费金额：

二、练习题参考答案

（一）中英文术语、短语互译

1. 中译英

(1) Shipper 或 Consignor
(2) Consignee
(3) Deliver Order
(4) Partial Shipment
(5) Original B/L
(6) Shipping Note (Booking Note)
(7) Freight Prepaid
(8) Dock Receipt
(9) Shipping Marks
(10) Freight Collect

2. 英译中

(1) 目的地
(2) 装运期
(3) 托运单
(4) 转运
(5) 货物积载图
(6) 装运港
(7) 商品描述
(8) 装货单
(9) 集装箱装箱单
(10) 收货单

（二）单项选择题

1. A。理由：以 CIF ROTTERDAM 成交，即使货物的目的地是一内陆城市，若没有特别规定，托运单的目的港栏目应填写 CIF 后面的目的港。若填写为目的地，则卖方须支付从目的港运至目的地的运费。

2. C。理由：MADE OUT TO OUR ORDER 是指制成凭开证行的指示抬头。

3. B。理由：FCL：FULL CONTAINER LOAD 整箱货 LCL：LESS THAN CONTAINER LOAD 拼箱货。

4. A。理由：TO ORDER = TO ORDER OF SHIPPER 凭托运人指示。

5. C。理由：信用证同时列明 3 个起运港 XINGANG/QINHUANGDAO/TANGSHANG，受益人应根据 L/C 提供的港口，填写实际装运港的名称。

（三）多项选择题

1. ABD。理由：托运单属于非结汇单据。

2. BCD。理由：记名提单不能转让，指示提单可以经背书转让。

3. ABC。理由：提单编号、船名、船期由船公司填写。

4. ABCD。理由：除非信用证有特别要求，几乎所有的海运提单都不填写运费的数额，而只是表明运费是否已付清或什么时候付清。主要有：①运费已付——FREIGHT PAID；②运费预付——FREIGHT PREPAID；③运费到付——FREIGHT PAYABLE AT DESTINATION；④运费待付——FREIGHT COLLECT。

5. AC。理由：CY TO CY：集装箱堆场到集装箱堆场；CY TO CFS：集装箱堆场到集装箱货运站；DOOR TO CY：门到集装箱堆场；CFS TO CY：集装箱货运站到集装箱堆场。

（四）判断题

1. 错误。理由：如来证中要求两个或两个以上的公司为被通知人，若托运单栏内填写不下，可打＊号，并在下面空白处打＊号并标出余下的内容。

2. 正确。理由：托运人凭大副收据向船公司或船代理换取全套正本提单。

3. 错误。理由：空白指示是指写成 TO ORDER 形式。

4. 错误。理由：被通知人的职责是及时接受船方发出的到货通知但无权及时提货。

5. 正确。理由：托运单的数量应填最大包装的件数。

6. 错误。理由：如果买卖合同和信用证都没有规定唛头，则卖方可以自行选择一个合适的唛头。

7. 错误。理由：应先分别计算并填写每一种包装材料或每一货物毛重，然后合计全部的毛重。

8. 错误。理由：托运单中的货物允许只写大类名称或统称。

9. 错误。理由：托运单号码一般由托运人填写商业发票的号码，以便查寻与核查。而提单号码由船公司给出。

10. 错误。理由：若信用证中规定装运港为 Chinese main port，则在托运单中的装运港应填实际的装运港口。

（五）单据填制

1. 单据填制一

中　国　外　运　广　东　公　司
出口货物托运单

提单编号＿＿＿＿　托运日期 JAN. 2, 2005　托运单位编号 GD－TX－9057

合约编号 2004/2495

船　　名＿＿＿＿　船期＿＿＿＿　运往地点 DUBAI

托 运 人 GUANGDONG TEXTILES IMP AND EXP GRANDTON TRADING CO., LTD.
7/F., GUANGDONG TEXTILES MANSION, NO. 168 XIAOBEI ROAD, GUANGZHOU, CHINA

受 货 人 TO THE ORDER OF HABIB BANK AG ZURIURICH DUBAI U. A. E.

通　　知 AHARAJA DEIRA L. L. C, DUBAI (UAE).
P. O. BOX No. 6093, DUBAI (UAE), FAX NO. 263745

标记及号码	件数	货　名	重量（公斤）		容积吨
			净重	毛重	
MAHARAJA 264553 DUBAI NO. 1－400	400CTNS	LADIES LYCRA LONG PANT	4,800KGS	6,000KGS	24CBMS

合计　400CTNS　　共重　6,000KGS

特约事项	1. 配 1×20’集装箱，并标出集装箱号码。 2. 只能在香港转船。 3. 提单须标出信用证的号码。	

可否转船	允许			（托运人盖章）	
可否分批	允许	需要提单正本 3 份副本 3 份			
货物堆存地点	大松岗	装船期限	AT THE LATEST MARCH 27, 2005	结汇期限	MAR. 27, 2005
运费缴付方式	Freight Prepaid		运费账单开送		
信用证号码	SK/25067/2004	货　价	F. O. B.	C. I. F. USD99,960.00	
运往香港船名		实际装船日期			

运费吨：　　　运费率：　　　运费金额：

2. 单据填制二

中 国 外 运 广 东 公 司
出口货物托运单

提单编号______ 托运日期 OCT. 20, 1997 托运单位编号 GDF－97－2503

合约编号 GDF－97－44011128

船 名______ 船期______ 运往地点 TOKYO

托 运 人 GUANGDONG ARTS AND CRAFTS IMP. AND EXP. CORP. (GROUP) 318 DADE ROAD, GUANGZHOU, CHINA

受 货 人 TO ORDER OF THE CHINA AND SOUTH SEA BANK LTD.

通 知 SUNNY TRADE ENTERPRISE
UNIT A 8/F CHINA TRADE CTR 122 WAI YIP ST KWUN TONG KOWLOON, JAPAN

标记及号码	件数	货 名	重量（公斤）		容积吨
			净	毛	
SUNNY TOKYO NO. 1－200	200CTNS	ENERGY SAVING LAMPS LES9W2U	1,600KGS	2,000KGS	8.39CBMS

合计 200CTNS 共重： 2,000KGS

特约事项	
	1. 配1×20’集装箱，并标出集装箱号码。 2. 提单标出东京货代的名称、地址和电话号码。 ABC SHIPPING CO., LTD. 222 ROSE STREET, TOKYO, JAPAN TEL: 222888

可否转船	允许			（托运人盖章）	
可否分批	允许	需要提单正本 3 份副本 3 份			
货物堆存地点		装船期限	97/10/25	结汇期限	97/11/10
运费缴付方式	FREIGHT PREPAID	运费账单开送			
信用证号码	D－22－P31029	货 价	F. O. B.	C. I. F. USD30,000.00	
运往香港船名		实际装船日期			

运费吨： 运费率： 运费金额：

第五章
报　关　单

一、练习题

（一）单项选择题

1．某进出口公司向某国出口500吨散装小麦，该批小麦分装在一条船的三个船舱内。海关报关单上的“件数”和“包装种类”两个项目填报正确的应是（　　）。

A．件数为500，包装种类为“吨”

B．件数为1，包装种类为“船”

C．件数为3，包装种类为“船舱”

D．件数为1，包装种类为“散装”

2．海关规定进口货物的进口日期是指(　　)。

A．申报货物办结海关进口手续的日期

B．向海关申报货物进口的日期

C．运载货物的运输工具申报进境的日期

D．所申报货物进入海关监管场地或仓库的日期

3．我国某进出口公司从香港购进一批SONY牌电视机，该电视机为日本品牌，其中显像管由韩国生产，集成电路板由新加坡生产，其他零件均由马来西亚生产，最后由韩国组装成整机。该公司向海关申报进口该电视机时，原产地应填报为(　　)。

A．日本　　B．韩国

C．新加坡　　D．马来西亚

4．海关规定对在海关注册登记的企业给予十位数代码编号，称为“经营单位代码”。下列选项中十位数代码的正确组成顺序是(　　)。

A．地区代码、企业性质代码和顺序代码

B．企业详细地址代码、特殊地区代码、企业性质代码和顺序代码

C．企业所在省、直辖市代码，特殊地区代码，企业性质代码和顺序代码

D．企业所在省、直辖市代码及省辖市、县、计划单列市、沿海开放城市代码，企业性质代码，特殊地区代码和顺序代码

5．某外资企业出口一批男式全羊毛西服，该批西服分别用约85%的进料加工料件和15%的国产原料加工而成。请问该企业在向海关办理出口申报手续时应填写的报关单是(　　)。

A. 进料加工专用出口货物报关单

B. 一般贸易用出口货物报关单

C. 外商投资企业专用出口货物报关单

D. 来料加工和补偿贸易专用出口货物报关单

6. 某外贸总公司（甲方）与日本某公司（乙方）签订了一项合同。合同规定，由乙方卖给甲方价值 4 000 美元用于制作服装的辅料，甲方用该辅料和国产主料加工成价值 40 万美元的西服返销给乙方。在填制进出口货物报关单贸易方式栏时应填写(　　)。

A. 进口、出口均为“进料对口”

B. 进口为“进料对口”，出口为“一般贸易”

C. 进口、出口均为“一般贸易”

D. 进口为“一般贸易”，出口为“进料对口”

7. 联合国救灾协调员办事处在美国市场采购原产于加拿大的冰雪救灾物资无偿援助我国，该批物资在洛杉矶装船，在日本东京中转后运抵我国，这种情况其报关单“起运国（地区）”栏目应填写为(　　)。

A. 日本　　B. 加拿大

C. 美国　　D. 联合国

8. 大连某中日合资企业委托辽宁省机械设备进出口公司与日本三菱重工签约进口工程机械，并委托大连外运公司代理报关，在填制进口报关单时，“经营单位”一项应填写(　　)。

A. 该中日合资企业　　B. 辽宁省机械设备进出口公司

C. 日本三菱重工　　D. 大连外运公司

9. 某服装进出口公司自日本进口一批工作服样装，在向海关申报时，其报关单“贸易方式”栏应填报为(　　)。

A. 一般贸易　　B. 货样广告品

C. 货样广告品 A　　D. 货样广告品 B

10. 报关单“贸易方式”栏目应填报为“进料非对口”的是（　　）。

A. 原进料加工项下的成品或半成品，已在海关办理结转手续不直接出口，而是转让给境内其他承接进口料件加工复出口业务的单位进行再加工装配的贸易方式

B. 我方有外贸进出口经营权的企业动用外汇购买进口料件，加工成品或半成品后返销出口的贸易方式

C. 进料加工贸易进口料件，经批准转为内销的贸易方式

D. 特定用途以进料加工形式进口料件加工的成品不返销出境而供应国内市场的贸易方式

（二）多项选择题

1. 根据海关对报关单上“运输方式”项目的分类规定，“其他运输”是指下列(　　)运输方式。

A. 管道运输　　B. 驮畜运输

C. 自行车装运　　D. 人力扛运

2. 下列哪种类型的单位可以作为经营单位进行填报。(　　)

A. 对外签订合同但并非执行合同的单位

B. 非对外签订合同但具体执行合同的单位

C. 委托外贸公司对外签订并执行进口投资设备合同的外商投资企业

D. 接受并办理进口溢卸货物报关纳税手续的单位

3. 在填制报关单时，海关根据进出口商品的不同情况，对商品数量的填报作出了一些规定，请选择下列规定哪些是符合海关规定的。(　　)

A. 规范的数量和单位，应以海关统计商品目录上规定的数量和单位填写

B. 与海关规范的数量和单位不一致的实际成交的数量和单位也可填在报关单上

C. 不能把整机和零件的数量加在一起填报数量

D. 不能把类似"一卷"、"一箱"、"一捆"等较笼统的数量和单位填在报关单上

4. 某公司从日本进口联合收割机 10 台及部分附件，分装 30 箱，发票注明每台单价为 CIF Shanghai US $ 22 400，总价为 US $ 224 000，附件不另计价。进口货物报关单以下栏目正确填报的为(　　)。

A. 成交方式：海运　　B. 件数：30

C. 商品名称：联合收割机及附件　　D. 单价：22 400

5. 进口货物报关单有若干联，请指出下列报关单中的哪几联属于报关单的基本联。(　　)

A. 海关留存联　　B. 企业留存联

C. 海关核销联　　D. 海关统计联

6. 某进出口公司报关员在制作一份进口报关单时，在"标记唛码及备注"栏目内添入了以下内容，请选出哪些内容是正确的。(　　)

A. NO MARK 字样　　B. 付汇核销单编号

C. 商检证 1 份及其编号　　D. 进料加工合同共 2 本手册及全部编号

7. 根据海关规定，在填写进出口货物报关单的"贸易方式"时，有未名的贸易方式填写为"其他贸易"。在下列几种贸易方式中，不可填写为"其他贸易"的是(　　)。

A. 溢卸货物　　B. 货样、广告品

C. 暂时进口货物　　D. 对台直接贸易

8. 某合资企业从韩国进口一批作为投资的机器设备，该公司委托 A 进出口公司对外签订进口合同，并代办进口手续。A 进出口公司与外商订货后，随即委托 B 公司具体办理货物运输事宜，同时委托上海 C 报关公司负责办理进口报关手续。请选择下列出现在报关单有关栏目内的单位哪些是填写错误的。(　　)

A. 经营单位：A 进出口公司　　B. 收货单位：某合资企业

C. 申报单位：B 公司　　D. 收货单位：A 进出口公司

9. 某合资企业从英国进口一批作为投资的机器设备，该企业委托 A 进出口公司对外签订进口合同，并代办进口手续，A 进出口公司与外商订货后，随即委托 B 公司具体办理货物运输事宜，下列出现在报关单栏目内的单位，哪些是错误的。(　　)

A. 经营单位：A 进出口公司　　B. 收货单位：某合资企业

C. 申报单位：B 公司　　D. 收货单位：A 进出口公司

10. 请指出下列哪种贸易行为应填写出口货物报关单。(　　)

A. 非保税区运入保税区供加工生产产品用

B. 加工贸易深加工结转

C. 加工贸易成品转内销

D. 保税仓库货物复出口

(三) 判断题

1. 报关单上的“杂费”指成交价格以外的、应计入完税价格或从完税价格中扣除的费用，如手续费、佣金、回扣等。(　　)

2. 某进口单位在申报进口租赁期在一年以上的租赁贸易货物时，只填制了一份贸易方式为“租赁贸易”的报关单，海关认为其申报有误。(　　)

3. 报关单上的“收货单位”应为进口货物在境内的最终消费，使用的单位名称，“发货单位”应为出口货物在境内的生产或销售的单位名称。(　　)

4. 某租赁有限公司从事国内租赁业务。该公司委托广州某对外贸易公司从日本进口50台水泥搅拌车，用于租借给国内的建筑公司。由广州某对外贸易公司对外订货，向海关办理进口报关手续时，该批用于租赁货物的贸易方式应填报为“一般贸易”。(　　)

5. 报关单上“商品名称、规格型号”栏目，正确的填写内容应有中文商品名称、规格型号，商品的英文名称和品牌，缺一不可。(　　)

6. 某外贸公司与境外贸易商以 FOB 价、即期信用证方式结算订立出口棉麻衬衣的一般贸易出口合同，按规定申报时应填写一式四联报关单，分别是海关留存联、海关统计联、企业留存联、出口退税专用联。(　　)

7. 北京煤炭进出口总公司对巴基斯坦签约出口“水洗炼焦煤”10 万吨，由唐山煤炭分公司执行合同，组织货源，并安排出口。在这一情况下报关单“经营单位”栏目应填报为“北京煤炭进出口总公司”11091×××××北京煤炭进出口总公司的编号。(　　)

8. 经海关批准，从保税仓库内提取一批货物在国际市场上销售，由于该批货物原进入保税仓库时是空运进口的，故该货出仓库时在报关单上“运输方式”栏应填报“航空运输”。(　　)

9. 一批精密仪表在大连机场海关申报出口并转关运输至北京出境，其出口报关单“出口口岸”栏应按实际申请海关所在地填为“大连机场”。(　　)

10. 某仪器出口公司从日本购得分属三个合同的同样规格、不同数量的精密仪器，并同一船同时运达。这些货物品种单一且数量不大，申报时可用一份进口货物报关单，准备、真实、齐全地向海关填报。(　　)

(四) 单据填制

1. 单据填制一

根据以下资料填制进口货物报关单。

北京水晶电子进出口公司经北京市机电办批准（批文号码为京机批第 00256 号），与美国一家公司签订了购买一台 400 千瓦日本产直流发电机（合同号码为 97－Y1－1002），成交价为 CIF3 000 美元，标记唛码为 Y1 - 1002/BJ，于 1997 年 6 月 10 日装“大东丸”船由东京抵天津新港（0202），提单号为 CB - 1647，由一个木箱包装，包装重量 1 500 千克，电机自重 1 400 千克，经办理转关运输手续后该公司于 6 月 15 日向北京海关办理进出口报关手续。

随附单证（发票、装箱单、提单、商检证），总运费：600 美元

经营单位代码：1101910077　　　　商品编码：85013300

中华人民共和国海关进口货物报关单

预录入编号：002102133　　　　海关编号：

进口口岸	备案号 ×××	进口日期	申报日期
经营单位	运输方式	运输工具名称	提运单号
收货单位	贸易方式	征免性质 一般征税	征税比例
许可证号	起运国(地区)	装货港	境内目的地

批准文号 0108759	成交方式	运费	保费 502/50/3	杂费 ×××
合同协议号	件数	包装种类	毛重(公斤)	净重(公斤)

集装箱号 ×××	随附单据	用途 外贸自营内销

标记唛码及备注

项号	商品编码	商品名称、规格型号	数量及单位	原产国(地区)	单价	总价	币制	征免

税费征收情况 ×××

录入员　　录入单位	兹声明以上申报无讹并承担法律责任	海关审单批注及放行日期(签章) 审单　　审价
报关员 ××× 单位地址 ××× 邮编×××　电话×××	申报单位(签章) 填制日期	征税　　统计 查验　　放行

2. 单据填制二

下面是一份出口货物报关单，有些项目没有填写，请根据所提供的原始单证，将没有填写的项目按海关规定在报关单上补充填制完整。

RONGHUA TRADE DEVELOPMENT CO., LTD.

厦门荣华贸易发展公司

中国厦门

INVOICE

L/C NO.: 212948

INVOICE NO.: SF732B1397/12　　DATE: DEC. 10, 2003

MESSRS.: J. Y. CONSULTANT CO., LTD.

S/C No.: 03RH88704　ADDRESS: 1—7—20 OTEMON CHUO—FUKUOKA, JAPAN

PER S. S.: SU YUE V. 9801　　DATE OF DEPARTURE: DEC. 30, 2003

FROM SHANGHAI　　TO MOJI

MARK	PACKAGE	DESCRIPTION	QUANTITY	UNIT PRICE	AMOUNT
				(USD/KG)	(USD)
N/M	900 CTNS	鲜冬笋 WINTER BAMBOO SHOOTS HS CODE 07099010	9,000KGS 计量单位：千克	1.40	CFR 12,600.00
	3,592 CTNS	鲜香菇 FRESH MUSHROOM HS CODE 07095190	17,960KGS 计量单位：千克	1.80	32,328.00
		外汇核销单编号：35/0591540 经营单位海关注册编号：3502110278 发货单位与经营单位相同 预录入编号：587112114 随附：商检证、动植物检疫证			F: USD 2,250.00

GW 29,656Kgs　NW 26,960Kgs

B/L NO.: CSLMJ180180

CONTAINER NO.: CCLU 1000752 (20'), CCLU 8501143 (40'), CCLU 8505004 (40')

2003.12.28 由上海航联报关公司向上海浦江海关（2202）申报，当月 30 日装运出口。

中华人民共和国海关出口货物报关单

预录入编号：　　　　　　　　　　海关编号：

出口口岸	备案号 ×××	出口日期	申报日期
经营单位	运输方式	运输工具名称	提运单号
发货单位	贸易方式	征免性质	结汇方式
许可证号 ×××	运抵国(地区)	指运港	境内货源地 厦门特区

批准文号	成交方式	运费 502/5300/3	保费 ×××	杂费 ×××
合同协议号	件数	包装种类	毛重(公斤)	净重(公斤)

集装箱号	随附单据 B. C	生产厂家 厦门荣华贸易发展公司

标记唛码及备注

项号	商品编码	商品名称、规格型号	数量及单位	最终目的国	单价	总价	币制	征免

税费征收情况

录入员　　录入单位	兹声明以上申报无讹并承担法律责任	海关审单批注及放行日期(签章) 审单　　审价
报关员 ××× 单位地址 ×××	申报单位(签章)	征税　　统计
邮编×××　电话×××	填制日期	查验　　放行

二、练习题参考答案

（一）单项选择题

1. D。理由：根据中华人民共和国海关报关单填写规范的要求填写。

2. C。理由：进口日期是指运载进口货物的运输工具申报进境的日期。

3. B。理由：原产国是指进口货物生产、开采或加工制造的国家。对产品经过两个及两个以上的国家加工后进口，应以最后进行经济上可以视为实质性加工的国家为原产国。

4. D。理由：对已在海关注册的有权经营进出口业务的企业，由海关分别设置代号，此代号在全国范围内是唯一的、始终不变的。

5. C。理由：外商投资企业出口本企业生产的产品时，企业或其代理人应填写外商投资企业专用的出口货物报关单（浅蓝色报关单）向出境地海关办理申报出口手续。

6. D。理由：进料对口指买卖双方分别签订进出口对口合同，料件进口时，我方先付料件款，加工成品出口时再向对方收取出口成品款项的交易形式；一般贸易是指我国境内有进出口经营权的企业单边出口或单边进口的贸易。

7. C。理由：起运国（地区）指进口货物起始发出的国家（地区），对发生运输中转的货物，如中转地未发生任何商业性交易，起运国（地区）不变。如果中转地发生商业性交易，则以中转地作为起运国填报。

8. A。理由：根据中华人民共和国海关报关单填写规范的要求，填制进口报关单时，进口经营单位一项应为实际进口单位。

9. C。理由：按照报关单填写规范的规定，有对外贸易经营权的单位进出口的货样广告品在报关单“贸易方式”栏应填写“货样广告品 A”代码 3010。

10. B。理由：根据报关单填制规范的要求，我方有外贸进出口经营权的企业动用外汇购买进口料件，加工成品或半成品后返销出口的贸易方式成交的贸易，报关单“贸易方式”栏目应填报为“进料非对口”。

（二）多项选择题

1. ABCD。理由：按海关现行规定，其他运输方式是指利用人扛、驮畜、输油、输水管道和输电网等方式进口货物的运输方式。

2. BCD。理由：经营单位是指从事对外贸易活动的法人和其他组织。

3. ABC。理由：根据中华人民共和国海关报关单填写规范的要求填写。

4. BCD。理由：根据中华人民共和国海关报关单填写规范的要求填写。

5. ABD。理由：一般的进出口货物应填制报关单一式三联，俗称基本联。其中第一联为海关留存联，第二联为海关统计联，第三联为企业留存联。

6. AB。理由：“标记唛码及备注”栏目下部供打印随附单据栏中监管证件的编号。

7. ABCD。理由：各选项均属海关规定的《贸易方式代码表》中列明的贸易方式，应对照代码表填写相应简称或代码。

8. ACD。理由：根据报关单填写规范的要求，经营单位是指对外签订并执行进出口贸易合同的中国境内企业或单位。如果对外签约和执行合同的不是一个单位，则以执行合同的单位为准；收货单位是指已知的进口货物在境内的最终消费、使用单位。

9. ACD。理由：根据中华人民共和国进出口货物报关单的填制规范的规定，经营单位应填签订并执行进出口贸易合同的中国境内企业或单位。收货单位应填已知的进口货物在境内的最终消费、使用单位。

10. ABD。理由：除转内销的不用填写出口报关单外，其余几种情况都应填写出口报关单。

（三）判断题

1. 正确。理由：根据中华人民共和国海关报关单填制规范的规定，杂费是指成交价格以外的、应记入完税价格或应从完税价格中扣除的费用，如手续费、佣金、回扣等，可按杂费总价或杂费率两种方式之一填报，同时注明杂费标记，并按海关规定的《货币代码表》选择填报相应的币种代码。

2. 正确。理由：为了统一、规范对租赁进口货物征税、统计作业规程，自 1997 年 1 月 1 日起增加一新的贸易方式，即租赁征税。有关企事业单位在填报进口租赁期在一年以上的租赁货物时，应填报两张进口报关单。

3. 正确。理由：根据报关单填写规范的要求，收货单位是指进口货物在境内最终消费、使用的单位，包括：①自行从境外进口货物的单位；②委托有外贸进出口经营权的企业进口货物的单位。发货单位是指出口货物在境内的生产或销售单位，包括：①自行出口货物的单位；②委托有外贸进出口经营权的企业出口货物的单位。

4. 正确。理由：按现行规定，以下方式进出口的货物，贸易方式均填一般贸易：国内经营租赁业务的企业购进供租用的货物。

5. 错误。理由：报关单上的商品名称、规格型号的填写要求如下：商品名称应当填写规范的中文名称，必要时可加注原文。规格型号应当足够详细，以能满足海关归类、审价以及监管的要求为准。禁止、限制进出口等实施特殊管制的商品，其名称必须与交验的批准证件上的商品名称相符。

6. 错误。理由：申请出口产品退税的企业，在向海关办理出口退税手续时，除应按规定填制报关单和随附单证之外，还应填制一份与普通出口报关单格式一致的浅黄色"出口退税报关单"，而并非一式四联。

7. 错误。理由：根据报关单填写规范的要求，经营单位一栏应填对外签订并执行进出口贸易合同的境内企业或单位。如果对外签约和执行合同的不是同一单位，则以执行合同的单位为准。

8. 错误。理由："保税区"表明是保税区运往非保税区的货物。"保税仓库"表明是保税仓库转内销的货物。都是用于标识境内进出和退回保税区、存入保税区的货物。

9. 错误。理由：根据报关单填制规范的要求，出口转关运输货物的出口口岸应填报货物出境地海关名称及代码；按转关运输方式跨关区深加工结转货物，出口报关单填报转出地海关名称及代码，进口报关单填报转入地海关名称及代码。

10. 错误。理由：根据海关对进出口货物报关单填制要求，一张报关单上如果有不同商品，应分别填报清楚，但一张报关单最多不能超过五项海关统计商品编号的货物。

（四）单据填制

1. 单据填制一

中华人民共和国海关进口货物报关单

预录入编号：　　　　　　　　海关编号：

进口口岸 天津新港(0202)	备案号 × × ×	进口日期 97.06.10	申报日期 97.06.15

经营单位 北京水晶电子进出口公司 (1101910077)	运输方式 海运/江海	运输工具名称 大东丸	提运单号 CB－1647
收货单位 北京水晶电子进出口公司	贸易方式 一般贸易	征免性质 一般征税	征税比例
许可证号 京机批第00256号	起运国(地区) 日本	装货港 东京	境内目的地 北京

批准文号 0108759	成交方式 CIF	运费 502/600/3	保费 502/50/3	杂费 × × ×
合同协议号 97－Y1－1002	件数 1	包装种类 台	毛重(公斤) 1 500	净重(公斤) 1 400

集装箱号 × × ×	随附单据 商检证	用途 外贸自营内销

标记唛码及备注
Y1－1002/BJ

项号	商品编码	商品名称、规格型号	数量及单位	原产国(地区)	单价	总价	币制	征免
01	85013300	直流发电机(400千瓦)	1台	日本	3 000	3 000	美元	照章

税费征收情况
× × ×

录入员　　录入单位	兹声明以上申报无讹并承担法律责任	海关审单批注及放行日期(签章) 审单　　审价	
报关员 × × × 单位地址 × × × 邮编× × ×　电话× × ×	申报单位(签章) 北京水晶电子进出口公司报关专用章 填制日期　97.06.15	征税　　统计 查验　　放行	

中华人民共和国海关出口货物报关单

预录入编号：　　　　　　　　海关编号：

出口口岸 上海浦江海关(2202)	备案号 ×××	出口日期 03.12.30	申报日期 03.12.28
经营单位 厦门荣华贸易发展公司 (3502110278)	运输方式 江海	运输工具名称 SU YUE V.9801	提运单号 CSLMJ180180
发货单位 厦门荣华贸易发展公司	贸易方式 一般贸易	征免性质 一般征税	结汇方式 信用证
许可证号 ×××	运抵国(地区) 日本	指运港 门司	境内货源地 厦门特区

批准文号 35/0591540	成交方式 CFR	运费 502/5300/3	保费 ×××	杂费 ×××
合同协议号 03RH88704	件数 4492	包装种类 纸箱	毛重(公斤) 29 656	净重(公斤) 26 960

集装箱号 CCLU1000752 * 3(5)	随附单据 B. C	生产厂家 厦门荣华贸易发展公司

标记唛码及备注
N/M
CCLU8501143
CCLU8505004

项号	商品编码	商品名称、规格型号	数量及单位	最终目的国	单价	总价	币制	征免
01	07099010	鲜冬笋	9 000 千克	日本	1.40	12 600.00	美元	照章
02	07095190	鲜香菇	17 960 千克	日本	1.80	32 328.00	美元	照章

税费征收情况

录入员　　录入单位	兹声明以上申报无讹并承担法律责任	海关审单批注及放行日期(签章) 审单　　审价
报关员 ××× 单位地址 ×××	申报单位(签章) 上海航联报关 有限责任公司报关专用章	征税　　统计
邮编×××　电话×××	填制日期　03.12.28	查验　　放行

第六章
出口收汇核销单

一、练习题

（一）单项选择题

1．出口收汇核销单由(　　)制发。

A．中国银行　　B．中国人民银行

C．国家外汇管理局　　D．海关

2．有出口收汇的单位，应到当地外汇管理部门领取外汇管理部门加盖(　　)印章的核销单。

A．外汇管理　　B．已核销

C．验讫章　　D．监督收汇章

3．远期出口项下，企业应当在合同规定收汇日起(　　)内到外汇管理局办理核销手续。

A．10 天　　B．20 天

C．30 天　　D．40 天

4．国家外汇管理局和海关总署联合开发了电子口岸“出口收汇系统”于(　　)起在全国范围内试行。

A．2000 年 1 月 1 日　　B．2001 年 1 月 1 日

C．2000 年 6 月 1 日　　D．2001 年 6 月 1 日

5．即期出口项下，出口单位办理报关后，应当自报关之日起(　　)内，凭核销单及加盖海关“验讫章”的出口报关单等到外汇管理局办理核销手续。

A．60 天　　B．30 天

C．100 天　　D．90 天

6．出口单位应当在收到外汇之日起(　　)内凭核销单、银行出具的“出口收汇核销专用联”到外汇管理局办理出口收汇核销。

A．60 天　　B．30 天

C．15 天　　D．90 天

7．出口收汇率达到 70%（含 70%）至 95% 之间的，评为(　　)

A．出口收汇荣誉企业　　B．出口收汇达标企业

C．出口收汇风险企业　　D．出口收汇高风险企业

8. 来料加工项下的出口收汇核销是按照(　　)办理出口收汇核销的。

A. 货物总值　　B. 料件值

C. 工缴费　　D. 外汇局规定的货物总值的百分比

9. 进口单位在外汇指定银行办理付汇手续后，应当将退回的核销单留存联与其他付汇单证一并留存(　　)备查。

A. 3 年　　B. 4 年

C. 5 年　　D. 6 年

10. “口岸电子执法系统”于(　　)起在全国正式运行。

A. 2001 年 6 月 1 日　　B. 2001 年 1 月 1 日

C. 2001 年 9 月 1 日　　D. 2001 年 8 月 1 日

（二）多项选择题

1. 进行网上核销后，核销员需将(　　)送交外汇管理部门办理核销手续。

A. 已报关的核销单　　B. 报关单的核销联

C. 银行结汇水单　　D. 出口发票

2. 下列贸易方式无须凭核销单办理报关的是(　　)。

A. 易货贸易　　B. 广告品

C. 援外项目物资　　D. 暂时出口货物

3. 核销单领取后应(　　)，才能办理报关手续。

A. 加盖公章　　B. 进行网上备案

C. 法人代表签名　　D. 加盖报关章

4. 出口收汇核销的单位通常是(　　)。

A. 生产企业　　B. 银行

C. 外商投资企业　　D. 外贸公司

5. 出口单位有(　　)行为的，由外汇管理局给予警告、通报批评、没收违法所得，并处以 5 万元以上 30 万元以下的罚款。

A. 借用、冒用、转让或者买卖核销单的

B. 虚报核销单丢失的

C. 从领单之日起 4 个月内未向外汇管理局送交核销单存根的

D. 重复使用银行出具的出口收汇核销专用联的

（三）判断题

1. 货物出口后，无论是哪种方式出口，都必须持海关签章后的核销单、报关单及其他有关单证送银行办理收汇手续。(　　)

2. 某茶叶进出口公司因出货报关急需，向轻工业品进出口公司借了一份核销单向海关申报。(　　)

3. 某企业申领到新版核销单后，无须备案即可到海关报关出口。(　　)

4. 货物出口后，企业应及时将海关签章的核销单、报关单以及银行出具的结汇水单等资料到外汇管理局办理核销手续。(　　)

5. 核销单遗失后，应当立即自行网上挂失或向外汇管理局申请挂失。(　　)

6. 有进出口经营权的企业如果需要核销单报关出口，无须办理网上申领，即可直接到外汇管理局申领核销单。(　　)

7. 代理出口项下的核销手续，应当由委托方领取核销单、办理出口报关及出口收汇核销手续。(　　)

8. 出口单位遗失报关单的，应当凭银行签发的未核销证明，向海关申请补办。(　　)

9. 出口单位遗失出口收汇核销专用联的，应当先向外汇管理局提出申请补办，然后凭外汇管理局签发的出口收汇核销专用联补办批准件，到银行补办出口收汇核销专用联。(　　)

10. 出口收汇考核分为季度考核和年度考核，是指对企业的交单率进行考核。(　　)

（四）案例分析

2004 年 3 月 5 日，达成家具厂有一批家具需出口到迪拜，但该厂没有进出口权，不能向外汇管理局申领核销单，因此向联兴进出口公司买了一份核销单报关出口，货物出口后联兴进出口公司一直对该核销单未能按时收汇核销。请问此例属于什么现象？联兴进出口公司卖出核销单的做法对吗？应如何处理？

（五）单据填制

2002 年 4 月 20 日，HT 进出口公司（法人代码：19034346－8）与香港资信有限公司通过友好协商，就出口普洱茶事宜在惠州签订了一份出口合同。2002 年 5 月 27 日，HT 进出口公司备好了货物，到惠州海关办理报关出口手续。货物具体情况如下：普洱茶 6 000千克，共 120 箱，用纸箱包装，毛重 6 060 千克，价格为 FOB 深圳每千克 USD1. 22，采用即期 D/P 方式支付。报关单打印出来后的编号为：5162545658。请按照上述资料填写一份核销单。

未经核销此联不得撕开

出口收汇核销单
存根

(粤)编号：44G288190

出口单位：
单位代码：
出口币种总价：
收汇方式：
预计收款日期：
报关日期：
备注：
此单报关有效期截止到

(出口单位盖章)

出口收汇核销单

(粤)编号：44G288190

出口单位：				
单位代码：				
银行签注栏	类别	币种金额	日期	盖章
海关签注栏：				
外汇局签注栏： 年　月　日(盖章)				

(出口单位盖章)

(海关盖章)

出口收汇核销单
出口退税专用

(粤)编号：44G288190

出口单位：		
单位代码：		
货物名称	数量	币种总价
报关单编号：		
外汇局签注栏： 年　月　日(盖章)		

二、练习题参考答案

（一）单项选择题

1. C　2. D　3. A　4. A　5. C
6. B　7. B　8. C　9. C　10. D

（二）多项选择题

1. ABC　2. BCD　3. AB　4. CD　5. ABD

（三）判断题

1. 错误。理由：信用证、托收方式出口，可以不凭核销单向银行交单议付，但必须提供一联注有核销单编号的发票。

2. 错误。理由：核销单规定“谁单谁用”，不能相互借用。

3. 错误。理由：核销单申领后必须经过备案后才能使用。

4. 正确。

5. 正确。

6. 错误。理由：企业申领核销单，必须预先办理网上申领后才能到外汇管理局领取。

7. 错误。理由：应当由代理方领取核销单、办理出口报关及出口收汇核销手续。

8. 错误。理由：应当凭外汇管理局签发的未核销证明向海关申请补办。

9. 正确。

10. 错误。理由：是指对企业的出口收汇率进行考核。

（四）案例分析

答：此现象属于出口买单行为，也就是外汇汇入买单出口公司，而外贸公司根本就收不到外汇核销。外汇管制要求谁核销，谁就出口收汇。而买单根本就不会将外汇汇到提供核销单的外贸公司，造成外汇管理混乱。因此联兴进出口公司卖出核销单的做法不符合外汇管理规定，正确的做法可以采用代理出口方式，用本公司的核销单报关出口，按时收取外汇核销，再划款给达成家具厂，收取一定的代理费。

（五）单据填制

出口收汇核销单

出口退税专用

（粤）编号：44G288190

（出口单位盖章）

出口单位：HT 进出口公司		
单位代码：19034346－8		
货物名称	数量	币种总价
普洱茶	120 箱	7 320 美元
报关单编号：5162545658		
外汇局签注栏： 年　月　日（盖章）		

（海关盖章）

出口收汇核销单

（粤）编号：44G288190

（出口单位盖章）

出口单位：HT 进出口公司				
单位代码：19034346－8				
银行签注栏	类别	币种金额	日期	盖章
海关签注栏：				
外汇局签注栏： 年　月　日（盖章）				

出口收汇核销单

存根

（粤）编号：44G288190

出口单位：HT 进出口公司
单位代码：19034346－8
出口币种总价：USD65 800.00
收汇方式：即期 D/P
预计收款日期：
报关日期：2002 年 5 月 27 日
备注：
此单报关有效期截止到

未经核销此联不得撕开

第七章
出口企业退税及有关单证

一、练习题

（一）单项选择题

1. 一般情况下，出口企业应在出口后(　　)内向主管出口退税的税务机关提供“出口收汇已核销证明”。

A. 3个月　　B. 6个月　　C. 9个月　　D. 10个月

2. 对于要求补办出口退税专用联的，在办理出口核销手续后，出口单位应当凭税务部门签发的与该核销单对应的出口未退税证明，向(　　)书面申请办理“出口收汇核销单退税联补办证明”。

A. 外汇管理局　　B. 结汇银行　　C. 税务局　　D. 海关

3. 出口申请退税单位在会计核算上作出销售处理后，(　　)向外经贸部门填报《出口货物退（免）税申报表》。

A. 按单　　B. 按月　　C. 按年　　D. 可随时

4. 凡经营出口产品的企业，均应填具(　　)，报经所在地主管出口退税的税务机关审核后批准执行。

A. 出口货物报关单　　B. 出口产品退税鉴定表

C. 出口货物退（免）税申报表　　D. 出口收汇已核销证明

5. 凡属于工业企业直接出口或委托代理出口的出口发票，应审核产品的(　　)，确定退税的计税依据。

A. FOB价　　B. CIF价　　C. CFR价　　D. FCA价

（二）多项选择题

1. 以下不能申请退税的是(　　)。

A. 来料加工厂出口一批服装

B. 易货贸易下出口一批小麦

C. 捐赠一批速食面给泰国

D. 没有出口经营权的某企业出口一批货物

2. 外贸公司向当地税务局申请退税，应提供的证明资料有(　　)。

A. 盖有海关验讫章的出口货物报关单　B. 出口销售发票

C. 进货发票　　D. 银行结汇水单

3. 属于生产企业直接出口的自制产品，凡以 CIF 价结算的，除了两单两票外，还需提供(　　)。

A. 银行结汇水单　　B. 代理出口协议书

C. 出口货物货运单　　D. 出口保险单

(三) 判断题

1. 红星食品厂生产一批食品，并直接出口，则该商品出口前应缴纳增值税和消费税，并在出口后集齐所有单据向税务部门申请退税。(　　)

2. 办理出口退税时，须提供的两单两票是指出口货物报关单出口退税专用联、出口结汇水单、出口发票、出口产品增值税发票。(　　)

3. 报关单位如需申请退税的，应增填一份“出口货物报关单”，并在右上角盖上“申请出口产品退税专用联”。(　　)

4. 凡属于转关出口产品要求退税的，可在出境地海关办理出口手续后，直接在“出口货物报关单”上批注，以便办理退税。(　　)

5. 当企业将不同税率的出口产品放在一起核算时，由企业将不同的产品按适用的税目、税率计算，划分不清的，退税税率一律按从高的原则办理。(　　)

6. 根据《国家税务总局关于出口货物退（免）税管理有关问题的通知》规定：出口企业应在货物报关出口之日起 90 日内，向退税部门申报办理出口货物退（免）税手续。(　　)

二、练习题参考答案

(一) 单项选择题

1. B　2. A　3. B　4. B　5. A

(二) 多项选择题

1. ACD。理由：除易货贸易外，其他三种贸易均不能退税。

2. ABC。理由：工贸公司自营出口申请退税才需提供银行结汇水单。

3. AC。理由：工贸公司自营出口申请退税时须提供银行结汇水单，委托代理出口产品时须提供出口货物货运单。

(三) 判断题

1. 错误。理由：按规定，出口商品直接由生产厂家出口，则该商品既不征税，也不退税。

2. 错误。理由：出口结汇水单应改为出口收汇核销单出口退税专用联。

3. 正确。

4. 错误。理由：应在起运地海关办理。

5. 错误。理由：应该按从低的原则办理。

6. 正确。

第八章
信用证申请书

一、练习题

（一）中英文术语、短语互译

1. 中译英

（1）议付　　（2）延期付款

（3）开证人　　（4）受益人

（5）转运　　（6）分运

（7）空运单　　（8）账号

（9）通知行　　（10）到期日

2. 英译中

（1）Airmail　　（2）Acceptance

（3）Sight Payment　　（4）Price Term

（5）Tolerance of Amount　　（6）Latest Date of Shipment

（7）Express Delivery　　（8）Banking Charges

（9）For Beneficiary's Account　　（10）Transacted By

（二）单项选择题

1. 若在信用证申请书中的金额前加上 about、approximately、circa 等词语，根据《UCP600》，允许有（　　）的金额增减幅度。

A. 3%　　B. 5%

C. 10%　　D. 15%

2. 若规定货物装船后 30 天付款，则在信用证申请书中汇票的付款期限应填为（　　）。

A. AT 30 DAYS SIGHT　　B. AT 30 DAYS AFTER B/L DATE

C. AT 30 DAYS FROM INVOICE DATE　　D. AT * * * SIGHT

3. 若信用证的申请书中，要求到期日为 5 月 30 日，但未规定在装运日后必须交单的规定期限。则当受益人 5 月 8 日取得提单后，则其最迟应于（　　）前向银行交单。

A. 5 月 9 日　　B. 5 月 23 日

C. 5 月 29 日　　D. 5 月 30 日

4. 开证时要注意(　　)一致。

A. 证同　　B. 单证

C. 单单　　D. 证货

5. 在信用证申请书中汇票的付款人应填为(　　)

A. 开证人　　B. 开证行或指定付款行

C. 通知行　　D. 受益人

6. 某公司从英国的纽卡斯尔进口一批货物到广州，则申请书中的 LOADING ON BOARD FROM 后应填为(　　)。

A. GUANGZHOU　　B. ENGLAND

C. NEWCASTLE　　D. NEWCASTLE ENGLAND

7. 下列说法不正确的是(　　)。

A. 开立信用证时，进口人应向银行交付保证金

B. 开证行根据合同开立信用证

C. 开证后，银行的权利和义务只限于信用证的规定，只对信用证负责

D. 开证后，银行的权利和义务还要受到合同的约束

8. 下列关于信用证修改的说法错误的是(　　)。

A. 修改应由开证人办理

B. 经开证行、受益人同意，才能生效

C. 受益人可对一份修改通知书中的内容有选择地接受

D. 原证的条款，在受益人向通知行发出接受修改前仍对受益人有效

(三) 多项选择题

1. 若在信用证申请书中无明确规定，根据《UCP600》的规定，应视为允许的有(　　)。

A. 分运　　B. 转运

C. 接受第三者装运单据　　D. 可撤销信用证

2. 信用证申请书上常见的付款方式有(　　)。

A. 即期支付　　B. 承兑支付

C. 议付　　D. 延期支付

3. 申请开立信用证的具体手续有(　　)。

A. 递交有关合同的副本及附件　　B. 填写开证申请书

C. 缴付保证金　　D. 递交发票

4. 信用证申请书中，下列(　　)不是由开证人填写。

A. 开证日　　B. 到期日

C. L/C 号码　　D. 通知行

5. 如使用(　　)术语时，应在信用证申请书中的保单条款前的括号打“×”。

A. CIF　　B. FOB

C. CFR　　D. CIP

(四) 判断题

1. 信用证申请书已印好常见单据要求，如不需要某些单据，则在其前面的括号打“×”。(　　)

2. 若合同中有装运期的起止日期，则最迟必须让卖方在装运期的最后一天就能收到信用证。(　　)

3. 合同中规定要在信用证上明确定条款，如内容较多，可使用“参阅第×××号合同”或“第×××号合同项下货物”等条款，或将有关合同作为信用证附件附在信用证后。(　　)

4. 进口人对卖方的要求，在申请开证时，应按合同有关规定转化成有关单据，具体规定在信用证中。(　　)

5. 如在信用证申请书中采用延期付款方式，则卖方一般将使货价比采用承兑支付方式高。(　　)

6. 一般情况下，为避免风险，买卖双方都不应轻易接受“提交2/3套的正本提单，另一份正本提单径寄给买方”。(　　)

7. 如合同规定该笔货款由信用证和托收两种方式各付50%，则应在信用证申请书中汇票金额中填写50% of invoice value。(　　)

8. 如在信用证申请书中没注明是否允许转让，则开证行将视为申请可转让的信用证。(　　)

9. 如要求受益人提交两份正本发票，可在发票条款份数中注明“DUPLICATE”。(　　)

10. 在信用证申请书的装运期中，开证人可通过使用诸如“迅速”、“立即”、“尽快”之类的词语，以促使受益人尽快完成装运。(　　)

(五) 单据填制

1. 单据填制一

请根据以下材料填制信用证申请书(申请开证时间为1998年4月26日)。

售 货 合 同
SALES CONTRACT

卖 方:

Sellers: ABC CORP.

Contract No.: 98SGQ468001

Date: APR. 22, 1998

地址:

Signed at: GUANGZHOU

Address: AKEDSANTERINK AUTO P. O. BOX. 9, FINLAND

Telex: 0835

Fax: 83556688

Buyers: GUANGDONG LIGHT ELECTRICAL APPLANCES CO., LTD.

Address: 52, DEZHENG ROAD SOUTH, GUANGZHOU, CHINA.

Telex:

Fax:

This Sales Contract is made by and between the Sellers and the Buyers, whereby the sellers agree to sell and the Buyers agree to buy the under-mentioned goods according to the terms and conditions stipulated below:

(1) 货号、品名及规格 Name of Commodity and Specifications	(2) 数量 Quantity	(3) 单位 Unit	(4) 单价 Unit Price	(5) 金额 Amount
HALOGEN FITTING W500 5% more or less both in amount and quantity allowed	9,600PCS	PC	CIF GUANGZHOU USD3.80/PC	USD36,480.00
	Total Amount			USD 36,480.00

(6) Packing: 30PCS/CARTON (7) Delivery from HELSINKI to GUANGZHOU

(8) Time of Shipment: Within 30 days after receipt of L/C. allowing transshipment and partial shipment.

(9) Terms of Payment: By irrevocable Letter of Credit in favor of the Sellers to be available by sight draft to be opened and to reach FINLAND before MAY 15, 1998 and to remain valid for negotiation in FINLAND until the 15th days after the foresaid Time of Shipment.

L/C must mention this contract number. All banking Charges outside China (the mainland of China) are for account of the Beneficiary

(10) Insurance: To be effected by Sellers for 110% of full invoice value covering F. P. A. up to GUANGZHOU

~~To effected by buyers~~

(11) Arbitration: All dispute arising from the execuion of or in connection with this contract shall be settled amizedly by negotiation. In case of settlement can be reached through negotiation the case shall then be submit China International Economic & Trade Arbitration Commision. In Shenzhen (or in Beijing) for arbitration in act with its sure of procedures. The arbitral award is final and binding upon both parties.

The Seller ABC CORP.

The Buyer GUANGDONG LIGHT ELECTRICAL APPLANCES CO., LTD.

IRREVOCABLE DOCUMENTARY CREDIT APPLICATION

TO: **Date:**

Beneficiary(full name and address)	L/C NO. Ex - Card No. Contract No.
	Date and place of expiry of the credit
Partial shipments □ allowed □ not allowed Transshipment □ allowed □ not allowed	□ Issue by airmail □ With brief advice by teletransmission □ Issue by express delivery □ Issue by teletransmission(which shall be the operative instrument)
Loading on board/ dispatch/ taking in charge at/ from not later than for transportation to	Amount (both in figures and words)
Description of goods: Packing:	Credit available with □ by sight payment □ by acceptance □ by negotiation □ by deferred payment at against the documents detailed herein □ and beneficiary's draft for % of the invoice value at on
	□ FOB □ C&F □ CIF □or other terms

Documents required:(marked with ×)

1. ( ) Signed Commercial Invoice in copies indicating L/C No. and Contract No.
2. ( ) Full set of clean on board ocean Bills of Lading made out to order and blank endorsed, marked "freight[ ]to collect/[ ]prepaid[ ]showing freight amount" notifying applicant.
3. ( ) Air Waybills showing "freight[ ]to collect/[ ]prepaid[ ]indicating freight amount" and consigned to
4. ( ) Memorandum issued by consigned to
5. ( ) Insurance Policy/Certificate in copies for % of the invoice value showing claims payable in China in currency of the draft, blank endorsed, covering([ ]Ocean Marine Transportation /[ ]Air Transportation /[ ]Over Land Transportation) All Risks, War Risks.
6. ( ) Packing List/ Weight Memo in copies issued by quantity/ gross and net weights of each package and packing conditions as called for by the L/C.
7. ( ) Certificate of Quantity /Weight in copies issued by an independent surveyor at the loading port, indicating the actual surveyed quantity/ weight of shipped goods as well as the packing condition.
8. ( ) Certificate of Quantity in copies issued by [ ] manufacturer /[ ]public recognized surveyor /[ ]
9. ( ) Beneficiary's certified copy of cable/ telex dispatched to the accountees within hours after shipment advising[ ]name of vessel/[ ]flight No. /[ ]wagon No. , date, quantity, weight and value of shipment.
10. ( ) Beneficiary's Certificate certifying that extra copies of the documents have been diapatched according to the contract terms.
11. ( ) Shipping Co.'s Certificate attesting that the carrying vessel is chartered or booked by accountee or their shipping agents.
12. ( ) Other documents, if any:

Additional instructions:

1. ( ) All banking charges outside the opening bank are for beneficiary's account.
2. ( ) Documents must be presented within days after the date of issuance of the transport documents but within the validity of this credit.
3. ( ) Third party as shipper is not acceptable. Short Form/ Blank Back B/L is not acceptable.
4. ( ) Both quantity and amount % more or less are allowed.
5. ( ) Prepaid freight drawn in excess of L/C amount is acceptable against presentation of original charges voucher issued by shipping Co. / Air Line/ or it's agent.
6. ( ) All documents to be forwarded in one cover, unless otherwise stated above.
7. ( ) Other terms, if any:

Account No. : with ______________________ (name of bank)

Transacted by: (Applicant: name, signature of authorized person)

Telephone No. : (with seal)

2. 单据填制二

请根据以下材料填制信用证申请书(申请开证时间为 2001 年 3 月 1 日)。

售 货 合 同

SALES CONTRACT

卖 方:
Sellers: ABC CORPORATION

地址:
Address: OSAKA,JAPAN OSACY SECTION.

Contract No. : 2001 - 107
Date: JAN. 5,2001
Signed at: SHANGHAI
Telex: 0835
Fax: 83556688

买 方:
Buyers: SHANGHAI TEXTILES IMP AND EXP. CORP.
Address: 27 ZHONGSHAN ROAD,SHANGHAI,CHINA.

Telex: 44371
Fax: (020)82673475

WE HEREBY THE SELLERS AGREE TO SELL AND THE BUYERS TO BUY THE COMMODITY/IES MENTIONED IN THIS CONTRACT SUBJECT TO THE TERMS AND CONDITIONS STIPULATED AS FOLLOWS:

NAME OF COMMODITY & SPECIFICATION, PACKING AND SHIPPING MARK	QUANTITY (PCS.)	UNIT PRICE	AMOUNT
100% PURE COTTON TOWEL		CIF SHANGHAI	
ART. NO. 49394 (014428)	3,000	USD1.00	USD3,000.00
ART. NO. 49393(014428)	3,000	USD1.00	USD3,000.00
ART. NO. 55306(014429)	2,000	USD1.25	USD2,500.00
REMARKS: 1) EACH IN PLASTIC BAGS, 10 BAGS TO A CARTON TOTAL 800 CARTONS 2) SHIPPING MARK: ITOCHU SHANGHAI NO. 1 - 800		TOTAL:	USD8,500.00
TOTAL VALUE: SAY US DOLLARS EIGHT THOUSAND FIVE HUNDRED ONLY.			

TIME OF SHIPMENT: Within 45 days of receipt of letter of credit and not later than the month of MAY 2001 with partial shipments and transshipment allowed.

PORT OF LOADING: OSAKA JAPAN

PORT OF DESTINATION: SHANGHAI

TERMS OF PAYMENT: By 100% Irrevocable Sight Letter of Credit Opened by the Buyer to reach the Seller not later than APRIL 15th, 2001 and to be available for negotiation in JAPAN until the 15th day after the date of shipment. In case of late arrival of the L/C, the Seller shall not be liable for any delay in shipment and shall have the right to rescind the contract and /or claim for damages.

INSURANCE: To be effected by the Seller for 110% of the CIF invoice value covering ALL RISKS AND WAR RISK only as per China Insurance Clauses.

TERMS OF SHIPMENT: To be governed by "INCOTERMS 2000". For transactions concluded on CFR or CIF terms, all surcharges including port congestion surcharges, etc. levied by the shipping company, in addition to freight, shall be for the Buyer's account.

The Buyer
SHANGHAI TEXTILES IMP.
AND EXP. CORPORATION
(签名)

The Seller
ABC CORPORATION
(签名)

IRREVOCABLE DOCUMENTARY CREDIT APPLICATION

TO: **Date**:

Beneficiary (full name and address)	L/C NO. Ex - Card No. Contract No.
	Date and place of expiry of the credit
Partial shipments ☐ allowed ☐ not allowed / Transshipment ☐ allowed ☐ not allowed	☐ Issue by airmail ☐ With brief advice by teletransmission ☐ Issue by express delivery ☐ Issue by teletransmission (which shall be the operative instrument)
Loading on board/ dispatch/ taking in charge at/ from not later than for transportation to	Amount (both in figures and words)
Description of goods: Packing:	Credit available with ☐ by sight payment ☐ by acceptance ☐ by negotiation ☐ by deferred payment at against the documents detailed herein ☐ and beneficiary's draft for % of the invoice value at on
	☐ FOB ☐ C&F ☐ CIF ☐ or other terms

Documents required: (marked with ×)

1. ( ) Signed Commercial Invoice in copies indicating L/C No. and Contract No.
2. ( ) Full set of clean on board ocean Bills of Lading made out to order and blank endorsed, marked "freight[ ]to collect/[ ]prepaid[ ]showing freight amount" notifying applicant.
3. ( ) Air Waybills showing "freight[ ]to collect/[ ]prepaid[ ]indicating freight amount" and consigned to
4. ( ) Memorandum issued by consigned to
5. ( ) Insurance Policy/Certificate in copies for % of the invoice value showing claims payable in China in currency of the draft, blank endorsed, covering([ ]Ocean Marine Transportation /[ ]Air Transportation /[ ]Over Land Transportation) All Risks, War Risks.
6. ( ) Packing List/ Weight Memo in copies issued by quantity/ gross and net weights of each package and packing conditions as called for by the L/C.
7. ( ) Certificate of Quantity /Weight in copies issued by an independent surveyor at the loading port, indicating the actual surveyed quantity/ weight of shipped goods as well as the packing condition.
8. ( ) Certificate of Quantity in copies issued by [ ] manufacturer /[ ]public recognized surveyor /[ ]
9. ( ) Beneficiary's certified copy of cable/ telex dispatched to the accountees within hours after shipment advising[ ]name of vessel/[ ]flight No. /[ ]wagon No. , date, quantity, weight and value of shipment.
10. ( ) Beneficiary's Certificate certifying that extra copies of the documents have been diapatched according to the contract terms.
11. ( ) Shipping Co. 's Certificate attesting that the carrying vessel is chartered or booked by accountee or their shipping agents.
12. ( ) Other documents, if any:

Additional instructions:

1. ( ) All banking charges outside the opening bank are for beneficiary's account.
2. ( ) Documents must be presented within days after the date of issuance of the transport documents but within the validity of this credit.
3. ( ) Third party as shipper is not acceptable. Short Form/ Blank Back B/L is not acceptable.
4. ( ) Both quantity and amount % more or less are allowed.
5. ( ) Prepaid freight drawn in excess of L/C amount is acceptable against presentation of original charges voucher issued by shipping Co. / Air Line/ or it's agent.
6. ( ) All documents to be forwarded in one cover, unless otherwise stated above.
7. ( ) Other terms, if any:

Account No. : with ______________________ (name of bank)

Transacted by: (Applicant: name, signature of authorized person)

Telephone No. : (with seal)

二、练习题参考答案

（一）中英文术语、短语互译

1. 中译英

（1）Negotiation　（2）Deferred Payment

（3）Applicant　（4）Beneficiary

（5）Transshipment　（6）Partial Shipment

（7）Airway Bills　（8）Account No.

（9）Advising Bank　（10）Expiry Date

2. 英译中

（1）航空邮件　（2）承兑

（3）即期付款　（4）价格术语

（5）金额增减幅度　（6）最迟装运日

（7）快件　（8）银行费用

（9）由受益人承担　（10）由……执行

（二）单项选择题

1. C。理由：根据《UCP600》，允许有10%的金额增减幅度。

2. B。理由：装船日后30天即取得提单后的30天。

3. C。理由：若未规定在装运日后按信用证规定必须交单的特定期限，则银行不接受迟于装运日期后21天提交的单据。

4. A。理由：开证时必须以对外签订的正本合同为依据。

5. B。理由：根据《UCP600》，汇票的付款人应为开证行或指定付款行。

6. D。理由：因世界上有较多的newcastle港口，所以需要在港口后面附上所在国家。

7. D。理由：开证后，银行的权利和义务只限于信用证的规定，只对信用证负责。

8. C。理由：根据《UCP600》，受益人不允许对一份修改通知书中的内容有选择地接受，只能全部接受或者全部不接受。

（三）多项选择题

1. ABC。理由：根据《UCP600》，在信用证申请书中无明确表示是否可撤销，应视为不可撤销信用证。

2. ABCD。理由：L/C申请书上常见的付款方式有即期支付、承兑支付、议付、延期支付。

3. ABC。理由：申请开立信用证的具体手续有：递交有关合同的副本及附件、填写开证申请书、缴付保证金。

4. CD。理由：L/C号码、通知行由开证行填写。

5. AD。理由：CIF、CIP是卖方负责保险的价格术语，需要提交保险单据。

（四）判断题

1. 错误。理由：在单据括号前面打×表示选择这些单据。

2. 错误。理由：若合同中有装运期的起止日期，则最迟必须让卖方在装运期的第一天就能收到信用证。

3. 错误。理由：因为信用证是一个独立的文件，不依附于合同。

4. 正确。理由：在信用证支付条件下，只要单据表面与信用证条款相符合，开证行就必须按规定付款。所以应按合同有关规定把进口人对卖方的要求转化成有关单据，具体规定在信用证中。

5. 正确。理由：延期付款不要求出口商开立汇票，不能贴现，所以卖方一般将使货价比采用承兑支付方式高。

6. 正确。理由：另一份正本提单径寄给买方，对卖方不利，因为买方可先提货，而到时不再付款赎单；对买方也不利，因为如果卖方没有将另一份正本提单径寄给买方，一样可以得到银行的议付。

7. 正确。理由：因为合同规定，由信用证付款 50%，所以在信用证申请书中汇票金额中填写 50% of invoice value。

8. 错误。理由：如在信用证申请书中没注明是否允许转让，则开证行将视为申请不可转让的信用证。

9. 错误。理由：如要求受益人提交两份正本发票，应注明 TWO ORIGINALS，因为 DUPLICATE 表示一式两份，对方可提交 1 份正本加一份副本。

10. 错误。理由：使用诸如“迅速”、“立即”、“尽快”之类的词语，银行将不予置理。

（五）单据填制

1. 单据填制一

IRREVOCABLE DOCUMENTARY CREDIT APPLICATION

TO： **BANK OF CHINA**　　　　**Date：APR.** 26, 1998

Beneficiary (full name and address) ABC CORP. AKEDSANTERINK AUTO P. O. BOX 9, FINLANDL/CNO.	L/C NO. Ex-Card No. Contract No. 98SGQ468001
	Date and place of expiry of the credit JUNE 10, 1998, FINLAND
Partial shipments ☒ allowed ☐ not allowed　　Transshipment ☒ allowed ☐ not allowed	☐ Issue by airmail　☐ With brief advice by teletransmission ☐ Issue by express delivery ☒ Issue by teletransmission (which shall be the operative instrument)
Loading on board/ dispatch/ taking in charge at/ from HELSTNKI not later than　MAY 26, 1998 for transportation to　GUANGZHOU	Amount (both in figures and words) USD36, 480. OO (SAY US DOLLARS THIRTY SIX THOUSAND FOUR HUNDRED AND EIGHTY ONLY.)
Description of goods: 9,600PCS OF HALOGEN FITTING W500 CIF GUANGZHOU USD3. 80 PER PC Packing: 30PCS/CARTON	Credit available with ☒ by sight payment　☐ by acceptance　☐ by negotiation ☐ by deferred payment at against the documents detailed herein ☒ and beneficiary's draft for 100% of the invoice value at SIGHT on
	☐ FOB　☐ C&F　☒ CIF ☐ or other terms

Documents required: (marked with ×)

1. (×) Signed Commercial Invoice in　3　copies indicating L/C No. and Contract No.
2. (×) Full set of clean on board ocean Bills of Lading made out to order and blank endorsed, marked "freight[ ]to collect/[×]prepaid[ ]showing freight amount" notifying applicant.
3. (　) Air Waybills showing "freight[ ]to collect/[ ]prepaid[ ]indicating freight amount" and consigned to
4. (　) Memorandum issued by　　　　consigned to
5. (×) Insurance Policy/Certificate in　2　copies for　110　% of the invoice value showing claims payable in China in currency of the draft, blank endorsed, covering([×]Ocean Marine Transportation /[ ]Air Transportation /[ ]Over Land Transportation) All Risks× War Risks× F. P. A. up to GUANGZHOU
6. (×) Packing List/ Weight Memo in　3　copies issued by quantity/ gross and net weights of each package and packing conditions as called for by the L/C.
7. (　) Certificate of Quantity /Weight in　copies issued by an independent surveyor at the loading port, indicating the actual surveyed quantity/ weight of shipped goods as well as the packing condition.
8. (　) Certificate of Quantity in　　copies issued by [ ] manufacturer /[ ]public recognized surveyor /[ ]
9. (　) Beneficiary's certified copy of cable/ telex dispatched to the accountees within　24　hours after shipment advising[ ]name of vessel/[ ]flight No. /[ ]wagon No. , date, quantity, weight and value of shipment.
10. (　) Beneficiary's Certificate certifying that extra copies of the documents have been diapatched according to the contract terms.
11. (　) Shipping Co.'s Certificate attesting that the carrying vessel is chartered or booked by accountee or their shipping agents.
12. (　) Other documents, if any:

Additional instructions:

1. (×) All banking charges outside the opening bank are for beneficiary's account.
2. (×) Documents must be presented within　15　days after the date of issuance of the transport documents but within the validity of this credit.
3. (　) Third party as shipper is not acceptable. Short Form/ Blank Back B/L is not acceptable.
4. (×) Both quantity and amount　5　% more or less are allowed.
5. (　) Prepaid freight drawn in excess of L/C amount is acceptable against presentation of original charges voucher issued by shipping Co. / Air Line/ or it's agent.
6. (×) All documents to be forwarded in one cover, unless otherwise stated above.
7. (　) Other terms, if any:

Account No. :4411700718678328　　with　BANK OF CHINA, GUANGZHOU BRANCH　(name of bank)

GUANGDONG LIGHT ELECTRICAL APPLICANCES CO. ,LTD.
（签名）

Transacted by: 张三　　　　(Applicant: name, signature of authorized person)

Telephone No. :020－3365＊＊＊＊　　　　(with seal)

2. 单据填制二

IRREVOCABLE DOCUMENTARY CREDIT APPLICATION

TO: **BANK OF CHINA** **Date: MAR.** 1, 2001

Beneficiary (full name and address) ABC CORPORATION OSAKA, JAPAN OSACY SECTION	L/C NO. Ex-Card No. Contract No. 2001 - 107 Date and place of expiry of the credit MAY 1, 2001 JAPAN
Partial shipments: ☒ allowed ☐ not allowed Transshipment: ☒ allowed ☐ not allowed	☐ Issue by airmail ☐ With brief advice by teletransmission ☐ Issue by express delivery ☒ Issue by teletransmission (which shall be the operative instrument)
Loading on board/ dispatch/ taking in charge at/ from OSAKA JAPAN not later than APR. 14, 2001 for transportation to SHANGHAI	Amount (both in figures and words) USD8, 500. 00 (SAY US DOLLARS EIGHT THOUSAND FIVE HUNDRED ONLY.)
Description of goods: 100% PURE COTTON TOWEL CIF SHANGHAI ART. NO. 49394(014428) 3,000PCS USD1.00/PC ART. NO. 49393(014428) 3,000PCS USD1.00/PC ART. NO. 55306(014429) 2,000PCS USD1.25/PC Packing: EACH IN PLASTIC BAGS, 10 BAGS TO A CARTON, TOTAL 800CARTONS SHIPPING MARK: ITOCHU/SHANGHAI/NO. 1 - 800	Credit available with ☒ by sight payment ☐ by acceptance ☐ by negotiation ☐ by deferred payment at against the documents detailed herein ☒ and beneficiary's draft for 100% of the invoice value at SIGHT on ☐ FOB ☐ C&F ☒ CIF ☐ or other terms

Documents required: (marked with ×)

1. (×) Signed Commercial Invoice in 3 copies indicating L/C No. and Contract No.
2. (×) Full set of clean on board ocean Bills of Lading made out to order and blank endorsed, marked "freight[ ]to collect/[×]prepaid[ ]showing freight amount" notifying applicant.
3. ( ) Air Waybills showing "freight[ ]to collect/[ ]prepaid[ ]indicating freight amount" and consigned to
4. ( ) Memorandum issued by consigned to
5. (×) Insurance Policy/Certificate in 2 copies for 110 % of the invoice value showing claims payable in China in currency of the draft, blank endorsed, covering([×]Ocean Marine Transportation /[ ]Air Transportation /[ ]Over Land Transportation) All Risks, War Risks.
6. (×) Packing List/ Weight Memo in 3 copies issued by quantity/ gross and net weights of each package and packing conditions as called for by the L/C.
7. ( ) Certificate of Quantity /Weight in copies issued by an independent surveyor at the loading port, indicating the actual surveyed quantity/ weight of shipped goods as well as the packing condition.
8. ( ) Certificate of Quantity in copies issued by [ ] manufacturer /[ ]public recognized surveyor /[ ]
9. ( ) Beneficiary's certified copy of cable/ telex dispatched to the accountees within 24 hours after shipment advising[ ]name of vessel/[ ]flight No. /[ ]wagon No. , date, quantity, weight and value of shipment.
10. ( ) Beneficiary's Certificate certifying that extra copies of the documents have been diapatched according to the contract terms.
11. ( ) Shipping Co. 's Certificate attesting that the carrying vessel is chartered or booked by accountee or their shipping agents.
12. ( ) Other documents, if any:

Additional instructions:

1. (×) All banking charges outside the opening bank are for beneficiary's account.
2. (×) Documents must be presented within 15 days after the date of issuance of the transport documents but within the validity of this credit.
3. ( ) Third party as shipper is not acceptable. Short Form/ Blank Back B/L is not acceptable.
4. (×) Both quantity and amount 5 % more or less are allowed.
5. ( ) Prepaid freight drawn in excess of L/C amount is acceptable against presentation of original charges voucher issued by shipping Co. / Air Line/ or it's agent.
6. (×) All documents to be forwarded in one cover, unless otherwise stated above.
7. ( ) Other terms, if any:

Account No. :441170071867 * * * * with BANK OF CHINA, SHANGHAI BRANCH (name of bank)

SHANGHAI TEXTILES IMP. AND EXP. CORPORATION.

(签名)

Transacted by: 李四　　(Applicant: name, signature of authorized person)

Telephone No. :021 - 857 * * * * *　　(with seal)

第九章 综合制单练习

按下列信用证的要求和给定的资料填制各套单据。

综合制单练习一

Output Message Type : ISSUE OF A DOCUMENTARY CREDIT
Sent by : HNBNKRSEA ××× HANA BANK, SEOUL
Output Date/Time : 050106/1617
Priority : NORMAL
HUR : 050106DJOS00179

---

27 : Sequence of Total
1/1
40A : Form of Documentary Credit
IRREVOCABLE
20 : Documentary Credit Number
M12CL601ES00032
31C : Date of Issue
050105 05-JAN-2005
31D : Date and Place of Expiry
050215 AT YOUR COUNTRY 15-FEB-2005
50 : Applicant
STORY SHARP CO., LTD.
NO. 502 GL PLAZA, 713-1
HEANGSHIN-DONG, DUCKYANG-GU,
GOYANG-SI, GYEONGGI-DO, KOREA
59 : Beneficiary-Name & Address
GUANGDONG FOREIGN TRADE IMP. & EXP. CORP.
15-18/F., GUANGDONG FOREIGN ECONOMIC AND
TRADE BUILDING 351 TIANHE ROAD
GUANGZHOU, CHINA
32B : Currency Code, Amount
USD43, 200. 00 US DOLLAR 43, 200. 00
39A : Percentage Credit Amt Tolerance
10/10
41D : Available With... By... —Name & Addr.

ANY BANK BY NEGOTIATION

42C : Drafts at...
BENEFICIARY DRAFTS AT SIGHT
FOR 100 PCT OF THE INVOICE VALUE

42A : Drawee-BIC
HNBNCNSH × × ×　　HANA BANK SHANGHAI BRANCH
SHANGHAI

43P : Partial Shipments
ALLOWED

43T : Transshipment
ALLOWED

44A : On Board/Disp/Taking Charge at/F
HONGKONG

44B : For Transportation to...
BUSAN, KOREA

44C : Latest Date of Shipment
050130　　30-JAN-2005

45A : Description of Goods &/or Services
ORIGIN CHINA
FOB HONGKONG
80G COLOUR PAPER LENGTH: 9,500M　　30MT @ USD1,440.00
WIDTH: 1,000MM
INSIDE ROLL DIA.: 75MM
OUTSIDE ROLL DIA.: 100CM-120CM

46A : Documents Required
1) FULL SET OF CLEAN ON BOARD OCEAN BILLS OF LADING MADE OUT TO THE ORDER OF HANA BANK, SEOUL MARKED FREIGHT COLLECT AND NOTIFY ACCOUNTEE
2) SIGNED COMMERCIAL INVOICE IN THREE FULDS
3) PACKING LIST IN THREE FOLDS
4) INSPECTION CERTIFICATE ISSUED BY STORY SHARP CO., LTD. STATING THE GOODS ARE COMPLETELY CONFORM TO THE BENEFICIARY'S URDER

47A : Additional Conditions
+CONFIRMATION CHGS, IF ANY, ARE FOR ACCOUNT OF BENEFICIARY.
+10PCT MORE OR LESS IN Q'TY AND AMOUNT ALLOWED.
+EXCEPT SO FAR AS OTHERWISE EXPRESSLY STIPULATED HEREIN,
ALL DOCUMENTS SHOULD BE INDICATED L/C NUMBER AND MUST BE
FORWARDED DIRECTLY TO US IN ONE LOT BY COURIER SERVICES.
+ADDRESS OF THE ISSUING BANK
9-10, EULJIRD, 2-KA, JUNG-GU, SEOUL, KOREA
ZIP CODE: 100-720
ATTN: INTERNATIONAL BUSINESS OPERATION CENTER

71B : Charges
+ALL BANKING CHARGES OUTSIDE KOREA AND REMITTANCE CHARGES

ARE FOR ACCOUNT OF BENEFICIARY.

48 : Period for Presentation
DOCUMENTS MUST BE PRESENTED WITHIN 10 DAYS AFTER THE DATE OF SHIPMENT BUT WITHIN EXPIRY DATE

49 : Confirmation Instructions
CONFIRM

53A : Reimbursing Bank – BIC
HANA BANK SHANGHAI BRANCH
SHANGHAI

78 : Instr to Payg/Accptg/Negotg Bank
BENEFICIARY DRAFT SHOULD BE FORWARED TO DRAWEE BANK.
+IF DOCUMENTS ARE PRESENTED WITH DISCREPANCIES,
A DISCREPANCY FEE OF USD60.00 (JPY7,000.00 OR EUR60.00)
OR EQUIVALENT SHOULD BE DEDUCTED TO BENEFICIARY.
+THE NEGOTIATING BANK/PRESENTING BANK MUST SENT AN ADDITIONAL SET OF EACH DOCUMENT TO US FOR OUT FILES ALONG WITH THE ORIGINAL DOCUMENTS. IF NOT, USD10.00 WILL BE DEDUCTED FROM PAYMENT.

57D : "Advise Through" Bank-Name&Addr
DONGSHAN SUB-BRANCH

72 : Sender to Receiver Information
+U.C.P. (1993 REVISION) I.C.C. PUBLICATION NO.500

此证分两批装运，销货合同号码为：CPU04SC140。

第一批制单资料：

发票号：CPU04SC140A　　发票日期：JAN. 18, 2005
提单号：50100289BUS　　提单日期：JAN. 21, 2005
船名：KMTC ULSAN V. 501N　　装船标记：N/M
集装箱号：MTU7045319/KB846421/20'
商品数量：14.188MTS　　合计：21 ROLLS
毛重：14.188MTS　　净重：14.188MTS
尺码：1 000×1 050 (MM) /ROLL　　总尺码：19.950 CBMS

第二批制单资料：

发票号：CPU04SC140B　　发票日期：JAN. 21, 2005
提单号：50200389BUS　　提单日期：JAN. 28, 2005
船名：HONG KONG STAR V. 036N　　装船标记：N/M
集装箱号：MTU7311070/KB846360/20'
商品数量：14.227MTS　　合计：23 ROLLS
毛重：14.227MTS　　净重：14.227MTS
尺码：1 000×936 (MM) /ROLL　　总尺码：21.528CBMS

综合制单练习二

MT 700	**ISSUE OF A DOCUMENTARY CREDIT**
Basic Header	F 01 BKCHCNVJA400 1202 869809
Application Header	700 041126ICRAITMMA0506567177837 2004-11-27 N * BANCA DI CREDITO COOPERATIVO DI * SORISOLE E LEPRENO * SORISOLE
Sequence of Total	1/1
Form of Cec. Credit	IRREVOCABLE
Doc. Credit Number	088696000825
Date of Issue	2004 - 11 - 15
Expiry	DATE 2005 - 01 - 24 PLACE CHINA
Applicant	SPIL BERG DI YONG KEE FUI VIA A. DE GASPERI 4 24018 VILLA D' ALME' (BG) ITALY
Beneficiary	CHINA PACKAGING UNION GUANGZHOU CO. , LTD. 7/F. , NO. 753 DONGFENGDONG RD. , GUANGZHOU, CHINA
Amount	CURRENCY USD AMOUNT 32,016.00
Pos. /Neg. Tol (%)	10/10
Available with/by	ANY BANK BY NEGOTIATION AGAINST THE DOCUMENTS DETAILED HEREIN AND BENEFICIARY'S DRAFTS AT SIGHT DRAWN ON US FOR FULL INVOICE VALUE.
Partial Shipments	NOT ALLOWED
Transshipment	ALLOWED
Loading in Charge	GUANGZHOU CHINA
For Transport to . . .	GENOA ITALY
Latest Date of Ship.	2005 - 01 - 15
Descript. of Goods	MYANMAR TEAK GRADE A (UNFINISHED) SP. 16MM MYANMAR TEAK INDUSTRIAL PARQUET SP. 14 MM AS PROFORMA INV. RGCI/PI004 (SPL - 001) DD NOV. 904 PRICE CFR GENOA
Documents Required	1) EIGHT COMMERCIAL INVOICES IN ORIGINAL 2) EIGHT PACKING LIST IN ORIGINAL 3) FULL SET CLEAN ON BOARD OCEAN BILL OF LADING ISSUED TO ORDER AND BLANCK ENDODRSED MARKED FREIGHT PREPAID NOTIFY APPLICANT. 4) EIGHT CERTIFICATES OF ORIGIN FORM A ISSUED AND LEGALIZED BY COMPETENT AUTHORITY.
Additional Cond.	1) REFERENCE TO THIS CREDIT NUMBER MUST BE SHOWN ON ALL DOCUMENTS. 2) DOCUMENTS MUST BE SENT BY SPECIAL COURIER AT THE FOLLOWING ADDRESS U. P. F. —VIA DALWAZIA, 2—24047 TREVGLIO

(BG) ATT. NE MAR AMATO ADRIANA

3) IF DOCUMENTS DON' T COMPLY WITH THE TERMS AND CONDITIONS OF PRESENT L/C, SERVICE CHARGES OF USD50. 00 WILL BE DEDUCTED FROM ANY REMITTANCE MADE UNDER THIS CREDIT.

Details of Charges	ALL CHARGES AND COMMS OUTSIDE ITALY ARE FOR BENEFICIARY'S ACCOUNT.
Presentation Period	WITHIN 7 DAYS AFTER B/L DATE BUT WITHIN THE CREDIT VALIDITY
Confirmation	WITHOUT
Advise through	BANK OF COMMUNICATION GUANGZHOU BRANCH, CHINA
Send. to Rec. Info.	THIS IS THE OPERATIVE INSTRUMENTS NO MAIL CONFIRMATION WILL FOLLOW THIS CREDIT IS SUBJECT TO UCP REVISION 1993 ICC PUBLICATION N0. 500. OTHER MATERIALS:

有关资料:

INV. NO.: RGCL2584　　INV. DATE: JAN. 7, 2005

B/L NO.: 100397　　B/L DATE: JAN. 12, 2005

S/C NO.: RGCL/PI004 (SPL-001)　　FORM A NO.: GZ081/205/086

NAME OF STEAMER: HUI YUE 11 HAO V. 5112S

SHIPPING MARKS: N/M

CONTAINER & SEAL NO.: TELU2390424 (20'GP) /5429086

GOODS:

MYANMAR TEAK GRADE A (UNFINISHED) SP. 16MM 860m^2 @USD32. 10/m^2

PACKING: 2. 5m^2/BAG N. W. 30KGS/BAG G. W. 31KGS/BAG

MYANMAR TEAK INDUSTRIAL PARQUET SP. 14MM 300m^2 @USD14. 7/m^2

PACKING: 1. 5m^2/BAG N. W. 22KGS/BAG G. W. 23KGS/BAG

TOTAL MEASUREMENT: 18. 022 CBMS

该货物是完全自产品

综合制单练习三

ISSUE OF A DOCUMENTARY CREDIT

Sender : IBSPITTM414
* SANPAOLO IMI S. P. A
* PAVIA ITALY

Receiver : SOGECN22×××
* SOCIETE GENERALE
* (GUANGZHOU BRANCH)
* GUANGZHOU, CHINA

==================== Message Text ================

27 : Sequence of Total
1/1

40A : Form of Documentary Credit

IRREVOCABLE

20　: Documentary Credit Number
3109/1065

31C　: Date of Issue
050206　FEB. 6, 2005

31D　: Date and Place of Expiry
050406　CHINA　APR. 6, 2005

50　: Applicant
ARELLA AND C. SPA
PIAZZA COLLEGIO CAIROLI N. 3
27100 PAVIA, ITALY

59　: Beneficiary
GUANGDONG TEA IMP. & EXP. CORP.
26 – 30/F., GUANGDONG FOREIGN ECONOMICS & TRADE BUILDING
351 TIANHE ROAD, GUANGZHOU, CHINA

32B　: Currency Code, Amount
USD (US DOLLAR)
USD37,636.00 (US DOLLARS THIRTY SEVEN THOUSAND SIX HUNDRED AND THIRTY SIX ONLY.)

39A　: Percentage Credit Amt Tolerance
10/10

41A　: Available with... by...
ANY BANK BY NEGOTATION AGAINST THE DOCUMENTS DETAILED HEREIN AND BENEFICIARY'S DRAFTS AT 60 DAYS SIGHT DRAWN ON US FOR 100 PCT OF THE INVOICE VALUE.

43P　: Partial Shipment
NOT ALLOWED

43T　: Transshipment
ALLOWED

44A　: Loading in Charge
CHINESE PORT

44B　: For Transportation to
LA SPEZIA PORT

44C　: Latest Date of Shipment
050320　MAR. 20, 2005

45A　: Descript. of Goods
4538 CHINA BLACK TEA ABT. 4,000 KGS. @ USD4.50/KG
5380 CHINA GREEN TEA ABT. 4,000 KGS. @ USD5.20/KG
CIFC3% LA SPEZIA PORT (1 × 20' FCL/200 PAPERSACKS)
PACKED IN PAPERSACKS, PALLETIZED AND CONTAINERIZED AS PER THE SALES CONFIRMATION NO. BTS78905.
THE PRICE IS TO BE UNDERSTOOD PER KILO NET SHIPPED WEIGHT CIF GENOVA LESS 3 PERCENT COMMISSION, INCLUDING PACKING.

46A　: Documents Required

1) SIGNED COMMERCIAL INVOICE, ORIGINAL PLUS TWO COPIES, EVIDENCING THAT THE GOODS SHIPPED COMPLY WITH THE S/C NO. BTS78905 DATED 050112
2) 3/3 CLEAN ON BOARD BILLS OF LADING MADE OUT TO THE ORDER OF ARELLA AND C. SPA MARKED FREIGHT PREPAID AND NOTIFY TO CASASCO AND NARDI – VIA DON GIOVANNI CALABRIA, 30 – 20132 MILANO PHONE 02 – 2729241
3) CERTIFICATE OF WEIGHT
4) CERTIFICATE OF ORIGIN FORM A ISSUED BY THE COMPETENT LOCAL AUTHORITY IN TWO COPIES
5) MARINE INSURANCE POLICY/CERTIFICATE COVERING ALL RISKS AND WAR RISK FOR 110 PERCENT OF THE CIF INVOICE VALUE

47A : Additional Conditions
+/– 10 PCT IN AMOUNT, QUANTITY AND WEIGHT IS ALLOWED
ALL DOCUMENTS MUST INDICATE THIS CREDIT NUMBER
PLEASE SEND DOCUMENTS TO:
SANPAOLO IMI SPA
VIA FABIO FILZI N. 2 – 27100 PAVIA (ITALY)

71B : Charges
ALL BANKING CHARGES AND COMMISSIONS OUTSIDE OF ITALY ARE FOR BENEFICIARY'S ACCOUNT

49 : Confirmation Instructions
WITHOUT

78 : Instr to Payg/Accptg/Negotg Bank
AT RECEIPT OF DOCUMENTS IN CONFORMITY WITH CREDIT TERMS, WE SHALL CREDIT YOU AS PER YOUR INSTRUCTIONS AT MATURITY DATE.

57D : "Advise Through" Bank-Name & Addr.
SOCIETE GENERALS-GUANGZHOU BRANCH
21ST FLOOR PEACE WORLD PLAZA
362 – 366 HUANSHI EAST RD., GUANGZHOU

72 : Sender to Receiver Information
SUBJECT TO ICC PUS 500, 1993 REVISION AND SUBJECT TO THE UNIFORM RULES FOR BANK TO BANK REIMBURSEMENT UNDER DOC. CREDIT ICC PUB 525.

有关资料:

INVOICE NO.: TAR20057149　　INVOICE DATE: MAR. 2, 2005
B/L NO.: GSG05 – 723　　B/L DATE: MAR. 15, 2005
FORM A NO.: GZ7/80067/0589　　POLICY NO.: TES3478921
SHIPPING MARK: N/M　　PACKED IN 200 PAPERSACKS
CONTAINER, SEAL NO.: TEXU3730336/KHS487605/20'
NAME OF STEAMER: PUDONG SENATOR V. 743
WEIGHT: N. W.: @40 KGS　G. W.: @40.7 KGS
该货物是完全自产品　　PORT OF LOADING: GUANGZHOU

综合制单练习四

Issue of a Documentary Credit

Application Header　JANBBDDHAJBD 2189 045834 040529 2009 N
* JANATA BANK
* DHAKA
* (LOCAL OFFICE)

User Header　Service Code　103:
Bank. Priority　113:
Msg. User. Ref. 108: ABUL
Info. From CI.　115:

Sequence of Total　: 1/1
Form of Coc. Credit: IRREVOCABLE
Doc. Credit Number: 0093040600308
Date of Issue　: 040525
Expiry　: Date 040615 Place IN CHINA
Applicant Bank　: JANBBDDHJBD
* JANATA BANK
* DHAKA
* (LOCAL OFFICE)

Applicant　: M/S. SPEEDWELL LIMITED
PLOT NO. M-4/2, ROAD NO. -7, SECTION-7,
MIRPUR, DHAKA-1216, BANGLADESH

Beneficiary　: GUANGDONG TEXTILES IMPORT & EXPORT COTTON, YARN & PIECE-GOODS COMPANY LTD. 8/F., GUANGDONG TEXTILES MANSION, 168 XIAOBEI ROAD, GUANGZHOU, CHINA

Amount　: Currency USD Amount 7,650.00
Available with/by　: ANY BANK IN CHINA BY NEGOTIATION
Drafts at...　: 120 DAYS SIGHT FROM THE DATE OF NEGOTIATION
Drawee　: JANBBDDHJBD
* JANATA BANK
* DHAKA
* (LOCAL OFFICE)

Partial Shipments　: ALLOWED
Transshipment　: ALLOWED
Loading in Charge　: ANY SEA PORT OF CHINA
For Transport to...　: CHITTAGONG, BANGLADESH
Descript. of Goods　:

FABRICS FOR 100PCT EXPORT ORIENTED READYMADE GARMENTS INDUSTRY
4,500YDS 98/2 COTTON/SPANDE × CANVAS CONST: 21 + 12 × 16 + 16 + 70D 140 × 62
WIDTH 50/52INCH AT THE RATE OF USD1.70/YD AS PER PREFORMA INVOICE
NO. 2004CTHS02008 DATED 01-05-2004 OF THE BENEFICIARY.
TERMS OF DELIVERY: C N F CHITTAGONG

Documents Required:

A) ORIGINAL SIGNED INVOICE IN QUINTUPLICATE CERTIFYING MERCHANDISE TO BE OF CHINA ORIGIN.

B) FULL SET OF ORIGINAL CLEAN SHIPPED ON BOARD OCEAN BILL OF LADING DRAWN OR ENDORSED TO THE ORDER OF JANATA BANK, LOCAL OFFICE, DHAKA MARKED FREIGHT PREPAID NOTIFY OPENERS AND US GIVING FULL NAME AND ADDRESS.

C) CERTIFICATE OF ORIGIN ISSUED BY BENEFICIARY CERTIFYING MERCHANDISE OF CHINA ORIGIN.

D) BENEFICIARY'S CERTIFICATE TO THE EFFECT THAT THEY HAVE COMPLIED ALL TERMS AND CONDITIONS OF THEIR PROFORMA INVOICE NO. 2004CTHS02008 DT. 01 -05 -2004.

E) DETAILS PACKING, WEIGHT AND MEASUREMENT LIST REQUIRED IN TRIPLICATE.

Additional Cond. :

1) L/C AUTHORISATION FORM NO. 129306 AND H. S. CODE NO. 5208. 5200 TO APPEAR IN ALL INVOICES.

2) DOCUMENTS EVIDENCING SHIPMENTS MUST NOT BEFORE THE DATE OF OPENING OF THIS CREDIT.

3) SHIPMENT/TRANSSHIPMENT BY ISRAIL, MONTENIGRO AND SERBIA FLAG/VESSEL STRICTLY PROHIBITED.

4) THIRD PARTY, SHORT FORM, BLANK BACKED BILL OF LADING NOT ACCEPTABLE.

5) BILL OF LADING TO INDICATE GROSS AND NET WEIGHT AND CONTAINER NUMBER OF MERCHANDISE.

6) INTEREST WILL BE PAID BY OPENER USANCE PERIOD AT LIBOR FROM THE DATE OF NEGOTIATION.

7) EXCEPT OTHERWISE EXPRESSLY STATED, THIS CREDIT IS SUBJECT TO UNIFORM CUSTONS AND PRACTICE FOR DOCUMENTARY CREDIT (1993 REVISION) ICC PUBLICATION NO. 500.

8) L/C NO. 0093040600308 SHOULD APPEAR ON ALL DOCUMENTS.

9) THIS L/C IS OPENED AGAINST EXPORT L/C NO. 253011372706 - B DATED 10 - 06 - 2003 TO APPEAR ALL DOCUMENTS.

10) ALL EVIDIENCING SHIPMENT UNDER THIS CREDIT MUST BE ADVISED BY THE BENEFICIARY IMMEDIATELY AFTER SHIPMENT DIRECT TO M/S. CITY GENERAL INSURANCE CO. , LTD. LOCAL OFFICE, BAITUL HOSSATN BUILDING 3RD. FLOOR, 27, DILKUSHA C/A, DHAKA - 1000, BANGLADESH AND THE APPLICANT REFERRING TO INSURANCE COVER NOTE NO. CGIC/LO/MC - 191/05/ 04 DATED 25 - 05 - 2004 GIVING FULL DETAILS OF SHIPMENT AND A COPY TO THIS ADVICE ACCOMPANY EACH SET OF DOCUMENTS.

Details of Charges : ALL BANKING CHARGES ARE FOR THE BENEFICIARY'S ACCOUNT.
A FEE OF USD50. 00 WILL BE CHARGED IN CASE OF DISCRIPANT DOCUMENT.
REIMBURSEMENT CHARGE USD50. 00 WILL BE DEDUCTED AT THE TIME OF PAYMENT.

Presentation Period : WITHIN 15 DAYS OF SHIPEMNT BUT WITHIN THE VALIDITY OF CREDIT.

Confirmation : WITHOUT

Instructions　:

1) ORIGINAL AND DUPLICATE SET OF DOCUMENTS TO BE SENT BY SUCCESSIVE REGD. AIRMAIL/COURIER SERVICE IMMEDIATELY AFTER NEGOTIATION/PRESENTATION.

2) AMOUNT OF DRAFT (S) NEGOTIATED/PRESENTED SOULD BE ENDORSED ON REVERSE OF THIS CREDIT.

3) WE SHALL ARRANGE REMITTANCE OF THE PROCEEDS ON RECEIPT OF DOCUMENTS COMPLYING WITH THE TERMS OF THE CRDDIT.

Send. To Rec. Info. DRAFT TO BE DRAWN ON US AT 120 DAYS SIGHT FOR 100PCT
INVOICE VALUE.
DOCS TO BE FORWARDED TO: JANATA BANK
LOCAL KOFFICE, 1 - DILKUSHA C/A,
DHAKA - 1000, BANGLADESH.

有关资料:

INV. NO.: 24HS024018　　INV. DATE: MAY 28, 2004
B/L NO.: FYPX0403335CHI　　B/L DATE: MAY 31, 2004
PORT OF LOADING: SHANGHAI PORT
NAME OF VESSEL: MOL MAAS V. 571W
CONTAINER & SEAL NO.: APZU3028274/4014710

TOTAL QUANTITY: 4,491.4 YDS　　PACKING: 22 BALES
WEIGHT: N. W.: @77.3KGS/BALE　　G. W.: 75.0KGS/BALE
TOTAL MEASUREMENT: 3CBMS
MARKS & NUMBERS: SIRETCH CANVAS
COLOR:
BALS NO.:
MADE IN CHINA

综合制单练习参考答案

L/C（Ⅰ）

综合制单练习一（第一次装运全套单据）

F14

1

凭
Drawn under HANA BANK, SEOUL,KOREA

信用证 第 号
L/C No. M 12CL601ES00032

日期 年 月 日
dated 5 JAN., 2005

按 息 付 款
Payable with interest @ % per annum

号码 汇票金额 中国 广州 年 月 日
No. CPU04SC140A **Exchange** for USD20,430.72 Guangzhou, China 19

见票 日 后（本 汇 票 之 副 本 未 付）付
At *** *** sight of this FIRST of Exchange (Second of exchange being unpaid)
pay to the order of BANK OF CHINA,GUANGDONG BRANCH,GUANZHOU 或其指定人

金 额
the sum of U S DOLLARS TWENTY THOUSAND FOUR HUNDRED AND THIRTY AND CENTS SEVENTY TWO ONLY.

此致
To: HANA BANK SHANGHAI BRANCH,
SHANGHAI

GUANGDONG FOREIGN TRADE
IMP.&EXP.CORP.
（签章）

广东省对外贸易进出口公司

Guangdong Foreign Trade Imp. & Exp. Corp.

15－18/F., Guangdong Foreign Economic and Trade Building

351 Tianhe Road, Guangzhou, China

商业发票

COMMERCIAL INVOICE

Messrs.:		INVOICE NO.	: CPU04SC140A
STORY SHARP CO., LTD.		INVOICE DATE	: 18 JAN., 2005
NO. 502 GL PLAZA, 713－1		L/C NO.	: M12CL601ES00032
HEANGSHIN－DONG, DUCKYANG－GU		L/C DATE	: 5 JAN., 2005
GOYANG－SI, GYEONGGI－DO, KOREA		S/C NO.	: CUP04SC140

Exporter:

GUANGDONG FOREIGN TRADE IMP. & EXP. CORP.

Transport details:　　Terms of payment: BY L/C

FROM HONG KONG TO BUSAN, KOREA BY SEA

Marks & Numbers	Description of Goods	Quantity	Unit Price	Amount
	ORIGIN CHINA		PER MT	
	80G COLOUR PAPER	14.188 MTS	USD1,440.00	USD20,430.72
N/M	LENGTH: 9,500M			
	WIDTH: 1,000MM		FOB HONG KONG	USD20,430.72
	INSIDE ROLL DIA: 75MM			
	OUTSIDE ROLL DIA: 100CM-120CM			

TOTAL QUANTITY: 14.188 MTS PACKED IN 21 ROLLS

TOTAL WEIGHT: N. W.: 14.188MTS　G. W.: 14.188MTS

TOTAL US DOLLARS TWENTY THOUSAND FOUR HUNDRED AND THIRTY AND CENTS SEVENTY TWO ONLY.

GUANGDONG FOREIGN TRADE
IMP. & EXP. CORP.
（签章）

广东省对外贸易进出口公司

Guangdong Foreign Trade Imp. & Exp. Corp.

15－18/F., Guangdong Foreign Economic and Trade Building

351 Tianhe Road, Guangzhou, China

装箱单

PACKING LIST

ORIGINAL

Exporter:
GUANGDONG FOREIGN TRADE
IMP. & EXP. CORP.

INV. DATE: 18 JAN., 2005
INVOICE NO.: CPU04SC140A
B/L NO.: 50100289BUS
S/C NO.: CPU04SC140
L/C NO.: M12CL601ES00032

Transport details:
FROM HONG KONG TO BUSAN, KOREA BY SEA
SHIPPED PER KMTC ULSAN V. 501N

标记 Marks & numbers	件数 Quantity	货名 Description of goods	净重 Net weight	毛重 Gross weight	尺码 Measurement
		ORIGIN CHINA			
	21 ROLLS	80G COLOUR PAPER	14.188 MTS	14.188 MTS	@1,000×1,050(MM)
		LENGTH: 9,500M			
N/M		WIDTH: 1,000MM			
		INSIDE ROLL DIA.: 75MM			
		OUTSIDE ROLL DIA.: 100CM-120CM			
		TOTAL: 21 ROLLS	14.188 MTS	14.188 MTS	19.95 CBMS

TOTAL QUANTITY: 14.188 MTS
TOTAL TWENTY ONE ROLLS ONLY.

GUANGDONG FOREIGN TRADE
IMP. & EXP. CORP.
(签章)

BILL OF LADING

Shipper GUANGDONG FOREIGN TRADE IMP. & EXP. CORP.	B/L No. 50100289BUS
Consignee TO THE ORDER OF HANA BANK, SEOUL	**Combined Transport BILL OF LADING** RECEIVED in apparent good order and condition except as otherwise noted the total number of containers or other packages or units enumerated below for transportation from the place of receipt to the place of delivery subject to the terms and conditions hereof. One of the Bills of Lading must be surrendered duly endorsed to the Carrier by or on behalf of the Holder of the Bill of Lading, the rights and liabilities arising in accordance with the terms and conditions hereof shall, without prejudice to any rule of common law or statute rendering them binding on the Merchant, become binding in all respects between the Carrier and the Holder of the Bill of Lading as though the contract evidenced hereby had been made between them. IN WITNESS whereof the number of original Bills of Lading stated under have been signed. All of this tenor and date, one of which being accomplished, the other (s) to be void.
Notify Address STORY SHARP CO., LTD. NO. 502 GL PLAZA, 713 - 1 HEANGSHIN - DONG, DUCKYANG - GU GOYANG - SI, GYEONGGI - DO, KOREA	

Pre-carriage by	Place of receipt	For delivery of goods please apply to:
Ocean Vessel Voy. No. KMTC ULSAN V. 501N	Port of Loading HONG KONG	

Port of Discharge BUSAN, KOREA	Place of Delivery	Final Destination for the Merchant's Reference only

Particulars Furnished by Merchants

Container, Seal No. & Marks & Nos.	No. of Package & Description of Goods	Gross Weight Kgs	Measurement m^3
N/M	21 ROLLS 80G COLOUR PAPER	14, 188.00	19.95
	TOTAL TWENTY ONE ROLLS ONLY.	FREIGHT COLLECT	
MTU7045319 KB846421/20'			
	ON BOARD DATE: JAN. 21, 2005		
	L/C NO.: M12CL601ES00032		

FREIGHT & CHARGES	Revenue Tons.	Rate Per	Prepaid	Collect

	Prepaid at	Payable at BUSAN	Place and date of issue HONG KONG JAN. 21, 2005
	Total Prepaid	No. of Original B(s)/L THREE (3)	Stamp & Signature

LADEN ON BOARD THE VESSEL

Date

By................................

(TERMS CONTINUED ON BACK HEREOF)

综合制单练习一（第二次装运全套单据）

F14

1

凭
Drawn under HANA BANK, SEOUL,KOREA
信用证 第 号
L/C No. M12CL601ES00032
日期 年 月 日
dated 5 JAN.,2005
按 息 付 款
Payable with interest @ % per annum
号码 汇票金额 中国 广州 年 月 日
No. CPU04SC140B **Exchange** for USD20,486.88 Guangzhou, China 19
见票 日后（本汇票之副本未付）付
At *** *** sight of this FIRST of Exchange (Second of exchange being unpaid)
pay to the order of BANK OF CHINA,GUANGDONG BRANCH,GUANZHOU 或其指定人
金 额
the sum of U S DOLLARS TWENTY THOUSAND FOUR HUNDRED AND EIGHTY SIX AND CENTS EIGHTY EIGHT ONLY.

此致
TO: HANA BANK SHANGHAI BRANCH,
SHANGHAI

GUANGDONG FOREIGN TRADE
IMP.&EXP.CORP.
（签章）

广 东 省 对 外 贸 易 进 出 口 公 司

Guangdong Foreign Trade Imp. & Exp. Corp.

15 – 18/F., Guangdong Foreign Economic and Trade Building

351 Tianhe Road, Guangzhou, China

商业发票

COMMERCIAL INVOICE

Messrs.:

STORY SHARP CO., LTD.
NO. 502 GL PLAZA, 713 – 1
HEANGSHIN – DONG, DUCKYANG – GU
GOYANG – SI, GYEONGGI – DO, KOREA

INVOICE NO. : CPU04SC140B
INVOICE DATE : 21 JAN., 2005
L/C NO. : M12CL601ES00032
L/C DATE : 5 JAN., 2005
S/C NO. : CPU04SC140

Exporter:

GUANGDONG FOREIGN TRADE IMP. &
EXP. CORP.

Transport details:

FROM HONG KONG TO BUSAN, KOREA BY SEA

Terms of payment: L/C

Marks & Numbers	Description of Goods	Quantity	Unit Price	Amount
	ORIGIN CHINA		PER MT	
	80G COLOUR PAPER	14.227 MTS	USD1,440.00	USD20,486.88
N/M	LENGTH: 9,500M			
	WIDTH: 1,000MM		FOB HONG KONG	USD20,486.88
	INSIDE ROLL DIA.: 75MM			
	OUTSIDE ROLL DIA.: 100CM-120CM			

TOTAL QUANTITY: 14.227MTS PACKED IN 23 ROLLS
TOTAL WEIGHT: N.W.: 14.277MTS　G.W.: 14.227MTS
TOTAL US DOLLARS TWENTY THOUSAND FOUR HUNDRED AND EIGHTY SIX
AND CENTS EIGHTY EIGHT ONLY.

GUANGDONG FOREIGN TRADE
IMP. & EXP. CORP.
(签章)

广东省对外贸易进出口公司

Guangdong Foreign Trade Imp. & Exp. Corp.

15－18/F., Guangdong Foreign Economic and Trade Building

351 Tianhe Road, Guangzhou, China

装箱单

PACKING LIST

ORIGINAL

Exporter:
GUANGDONG FOREIGN TRADE
IMP. & EXP. CORP.

INV. DATE: 21 JAN., 2005
INVOICE NO.: CPU04SC140A
B/L NO.: 50200389BUS
S/C NO.: CPU04SC140
L/C NO.: M12CL601ES00032

Transport details:
FROM HONG KONG TO BUSAN, KOREA BY SEA
SHIPPED PER HONG KONG STAR V. 036N

标记 Marks & numbers	件数 Quantity	货名 Description of goods	净重 Net weight	毛重 Gross weight	尺码 Measurement
N/M	23 ROLLS	ORIGIN CHINA 80G COLOUR PAPER LENGTH: 9,500M WIDTH: 1,000MM INSIDE ROLL DIA.: 75MM OUTSIDE ROLL DIA.: 100CM-120CM	14.227MTS	14.227 MTS	@1,000×936(MM)
		TOTAL: 23 ROLLS	14.277 MTS	14.277 MTS	21.528 CBMS

TOTAL QUANTITY: 14.227 MTS
TOTAL TWENTY THREE ROLLS ONLY.

GUANGDONG FOREIGN TRADE
IMP. & EXP. CORP.
（签章）

BILL OF LADING

Shipper
GUANGDONG FOREIGN TRADE IMP. & EXP. CORP.

B/L No. 50200389BUS

Consignee
TO THE ORDER OF HANA BANK, SEOUL

Notify Address
STORY SHARP CO., LTD.
NO. 502 GL PLAZA, 713 – 1
HEANGSHIN – DONG, DUCKYANG – GU
GOYANG – SI, GYEONGGI – DO, KOREA

Combined Transport BILL OF LADING
RECEIVED in apparent good order and condition except as otherwise noted the total number of containers or other packages or units enumerated below for transportation from the place of receipt to the place of delivery subject to the terms and conditions hereof. One of the Bills of Lading must be surrendered duly endorsed to the Carrier by or on behalf of the Holder of the Bill of Lading, the rights and liabilities arising in accordance with the terms and conditions hereof shall, without prejudice to any rule of common law or statute rendering them binding on the Merchant, become binding in all respects between the Carrier and the Holder of the Bill of Lading as though the contract evidenced hereby had been made between them. IN WITNESS whereof the number of original Bills of Lading stated under have been signed. All of this tenor and date, one of which being accomplished, the other(s) to be void.

Pre-carriage by	Place of receipt	For delivery of goods please apply to:
Ocean Vessel Voy. No. HONG KONG STAR V. 036N	Port of Loading HONG KONG	

Port of Discharge	Place of Delivery	Final Destination for the Merchant's Reference only
BUSAN, KOREA		

Particulars Furnished by Merchants

Container, Seal No. & Marks & Nos.	No. of Package & Description of Goods	Gross Weight Kgs	Measurement m^3
N/M	23 ROLLS 80G COLOUR PAPER	14, 277. 00	21. 528
	TOTAL TWENTY THREE ROLLS ONLY.	FREIGHT COLLECT	
MTU7311070 KB846360/20'			
	ON BOARD DATE: JAN. 28, 2005		
	L/C NO.: M12CL601ES00032		

FREIGHT & CHARGES	Revenue Tons.	Rate Per	Prepaid	Collect

	Prepaid at	Payable at BUSAN	Place and date of issue HONG KONG JAN. 28, 2005
	Total Prepaid	No. of Original B(s)/L THREE (3)	Stamp & Signature

LADEN ON BOARD THE VESSEL

Date

By................................

综合制单练习二

F14

凭 Drawn under BANCA DI CREDITO COOPERATIVODI, SORISOLE, ITALY

信用证 L/C 第 No. 088696000825 号

日期 dated 年 月 日 NOV. 15, 2004

按 息 付款

Payable with interest @ % per annum

号码 No. RGCL2584 汇票金额 **Exchange** for USD32,016.00 中国 广州 Guangzhou, China 年 月 日 19

见票 At *** *** sight of this FIRST of Exchange (Second of exchange being unpaid) 日后（本汇票之副本未付）付

pay to the order of BANK OF CHINA, GUANGDONG BRANCH, GUANGZHOU 或其指定人

金额 the sum of US DOLLARS THIRTY TWO THOUSAND AND SIXTEEN ONLY.

此致

TO: BANCA DI CREDITO COOPERATIVO DI
SORISOLE E LEPRENO, SORISOLE,
ITALY

CHINA PACKAGING UNION
GUANGZHOU CO., LTD.
(签章)

广州中包联外经实业有限公司

China Packaging Union Guangzhou Co., Ltd.

7/F., No. 753 Dongfeng Rd., Guangzhou, China

商业发票

COMMERCIAL INVOICE

Messrs.:
SPIL BERG DI YONG KEE FUI
VIA A. DE GASPERI 4
24018 VILLA D' ALME' (BG)
ITALY

INVOICE NO. : RGCL2584
INVOICE DATE : JAN. 7, 2005
L/C NO. : 088696000825
L/C DATE : NOV. 15, 2004
S/C NO. : RGCL/PI004 (SPL-001)

Exporter:
CHINA PACKAGING UNION
GUANGZHOU CO., LTD.
7/F., NO. 753 DONGFENG RD.,
GUANGZHOU, CHINA

Transport details:
FROM GUANGZHOU TO GENOA, ITALY
BY VESSEL

Terms of payment: L/C

Marks & Numbers	Description of Goods	Quantity	Unit Price	Amount
N/M	MYANMAR TEAK GRADE A (UNFINISHED) SP. 16 MM	860m^2	USD32.10/m^2	USD27,606.00
	MYANMAR TEAK INDUSTRIAL PARQUET SP. 14 MM	300m^2	USD14.70/m^2	USD4,410.00
		1,160m^2	CFR GENOA	USD32,016.00

TOTAL QUANTITY: 1,160m^2　　PACKING: 544BAGS
TOTAL WEIGHT: N. W.: 14,720KGS　G. W.: 15,264KGS
TOTAL US DOLLARS THIRTY TWO THOUSAND AND SIXTEEN ONLY.

CHINA PACKAGING UNION
GUANGZHOU CO., LTD.
(签章)

Consignor CHINA PACKAGING UNION GUANGZHOU CO. , LTD. 7/F. , NO. 753 DONGFENGDONG RD. , GUANGZHOU, CHINA	FBL No. 100397 Country Code. HK HKNEGOTIABLE FIATA MULTIMODAL TRANSPORT BILL OF LADING Issued subject to UNCTAD/ICC Rules forMultimodal Transport Documents (ICC publication 481)
Consigned to order of TO ORDER	INTERGROUP SHIPPING (ASIA) LTD.
Notify address SPIL BERG DI YONG KEE FUI VIA A. DE GASPERI 4 24018 VILLA D'ALME'(BG), ITALY	3 Floor, Block 2 Tien Chu Centre. 1E Mok Cheong Street, Tokwawan, KowLoon, Hong Kong Tel: (852) 2760 8872 P. O. Box 20445 Hennessy Road Post Office Fax: (852) 2760 8442 Telex: 43429 INGRO HX Cable Address: HKINGROUP
Place of receipt	
Ocean vessel: HUI YUE 11 HAO V. 51125 / Port of loading: GUANGZHOU	
Port of discharge: GENOA, ITALY / Place of delivery	LICENCE NO.

Marks and numbers	Number and kind of packages	Description of goods	Gross weight	Measurement
N/M	344 BAGS	MYANMAR TEAK GRADE A (UNFINISHED) SP. 16MM	15,140KGS	18.022 CBMS
	200 BAGS	MYANMAR TEAK INDUSTRIAL PARQUET SP. 14MM		

TOTAL FIVE HUNDRED AND FORTY FOUR BAGS ONLY.

FREIGHT PREPAID

L/C NO. 088696000825

ON BOARD DATE: JAN. 12, 2005

according to the declaration of the consignor

ORIGINAL

Declaration of Interest the consignor in timely delivery (Clause 6. 2).	Declared value for ad valorem rate according to the declaration of the consignor(Clauses 7 and 8).

The goods and instructions are accepted and dealt with subject to the Standard Conditions printed overleaf. Taken in charge in apparent good order and condition, unless otherwise noted herein, at the palce of receipt for transport and delivery as mentioned above. One of these Multimodal Transport Bills of Lading must be surrendered duly endorsed in exchange for the goods. In Witness whereof the original Multimodal Transport Bills of Lading all of this tenor and date have been signed in the number stated below, one of which being accomplished the other (s) to be void.

Freight amount	Freight payable at	Place and date of issue GUANGZHOU, JAN. 12, 2005
Cargo Insurance through the undersigned ☐ not covered ☐ Covered according to attached Policy	Number of Original FBL's TWO	Stamp and signature

提单背书:　　CHINA PACKAGING UNION GUANGZHOU CO. , LTD.

（签章）

广州中包联外经实业有限公司
China Packaging Union Guangzhou Co. , Ltd.
7/F. , No. 753 Dongfeng Rd. , Guangzhou, China

装箱单
PACKING LIST

ORIGINAL

Exporter:
CHINA PACKAGING UNION
GUANGZHOU CO. , LTD.

INV. DATE : JAN. 7, 2005
INVOICE NO. : RGCL2584
B/L. NO. : 100397
S/C NO. : CPU04SC140
L/C NO. : M12CL601ES00032

Transport details:
FROM GUANGZHOU TO GENOA, ITALY BY SEA
Shipped per HUI YUE 11 HAO V. 51125

标记 Marks & numbers	件数 Quantity	货名 Description of goods	净重 Net weight	毛重 Gross weight	尺码 Measurement
	344BAGS	MYANMAR TEAK GRADE A	@30KGS	@31KGS	
N/M		(UNFINISHED) SP. 16MM	10, 200KGS	1, 0540KGS	
	200 BAGS	MYANMAR TEAK INDUSTRIAL	@22KGS	@23KGS	
		PARQUEST SP. 14MM	4, 400KGS	4, 600KGS	
		TOTAL: 544BAGS	14, 600KGS	15, 140KGS	18. 022CBMS

TOTAL QUANTITY: 1, 160m^2
TOTAL FIVE HUNDRED AND FORTY FOUR BAGS ONLY.

CHINA PACKAGING UNION
GUANGZHOU CO. , LTD.
(签章)

ORIGINAL

1. Goods consigned from (Exporter's business name, address, country)
CHINA PACKAGING UNION GUANGZHOU CO. ,LTD.
7/F. , NO. 753 DONGFENG DONG RD. ,
GUANGZHOU, CHINA

Reference No.
GZ081/205/086
GENERALIZED SYSTEM OF PREFERENCES
CERTIFICATE OF ORIGIN
(Combined declaration and certificate)
FORM A
issued in THE PEOPLE'S REPUBLIC OF CHINA
(COUNTRY)
See Notes over leaf

2. Goods consigned to(Consignee's name, address, country)
SPIL BERG DI YONG KEE FUI
VIA A. DE GASPERI 4
24018 VILLA D' ALME' (BG), ITALY

3. Means of transport and route (as far as known)
ON/AFTER JAN. 12, 2005
FROM GUANGZHOU TO GENOA, ITALY
BY SEA

4. For official use

5. Item number	6. Marks and numbers of packages	7. Number and kind of packages; description of goods	8. Origin criterion (see Notes over leaf)	9. Gross weight or other quantity	10. Number and date of invoices
01	N/M	(344) THREE HUNDRED AND FORTY FOUR BAGS OF MYANMAR TEAK GRADE A (UN-FINISHED) SP. 16MM	"P"	860m^2	RGCL2584 JAN. 7,2005
02		(200) TWO HUNDRED BAGS OF MYANMAR TEAK INDUSTRIAL PARQUET SP. 14MM	"P"	300m^2	
		* * * * * * * * * * * * * * * * L/C NO. 088696000825			

11. Certification
It is hereby certified, on the basis of control carried out, that the declaration by the exporter is correct.

GUANGZHOU, JAN. 9,2005(签章)

Place and date, signature and stamp of certifying authority

12. Declaration by the exporter
The undersigned hereby declares that the above detailsand statements are correct; that all the goods wereproduced in
CHINA
(country)
and that they comply with the origin requirements specified for those goods in the Generalized System of Preferences for goods exported to
ITALY
(importing country)
GUANGZHOU, JAN. 7,2005(签章)

Place and date, signature of authorized signatory

综合制单练习三

F14

1

凭 Drawn under SANPAOLO IMI S.P.A. PAVIA, ITALY

信用证 L/C 第 No. 3109/1065 号

日期 dated FEB.6,2005 年 月 日

按 息 付款

Payable with interest @ % per annum

号码 No. TAR20057149 汇票金额 **Exchange** for USD37,636.00 中国广州 Guangzhou, China 19 年 月 日

见票 At 60 DAYS 日后（本汇票之副本未付）付 sight of this SECOND of Exchange (Second of exchange being unpaid)

pay to the order of BANK OF CHINA, GUANGZHOU 或其指定人

金额 the sum of US DOLLARS THIRTY SEVEN THOUSAND SIX HUNDRED AND THIRTY SIX ONLY.

此致

To: SANPAOLO IMI S.P.A.
PAVIA, ITALY

GUANGDONG TEA IMP. & EXP.CORP.
（签章）

广东茶叶进出口公司

Guangdong Tea Imp. & Exp. Corp.

26 – 30/F., Guangdong Foreign Economics & Trade Building

351 Tianhe Road, Guangzhou, China

商业发票

COMMERCIAL INVOICE

Messrs.:

ARELLA AND C. SPA
PIAZZA COLLEGIO CAIROLI N. 3
27100 PAVIA, ITALY

INVOICE NO.　:　TAR20057149
INVOICE DATE　:　MAR. 2. 2005
L/C NO.　:　3109/1065
L/C DATE　:　FEB. 6, 2005
S/C NO.　:　BTS78905

Exporter:

GUANGDONG TEA IMP. & EXP. CORP.

Transport details:

FROM GUANGZHOU TO LA SPEZIA PORT BY SEA

Terms of payment: L/C

Marks & Numbers	Description of Goods	Quantity	Unit Price	Amount
N/M	4538 CHINA BLACK TEA	4,000 KGS	@USD4.50/KG	USD18,000.00
	5380 CHINA GREEN TEA	4,000 KGS	@USD5.20/KG	USD20,800.00
		CIFC 3% LA SPEZIA PORT		USD38,800.00
		LESS 3% COMISSION		USD1,164.00
		CIF LA SPEZIA PORT		USD37,636.00

TOTAL QUANTITY: 8,000 KGS　　PACKING: 200 PAPERSACKS
TOTAL WEIGHT: N. W.: 8,000 KGS　G. W.: 8,140 KGS
TOTAL US DOLLARS THIRTY SEVEN THOUSAND SIX HUNDRED
AND THIRTY SIX ONLY.
PACKING: IN PAPERSACKS, PALLETIZED AND
CONTAINERIZED INTO 1 × 20 FCL.

GUANGDONG TEA IMP. & EXP. CORP.
（签章）

广东茶叶进出口公司

Guangdong Tea Imp. & Exp. Corp.

26 - 30/F., Guangdong Foreign Economics & Trade Building

351 Tianhe Road, Guangzhou, China

CERTIFICATE OF WEIGHT

ORIGINAL

No.: TAR20057149　　Date: MAR. 2, 2005

Shipping Marks	Quantites & Descriptions of Goods	Net Weight	Gross Weight
N/M	4538 CHINA BLACK TEA	@40KGS	@40.7KGS
	100 PAPERSACKS	4,000KGS	4,070KGS
	5380 CHINA GREEN TEA	@40KGS	@40.7KGS
	100 PAPERSACKS	4,000KGS	4,070KGS
		8,000KGS	8,140KGS

TOTAL TWO HUNDRED PAPERSACKS ONLY.

L/C NO. 3109/1065

GUANGDONG TEA IMP. & EXP. CORP.
（签章）

Original

1. Goods consigned from (Exporter's business name, address, country)	Reference No.
GUANGDONG TEA IMP. & EXP. CORP. 26－30/F. ,GUANGDONG FOREIGN ECONOMICS & TRADE BUILDING 351 TIANHE ROAD, GUANGZHOU, CHINA	CZ7/80067/0589 GENERALIZED SYSTEM OF PREFERENCES CERTIFICATE OF ORIGIN (Combined declaration and certificate) FORM A issued in THE PEOPLE'S REPUBLIC OF CHINA (COUNTRY)
2. Goods consigned to (Consignee's name, address, country) ARELLA AND C. SPA PIAZZA COLLEGIO CAIROLI N. 3 2710 0 PAVIA, ITALY	See Notes over leaf
3. Means of transport and route (as far as known) ON/AFTER MAR. 15, 2005 FROM GUANGZHOU TO LA SPEZIA PORT BY SEA	4. For official use

5. Item number	6. Marks and numbers of packages	7. Number and kind of packages; description of goods	8. Origin criterion (see Notes over leaf)	9. Gross weight or other quantity	10. Number and date of invoices
01	N/M	(100) ONE HUNDRED PAPERSACKS OF 4538 CHINA BLACK TEA	"P"	4,070KGS	TAR20057149 MAR. 2,2005
02		(100) ONE HUNDRED PAPERSACKS OF 5380 CHINA GREEN TEA * * * * * * * * * * * * * * * * * L/C NO. 3109/1065	"P"	4,070KGS	

11. Certification	12. Declaration by the exporter
It is hereby certified, on the basis of control carried out, that the declaration by the exporter is correct. GUANGZHOU,MAR. 5,2005(签章) Place and date, signature and stamp of certifying authority	The ubdersigned hereby declares that the above detailsand statements are correct; that all the goods wereproduced in CHINA (country) and that they comply with the origin requirements specified for those goods in the Generalized System of Preferences for goods exported to ITALY (importing country) GUANGZHOU,MAR. 2,2005(签章) Place and date, signature of authorized signatory

PICC PROPERTY

中保财产保险有限公司
The people's insurance（Property）Company of China，Ltd．

发票号码
Invoice No. TAR20057149

保险单号次
Policy No. TES3478921

海 洋 货 物 运 输 保 险 单
MARINE CARGO TRANSPORTATION INSURANCE POLICY

被保险人：GUANGDONG TEA IMPORT & EXPORT CORP.
Insured：

中保财产保险有限公司（以下简称本公司）根据被保险人的要求，及其所缴付约定的保险费，按照本保险单承担险别和背面所载条款与下列特别条款承保下列货物运输保险，特签发本保险单。

This policy of Insurance witnesses that the People's Insurance（Property）Company of China，Ltd.（hereinafter called "the Company"），at the request of the Insured and in consideration of the agreed premium paid by the Insured，under takes to insure the undermentioned goods in transportation subject to the conditions of this Policy as per the Clauses printed overleaf and other special clauses attached hereon.

保险货物项目 Descriptions of Goods	包装　单位　数量 Packing Unit Quantity	保险金额 Amount Insured
4538 CHINA BLACK TEA 5380 CHINA GREEN TEA TOTAL 8,000KGS	100 PAPERSACKS 100 PAPERSACKS	USD41，400.00

承 保 险 别
Conditions

COVERING ALL RISKS AND WAR RISKS AS PER OCEAN MARINE CARGO CLAUSES（1/1/1981）（WAREHOUSE TO WAREHOUSE CLAUSE IS INCLUDED）AND OCEAN MARINE CARGO WAR RISK CLAUSE（1/1/1981）OF THE PEOPLE'S INSURANCE COMPANY OF CHINA

货 物 标 记
Marks of Goods

N/M

总 保 险 金 额：
Total Amount Insured：US DOLLARS FORTY ONE THOUSAND FOUR HUNDRED ONLY.

保费
Premium As arranged

载运输工具
Per conveyance S. S. PUDONG SENATOR V. 743

开航日期
Slg. on or abt MAR. 15，2005

起运港
From GUANGZHOU

目的港
to LA SPEZIA PORT

所保货物，如发生本保险单项下可能引起索赔的损失或损坏，应立即通知本公司下述代理人查勘。如有索赔，应向本公司提交保险单正本（本保险单共有　　份正本）及有关文件。如一份正本已用于索赔，其余正本则自动失效。

In the event of loss or damage which may result in a claim under this Policy，immediate notice must be given to the Company's Agent as mentioned hereunder. Claims，if any，one of the Original Policy which has been issued in 1 Original（s）together with the relevant do－cuments shall be surrendered to the Company. If one of the Original Policy has been accomplished，the others to be void.

中保财产保险有限公司
THE PEOPLE'S INSURANCE（PROPERTY）COMPANY OF CHINA，LTD.

赔款偿付地点
Claim payable at LA SPEZIA PORT

日期
Date MAR. 12，2005

在
at GUANGZHOU

地址：
Address：

保险单背书：　GUANGDONG TEA IMP. & EXP. CORP.

（签章）

BILL OF LADING

Shipper GUANGDONG TEA IMP. & EXP. CORP. 26－30/F., GUANGDONG FOREIGN ECONOMICS & TRADE BUILDING, 351 TIANHE ROAD, GUANGZHOU, CHINA	B/L No. GSG05－723
Consignee TO THE ORDER OF ARELLA AND C. SPA Notify Address CASASCO AND NARDI-VIA DON GIOVANNI CALABRIA, 30-20132 MILANO PHONE 02-2729241	Combined Transport BILL OF LADING RECEIVED in apparent good order and condition except as otherwise noted the total number of containers or other packages or units enumerated below for transportation from the place of receipt to the place of delivery subject to the terms and conditions hereof. One of the Bills of Lading must be surrendered duly endorsed to the Carrier by or on behalf of the Holder of the Bill of Lading, the rights and liabilities arising in accordance with the terms and conditions hereof shall, without prejudice to any rule of common law or statute rendering them binding on the Merchant, become binding in all respects between the Carrier and the Holder of the Bill of Lading as though the contract evidenced hereby had been made between them. IN WITNESS whereof the number of original Bills of Lading stated under have been signed. All of this tenor and date, one of which being accomplished, the other (s) to be void.

Pre-carriage by	Place of receipt	For delivery of goods please apply to:
Ocean Vessel Voy. No. PUDONG SENATOR V. 743	Port of Loading GUANGZHOU	
Port of Discharge LA SPEZIA PORT	Place of Delivery	Final Destination for the Merchant's Reference only

Particulars Furnished by Merchants

Container, Seal No. & Marks & Nos.	No. of Package & Description of Goods	Gross Weight Kgs	Measurement m^3
N/M	100 PAPERSACKS 4538 CHINA BLACK TEA 100 PAPERSACKS 5380 CHINA GREEN TEA	8, 140	
TEXU3730336 KHS487605/20'	TOTAL TWO HUNDRED PAPERSACKS ONLY.		
	L/C NO. 3109/1065 FREIGHT PREPAID		

FREIGHT & CHARGES	Revenue Tons.	Rate Per	Prepaid	Collect

Prepaid at	Payable at	Place and date of issue GUANGZHOU, MAR. 15, 2005
Total Prepaid	No. of Original B(s)/L THREE (3)	Stamp & Signature （签章）

LADEN ON BOARD THE VESSEL

Date

By ____________________

综合制单练习四

F14

1

凭
Drawn under JANATA BANK DHAKA (LOCAL OFFICE)

信用证 第 号
L/C No. 0093040600308

日期 年 月 日
dated MAY 25, 2004

按 息 付 款
Payable with interest @ % per annum

号码 汇票金额 中国 广州 年 月 日
No. Exchange for USD7,635.38 Guangzhou, China 19

见票 日 后（本 汇 票 之 副 本 未 付）付
At 120 DAYS sight of this FIRST of Exchange (Second of exchange being unpaid)

pay to the order of BANK OF CHINA, GUANGZHOU BRANCH, GUANGZHOU 或其指定人

金 额
the sum of US DOLLARS SEVEN THOUSAND SIX HUNDRED AND THIRTY FIVE AND CENTS THIRTY EIGHT ONLY.

此致
TO: JANATA BANK, DHAKA
(LOCAL OFFICE)

GUANGDONG TEXTILES IMPORT AND EXPORP
COTTON, YARN AND PIECE-GOODS COMPANY LTD.
(签章)

广东省纺织品进出口花纱布有限公司

GUANGDONG TEXTILES IMPORT & EXPORT
COTTON, YARN & PIECE-GOODS COMPANY LTD.

8/F., GUANGDONG TEXTILES MANSION, 168 XIAOBEI ROAD, GUANGZHOU, CHINA

商业发票
COMMERCIAL INVOICE

Messrs.:
M/S. SPEEDWELL LIMITED
PLOT NO. M-4/2, ROAD NO. -7, SECTION-7,
MIRPUR, DHAKA-1216, BANGLADESH

INVOICE NO.	:	24HS024018
INVOICE DATE	:	MAY 28, 2004
L/C NO.	:	0093040600308
L/C DATE	:	MAY 25, 2004
S/C NO.	:	2004CYHS02008

Exporter:
GUANGDONG TEXTILES IMPORT & EXPORT
COTTON, YARN & PIECE-GOODS CO., LTD.

Transport details:
FROM SHANGHAI PORT TO CHITTAGONG,
BANGLADESH BY SEA

Terms of payment: L/C

Marks & Numbers	Description of Goods	Quantity	Unit Price	Amount
STRETCH CANVAS	FABRICS FOR 100PCT EXPORT			
COLOR:	ORIENTED READYMADE GARMENTS			
BALS NO:	INDUSTRY. 92/2 COTTON/SPANDEX			C N F CHITTAGONG
MADE IN CHINA	CANVAS CONST: 21+12×16+70D			
	140×62 WIDTH 50/52 INCH	4,491.4YDS	@USD1.70/YD	USD7,635.38

TOTAL QUANTITY: 4,491.4YDS PACKED IN 22 BALES
TOTAL WEIGHT: N. W.: 1,650KGS G. W.: 1,700KGS
TOTAL US DOLLARS SEVEN THOUSAND SIX HUNDRED AND THIRTY FIVE
AND CENTS THIRTY EIGHT ONLY.

AS PER OUR PROFORMA INVOICE NO. 2004CTHS02008 DATED 01-05-2004
IT IS CERTIFY THAT MERCHANDISE ARE OF CHINA ORIGIN
L/C AUTHORISATION FORM NO. 129306 AND H. S. CODE NO. 5208.5200
THIS L/C IS OPENED AGAINST EXPORT L/C NO. 253011372706-B
DATED 10-06-2003.

GUANGDONG TEXTILES IMPORT & EXPORT
COTTON, YARN & PIECE-GOODS COMPANY LTD.
（签章）

BILL OF LADING

Shipper GUANGDONG TEXTILES IMPORT AND EXPORT COTTON, YARN AND PIECE - GOODS CO., LTD.	B/L No. FYPX0403335CHI
Consignee TO THE ORDER OF JANATA BANK, LOCAL OFFICE, DHAKA	Combined Transport BILL OF LADING RECEIVED in apparent good order and condition except as otherwise noted the total number of containers or other packages or units enumerated below for transportation from the place of receipt to the place of delivery subject to the terms and conditions hereof. One of the Bills of Lading must be surrendered duly endorsed to the Carrier by or on behalf of the Holder of the Bill of Lading, the rights and liabilities arising in accordance with the terms and conditions hereof shall, without prejudice to any rule of common law or statute rendering them binding on the Merchant, become binding in all respects between the Carrier and the Holder of the Bill of Lading as though the contract evidenced hereby had been made between them. IN WITNESS whereof the number of original Bills of Lading stated under have been signed. All of this tenor and date, one of which being accomplished, the other (s) to be void.
Notify Address 1) M/S. SPEEDWEL LIMITED PLOT NO. M-4/2 ROAD NO. -7, SECTION-7, MIRPUR, DHAKA-1216, BANGLADESH 2) JANATA BANK, LOCAL OFFICE, DHAKA	

Pre-carriage by	Place of receipt	For delivery of goods please apply to:
Ocean Vessel Voy. No. MOL MAAS V. 571W	Port of Loading SHANGHAI PORT	
Port of Discharge CHITTAGONG, BANGLADESH	Place of Delivery	Final Destination for the Merchant's Reference only

Particulars Furnished by Merchants

Container, Seal No. & Marks & Nos.	No. of Package & Description of Goods	Gross Weight Kgs	Measurement m³
SIRETCH COLOR: BALS NO.: MADE IN CHINA APZU3028274 4014710	22 BALES FABRICS FOR 100PCT EXPORT ORIENTED READYMADE GARMENTS INDUSTRY. 98/2 COTTON/SPANDES CANVAS TOTAL TWENTY TWO BALES ONLY. L/C AUTHORISATION FORM NO. 129306 AND H. S. CODE NO. 5208.5200 L/C NO. 0093040600308 THIS L/C IS OPENED AGAINST EXPORT L/C NO. 253011372706 - B DATED 10-06-2003 FREIGHT PREPAID SHIPPED ON BOARD DATE: MAY 31, 2004	1,700KGS NET WEIGHT 1,650KGS	3CBMS CFS TO CFS

FREIGHT & CHARGES	Revenue Tons.	Rate Per	Prepaid	Collect

Prepaid at	Payable at	Place and date of issue SHANGHAI, MAY 31, 2004
Total Prepaid	No. of Original B (s) /L THREE (3)	Stamp & Signature

LADEN ON BOARD THE VESSEL

Date

By................................

(TERMS CONTINUED ON BACK HERREOF)

广东省纺织品进出口花纱布有限公司

GUANGDONG TEXTILES IMPORT & EXPORT COTTON, YARN & PIECE-GOODS COMPANY LTD.

产地证明书

CERTIFICATE OF ORIGIN

发票号（INV. NO.）：24HS024018
L/C NO.：009304060308
日期（DATE）：MAY 28, 2004

兹证明下列商品系中华人民共和国生产/制造
(This is to certify that the under mentioned commodities were produced/manufactured in the People's Republic of China)

标记及号码 (Mark & No.)	品名 (Commodity)	数量 (Quantity)	重量 (Weight)
STRETCH CANVAS COLOR: BALS NO.: MADE IN CHINA	FABRICS FOR 100PCT EXPORT ORIENTED READYMADE GARMENTS INDUSTRY. 98/2 COTTON/SPANDE × CANVAS IT IS TO CERTIFY THAT MERCHANDISE ARE OF CHINA ORIGIN. L/C AUTHORISATION FORM NO. 129306 AND H. S. CODE NO. 5208.5200 THIS L/C IS OPENED AGAINST EXPORT L/C NO. 25301137206 - B DATED 10 - 06 - 2003	4,491.4 YDS (22 BALES)	NET WEIGHT 1,650 KGS GROSS WEIGHT 1,700 KGS

广东省纺织品进出口花纱布有限公司
GUANGDONG TEXTILES IMPORT & EXPORT COTTON, YARN & PIECE-GOODS COMPANY LTD.

8/F., GUANGDONG TEXTILES MANSION, 168 XIAOBEI ROAD, GUANGZHOU, CHINA

装船通知
SHIPPING ADVICE

To: M/S. CITY GENERAL INSURANCE CO., LTD., LOCAL OFFICE, BAITUL HOSSAIN BUILDING 3RD FLOOR, 27, DILKUSHA C/A, DHAKA - 1000, BANGLADESH	Inv. No. : 24HS024018
	Inv. Date : MAY 28. 2004
	Inv. Value : USD7, 635. 38
M/S. SPEEDWELL LIMITED PLOT NO. M-4/2, ROAD NO. -7, SECTION-7, MIRPUK, DHAKA-1216, BANGLADESH	L/C No. : 0093040600308
	S/C No. : 2004CTHS02008

Port of Shipment: SHANGHAI PORT, CHINA

Port of Destination: CHITTAGONG, BANGLADESH

Date of Shipment: MAY 31, 2004

Vessel's Name: MOL MAAS V. 571W

Commodity: FABRICS FOR 100PCT EXPORT ORIENTED READYMADE GARMENTS INDUSTRY
98/2 COTTON/SPANDE × CANVAS

Quantity: 4, 491. 4 YDS (22 BALES)

Weight: N. W.: 1, 650 KGS　G. W.: 1, 700 KGS

THE APPLICANT REFERRING TO INSURANCE COVER NOT NO. CGIC/LO/MC - 191/05/04 DATED 25 - 05 - 2004

L/C AUTHORISATION FORM NO. 129306 AND H. S. CODE NO. 5208. 5200

THIS L/C IS OPENED AGAINST EXPORT L/C NO. 253011372706 - B DATED 10 - 06 - 2003

GUANGDONG TEXTILES IMPORT & EXPORT
COTTON, YARN & PIECE-GOODS COMPANY LTD.
（签章）

广东省纺织品进出口花纱布有限公司

GUANGDONG TEXTILES IMPORT & EXPORT

COTTON, YARN & PIECE-GOODS COMPANY LTD.

8/F., GUANGDONG TEXTILES MANSION, 168 XIAOBEI ROAD, GUANGZHOU, CHINA

BENEFICIARY'S CERTIFICATE

Date: MAY 28, 2004

RE: INV. NO.: 24HS024018　L/C NO.: 0093040600308

WE HEREBY CERTIFY THAT THE EFFECT THAT THEY HAVE COMPLIED ALL TERMS AND CONDITIONS OF OUR PROFORMA INVOICE NO. 2004CTHS02008 DT. 01-05-2004.

GUANGDONG TEXTILES IMPORT & EXPORT

COTTON, YARN AND PIECE-GOODS COMPANY LTD.

(签章)

广东省纺织品进出口花纱布有限公司
GUANGDONG TEXTILES IMPORT & EXPORT
COTTON, YARN & PIECE-GOODS COMPANY LTD.
8/F., GUANGDONG TEXTILES MANSION, 168 XIAOBEI ROAD, GUANGZHOU, CHINA

DETAILS PACKING, WEIGHT AND MEASUREMENT LIST

NO. : 24HS024018
DATE : MAY 28, 2004

FABRICS FOR 100PCT EXPORT ORIENTED READYMADE GARMENTS INDUSTRY.

98/2 COTTON/SPANDEX CANVAS
CONST.: 21 + 12 × 16 + 16 + 70D　140 × 62　　WIDTH: 50/52 INCH

COLOUR: KHAKI

B/NO.	LOT NO.	QTY. (Y.)					TTL. (Y.)
——	——	——					——
1	A	105.0	78.7				183.7
2	A	107.2	91.9				199.1
3	A	113.7	89.7				203.4
4	A	123.6	108.3				231.9
5	A	109.4	37.2				146.6
6	A	114.8	79.8				194.6
							1 159.3

TTL.: 6 BALES—1, 159.3 YDS.

COLOUR: BROWN

B/NO.	LOT NO.	QTY. (Y.)					TTL. (Y.)
——	——	——					——
1	B	103.9	109.4				213.3
2	B	165.1	105.0				270.1
3	A	105.0	109.4				214.4
4	A	71.1	106.1	25.1			202.3
5	A	98.2	25.1				123.3
							1 023.4

TTL.: 5 BALES—1,023.4 YDS.

DETAILS PACKING, WEIGHT AND MEASUREMENT LIST

NO. : 24HS024018
DATE : MAY 28, 2004

COLOUR: GREY

B/NO.	LOT NO.	QTY. (Y.)					TTL. (Y.)
——	——	——					——
1	B	162.9	51.4	31.7			246.0
2	B	100.6	106.1				206.7
3	B	103.9	118.1				222.0
4	A	106.1	115.9	80.9			302.9
5	A	112.6	75.5	39.4			227.5
6	A	120.3	80.9				201.2
7	B	100.6	87.5				188.1
8	A	108.3					108.3
9	A	131.2	115.9				247.1
10	A	131.2	115.9				247.1
11	A	105.0	107.2				212.2
							2 409.1

TTL. : 11 BALES—2,409.1 YDS.

TOTAL : 22 BALES - 4,491.4 YDS.
G. WT.: @77.3/1,700 KGS
N. WT.: @75.0/1,650 KGS
MEAST.: 3.0 CBMS

AS PER PROFORMA INVOICE NO. 2004CTHS02008 DATED 01-05-2004 OF THE BENEFICIARY

L/C AUTHORISATION FORM NO. 129306 AND H. S. CODE NO. 5208.5200
L/C NUMBER: 0093040600308
THIS L/C IS OPENED AGAINST EXPORT L/C NO. 253011372706-B DATED 10-06-2003.
SHIPPPING MARK: STRETCH CANVAS
COLOR:
BALS NO. :
MADE IN CHINA

GUANGDONG TEXTILES IMPORT & EXPORT
COTTON, YARN & PIECE-GOODS COMPANY LTD.
(签章)

湖南茶叶进出口公司

HUNAN TEA IMPORT & EXPORT CORPORATION

WUYI ROAD, CHANGSHA, HUNAN, CHINA

商业发票

COMMERCIAL INVOICE

ORIGINAL

Messrs. :

INVOICE NO. :

INVOICE DATE :

L/C NO. :

L/C DATE :

Exporter:

S/C NO. :

Transport details:

Terms of payment:

Marks & Numbers	Description of Goods	Quantity	Unit Price	Amount

中国纺织品进出口公司
CHINA TEXTILES IMPORT & EXPORT CORP.
8 DONGAN ROAD, BEIJING, CHINA
商业发票
COMMERCIAL INVOICE　　ORIGINAL

Messrs.:

INVOICE NO. :
INVOICE DATE :
L/C NO. :
L/C DATE :
S/C NO. :

Exporter:

Transport details:

Terms of payment:

Marks & Numbers	Description of Goods	Quantity	Unit Price	Amount

大连威达贸易有限公司
DALIAN WEIDA TRADING CO. , LTD.
8 DONGAN ROAD, BEIJING, CHINA
商业发票
COMMERCIAL INVOICE

ORIGINAL

Messrs. :

INVOICE NO. :

INVOICE DATE :

L/C NO. :

L/C DATE :

S/C NO. :

Exporter:

Transport details:

Terms of payment:

Marks & Numbers	Description of Goods	Quantity	Unit Price	Amount

参考文献

1. 余世明. 国际商务单证实务. 广州：暨南大学出版社，2008.
2. 余世明. 报关员资格考试辅导. 广州：暨南大学出版社，2002.
3. 余世明. 全国外销员资格考试辅导. 广州：暨南大学出版社，2002.
4. 余世明. 国际贸易实务练习题及分析解答. 广州：暨南大学出版社，2004.
5. 余世明，冼燕华. 国际商务模拟实习教程. 广州：暨南大学出版社，2004.
6. 余世明. 国际货运代理员考试辅导. 广州：暨南大学出版社，2004.
7. 全国国际商务专业人员职业资格考试指定用书编委会. 国际商务基础理论与实务. 北京：中国对外经济贸易出版社，2003.
8. 中国国际货运代理协会. 国际航空货运代理理论与实务. 北京：中国商务出版社，2005.
9. 周树玲. 外贸单证实务. 北京：对外经济贸易大学出版社，2004.
10. 刘启萍，周树玲. 外贸英文制单. 北京：对外经济贸易大学出版社，2002.
11. 顾　民. 外贸制单与结汇. 北京：对外经济贸易大学出版社，2001.
12. 梅清豪. 外贸信用证实务. 上海：东方出版中心，1997.
13. 姚大伟. 国际贸易单证实务. 北京：中国对外经济贸易出版社，2002.
14. 黎孝先. 国际贸易实务. 北京：对外经济贸易大学出版社，1994.
15. 吴百福. 进出口贸易实务教程. 上海：上海人民出版社，2004.
16. 罗来仪，李乃军. 对外贸易业务问题集解. 北京：对外经济贸易大学出版社，2000.
17. 吴小平. 保险原理与实务. 北京：中国金融出版社，2003.
18. 陈海联等. 报关员考试习题精解. 北京：中国海关出版社，2002.
19. 国际商会. 2010 年国际贸易术语解释通则.